THE PERVERSE IMAGINATION
Sexuality and Literary Culture

every experience that is not converted
into a voluptuous one is a failure.

E. M. Cioran. *Précis de Décomposition* (1949)

The Perverse Imagination

Sexuality and Literary Culture

Edited by

IRVING BUCHEN

1970

New York   New York University Press

ACKNOWLEDGMENTS

"Satire and the Rhetoric of Sadism," by Joseph Bentley. Reprinted from *The Centennial Review* (Michigan State) (Summer, 1967) with permissions of the editors and the author. Copyright © *The Centennial Review*.

"The Resurrection of the Body," by Norman O. Brown. Reprinted from *Life against Death* (1959) with permission of Wesleyan University Press and Routledge & Kegan Paul, Ltd. Copyright © Wesleyan University Press.

"Sade: Prisoner of Consciousness," by Ihab Hassan. Excerpt reprinted from *TriQuarterly* (Spring, 1969) with permission of the editor and the author. Copyright © Ihab Hassan.

"The Enigma of Incest," by Georges Bataille. Excerpt reprinted from *Death and Sensuality* (1969) with the permission of Ballantine Books. Copyright © 1962 by Georges Bataille—all rights reserved.

"Philip Roth's Exact Intent—Interview," by George Plimpton. Reprinted from the New York *Times* (February 23, 1969) with the permission of the New York *Times* and the author. Copyright © 1969 by the New York Times Company.

"The Erotic Revolution," by Lawrence Lipton. Excerpt reprinted from the "Preface" to *The Erotic Revolution* (1965) with the permission of Sherbourne Press, Los Angeles 90035. Copyright © 1965 Lawrence Lipton.

"In Despite of Christendom," by Wayland Young. Excerpts reprinted from *Eros Denied* (1964) with the permissions of Grove Press, Inc., and George Weidenfeld & Nicolson. Copyright © 1964 Wayland Young.

"Pornography and the New Expression," by Richard Schechner. Reprinted from the *Atlantic* (January, 1967) with the permissions of the editor and the author. Copyright © 1966, by the Atlantic Monthly Company, Boston, Mass. Reprinted with permission.

"Attitudes Toward Sex in American 'High Culture,' " by Robert Boyers. Reprinted from *The Annals: The American Academy of Political and Social Science* (March, 1968) with the permission of the editors and the author.

"But He's a Homosexual . . ." from the book *Supergrow: Essays and Reports on Imagination in America* by Benjamin DeMott. Copyright © 1969, 1968 by Benjamin DeMott. Reprinted by permission of E. P. Dutton & Co., Inc., and Harold Ober Associates, Inc.

Excerpted from "Our Bedfellow, the Marquis de Sade," by Anthony Burgess. © Copyright 1969 by American Heritage Publishing Co., Inc. Reprinted by permission from the Winter 1969 issue of HORIZON magazine.

"On the Psychology of Erotic Literature." Reprinted from *Literature and Psychology,* XX (March, 1970), 22–9, with the permission of the editor and the author.

"Notes on Pornography" from *Reflections on a Sinking Ship* by Gore Vidal. Copyright © 1966 by Gore Vidal. Reprinted by permission of Little, Brown & Co. and *The New York Review of Books*.

"The Third Theater Revisited" by Robert Brustein. Reprinted with permission from the author and *The New York Review of Books*. Copyright © 1969 The New York Review.

"The New Immoralists" by William Phillips. Reprinted from *Commentary*, by permission, and with the permission of the author. Copyright © 1965 by the American Jewish Committee.

"Sexual Politics: Miller, Mailer, and Genet" taken from "Instances of Sexual Politics." Copyright © Kate Millett. From *Sexual Politics* by Kate Millett. Reprinted by permission of Doubleday & Company, Inc.

"The Cities of Night: John Rechy's *City of Night* and the American Literature of Homosexuality," by Stanton Hoffman. Reprinted with permission from *The Chicago Review*. Copyright © The Chicago Review.

"The Pornography of Death," by Geoffrey Gorer. Reprinted from *Death, Grief and Mourning*. Copyright © Geoffrey Gorer, 1965. Reprinted by permission of Doubleday & Company, Inc.

For my mother

PREFACE

During the academic year of 1968–69, I taught a course in "The Literature of Perversion." Contrary to melodramatic expectations, there was neither pressure from the administration nor protest from the local community. The course attracted many students—unfortunately, too many to be accommodated. It was the request of those who were excluded that I consider writing a book on sexual perversions in literature.

But what kind of book? In the course itself we ranged ambitiously from the *Kamasutra* to *Portnoy's Complaint*. We attended and discussed films and plays. We put our own fantasies in written form and studied them as a text. But much of what was good was so because it was sustained by the give-and-take of an interacting class, and that kind of dialogue could not be duplicated in a book. Nevertheless, I was convinced of the need to embody at least the literary issues and approach of the course in book form, if for no other reason than that no such coverage existed. Indeed, when I began to prepare for the course and to investigate the bibliography, what I found fell generally into three categories. The first and largest was books and articles dealing with the history of censorship, especially as it involved legal and constitutional matters. Then, there were a lesser number of surveys or anthologies of erotica, often elegantly printed and bound and occasionally illustrated, but almost always in special collections not available to the general public.* Finally, there

---

* In the "Preface" to the first edition of *Psychopathia Sexualis* (1906), Dr. R. von Krafft-Ebing states: "A scientific title has been chosen, and technical terms are used throughout the book in order to exclude the lay reader. For the same reason certain portions are written in Latin."

vii

were the psychological and sociological studies of deviant sexual behavior that performed autopsies on the diseased body of literature. In short, as many researchers have discovered, the absence of a book compelled its creation.

Although the bibliographical search yielded little of substance, it did make apparent a progressive pattern of change. Specifically, three general stages were discernible by which to measure all that has come about since the end of World War II to the present. The first period, which runs from 1945 to the mid-fifties, is summed up adequately by the favorite bibliographical category, "sex in literature." After the harsh proletarian struggles of the thirties and the equally grim realities of the war, post-war authors renewed a prior sexual focus. Although the renderings were far more explicit and clinical, it was for the most part a peaceful decade in the sense that the new Lawrences and Millers were for the most part just that and the opposition to their sexual liberties was couched in the familiar appeals to the higher callings of self-conscious literature. But from the mid-fifties to the mid-sixties the situation becomes unfamiliarly abrasive. The Beats emerge with a voice that is alternately howling and despairing. Gingerly-put questions of indecency now give way to out-right charges of obscenity. Homosexuality leaves the timid wings to occupy the center of the stage. The Grove Press begins to add reprints of Victorian pornographic samplers to its contemporary fare. *Playboy* appears as a magazine, philosophy, and way of life. Significantly, the bibliographical category of "sex in literature" is strained to the breaking point by the many cross references to both "obscenity in literature" and "pornography." Finally, from the mid-sixties to the present, pandemonium seems to break loose. The new is replaced by the radical; the literary becomes involved and even absorbed into the political; the underground, especially in drama and film, comes above ground. For the first time, unfamiliar and unexpected subjects like nudity, sexual anarchy, and perversion assault traditional categories; and for the first time, the bibliographical category of "sex in literature" competes for entries with a new one, "perversion in literature"; predictably, there is a revival of the Marquis de Sade. Depending upon one's point of view, one can sum up the three periods as an arc which moves from a high of order to a mid-point of confusion to a low of anarchy; or from a low of rigidity to a mid-point of flexibility to a high of liberation.

The last period requires special comment, not only because it is the seminal span out of which my own course and this book emerges, but also because it is the most problematical. Although the period is complex, two general voices are discernible. One is both vigorous and conciliatory, rational and quivering, flexible and betrayed, but determined that things have gone too far too fast and now there is need for serious pause. The other voice is both easy and hysterical, alternatively promiscuous and puritanical, urgent and impatient, but determined to demand a total revolution in the arts and society. As a critic and an editor I have sought to give expression to those voices calling for a new future. At the same time, I have tried to be responsive to the call for reevaluation. But I find—and I may not be alone here—that my own efforts are at odds with most reevaluative attempts.

The new focus—wrongly I think—for reconsideration seems to be pornography.† Obviously, there is nothing inherently amiss about discussing pornography seriously and thus filling a gap in literary history; but when the discussion seeks to persuade mature men and women to accept pornography as a safer version of perversion, then it is a dodge. What the chronological and bibliographical progression from sex to obscenity to perversion makes clear is that the impulse for futuristic change already has gone beyond the pornographic stage. For example, pornography can never serve as a comprehensive container because it exists in precisely the kind of inverse and subservient relationship to literature that the perverse imagination seeks to overturn. Even to endow pornography with respectability begs the question, for it presupposes a sexual revolution that is limited to sexuality and a literary revolution that is limited to literature. Above all, the reevaluation of pornography ignores or bypasses three crucial books, each of which appeared in each of the three periods and all of which collectively comprehend the entire span of change.

† At this writing, a book on *Perspectives on Pornography*, edited by Douglas A. Hughes, has just appeared and I have learned of another, Peter Michelson's, *Pornography: A Study of a Genre*, which is scheduled to appear later in 1970.

Herbert Marcuse's *Eros and Civilization* (1955), Norman O. Brown's *Life against Death* (1959) and Wayland Young's *Eros Denied* (1964) are truly re-evaluative in that pornography is treated not as a cause but as a symptom of a wider crisis of repressed sexuality and the assumptions of literary sexuality are examined not apart from, but integral with, the basic assumptions of civilization itself. That all three should more or less independently come to the same centrality of concern is striking enough, but that the coincidence should proceed through the diversity of Marcuse's heavy, germanic philosophy, Brown's fastidious classical orientation, and Young's exuberantly creative and societal style suggests that what is ultimately being reevaluated is nothing less than the entire image of man. After such efforts to invest the present with a pivotal role in history comparable to that of the times of Copernicus or Freud, to contain the turbulent newness in the tired and jaded sieve of pornography is to ask the past to be the present and to denude the now of its future. The strategy of substitution resembles the political game of trying to deal with a radical threat as if it were a familiar liberal challenge. Above all, it demonstrates a failure on the part of the critic to allow his confusion as a contemporary man to invade the sanctity of his traditional craft and to compel that craft to help work out his confusion. To do otherwise is to practice a craft which thrives on the separation of literature from reality and which is unresponsive to the coexistence of sensuousness and courage.

By necessity, then, these prefatory remarks have to bear the burden of indicating what this book is not. It is not another survey of the history of censorship on sexual grounds because that already has been done many times, and often well. Besides, although censorship is certainly not a dead issue, the problem today is not so much suppression as license. I am more concerned with the panderers passing themselves off as artists than with the purists setting themselves up as judges. I also have not set out to catalogue historical erotica. What does appear out of the past is here only to situate the present and the future, the real foci, in a double line of continuity and discontinuity. Then, too, there is no treatment of so-called hard core pornography, not because I consider it vile or beneath literary consideration (some of it, in fact, is well-written), but because again the issues have changed. Pornography as a secretive and peripheral aspect of culture is no longer secretive or peripheral. When D. H. Lawrence character- ized pornography as the dullard's way of degrading sex, he may have been accurately describing the smut of his day. But now although from Lawrence's point of view the degrading of sex may still be involved, writers like Genet, LeRoi Jones, James Baldwin, Nabokov and Philip Roth are clearly not dullards. No, we have to recognize that perversions in literature constitute no minor seamy trickle but a literary mainstream of sexual gothicism that is not limited to any one country or genre. Indeed, I hope that one of the yields of this volume will be to stimulate other studies both in print and in the classroom.

Finally, I reluctantly realized that I could and should not write this book myself. I could not because the range of material and expertise is enormous; and I should not because there is consider- able difference of opinion about the subject, and I am too set in my own views to be fair or comprehensive. So, I decided to edit rather than write this volume; and in that decision I came full circle to where it all began. For perhaps with this design, the give-and-take that hopefully I and my students valued in the classroom would be at least echoed in a book sustained and strained by diversity.

CONTENTS

THE PERVERSE IMAGINATION
Sexuality and Literary Culture

the taste for obscenity is universal and the appetite for reality rare and hard to cultivate.

James Baldwin. *Another Country.*

The only circumstance which popularly excuses the attempt of unpoetic people to write poetry is being in love. In the same way sexual fantasy is now almost the only topic which excites unliterary people to write. . . .

Alex Comfort. *Darwin and the Naked Lady.*

the obscene destroys form. That is why when the . . . form holds in spite of everything, the technical accomplishment is so astounding—and why so few obscene works of art succeed (either as art or obscenity, since—as Freud says of dirty jokes—the art makes the obscenity acceptable).

Bernard Keith Waldrop. *Aesthetic Uses of Obscenity in Literature.*

INTRODUCTION

One of the reasons I suspect we do not live forever or too long is that each generation only has a certain stretch to it. There is evidently just so much jarring change that a generation can absorb without feeling that whatever constitutes its collective identity is being distorted beyond recognition. There is so much in literature and life today that is radically discontinuous and stunningly futuristic that many already have either made peace with death or signed a pact with intransigence. Nor can these withdrawal or intractable symptoms be smugly assigned to a reactionary group alone. Even the most flexible, responsive and adventuresome must confess to being at least bewildered if not beset. And no wonder, for change has become not the exception but the rule; and the span of the strain as well as the strain of the span have been enormous.

In the space of one generation, for example, many writers, including most of the authors in this volume, have moved from a

position that war is justified (World War II) to that it is a necessary evil (Korean War) to that it is more evil than necessary
(Vietnam); and more to the point here, have witnessed a change
from the notion that sex is dirty, to that it is not, to that it is
polymorphous. Accustomed to the historical orientation of resisting the abuses of authority, many now find themselves also
confronting the abuses of freedom.[1] All the while we thought we
were extending the healthy momentum of Havelock Ellis, Freud,
D. H. Lawrence and Henry Miller and paving the way for a less
tortured, more joyous Blakean literature and life; the present generation, for whom much of this effort was made, seems to have
overleaped the New Morality for a New Perversity.[2] Onanism,
homosexuality, sadism, fetishism, sodomy, cannibalism, flagellation, exhibitionism, transvestitism, voyeurism, necrophilia, urolag-
nia, and even that apparently absolute taboo, incest—are no longer
subjects limited to pornography or paltry talents but increasingly
appear in "literature" by significant authors. How far we have
come in so short a time may be rapidly suggested by what has
happened to two earlier sexual prophets, Henry Miller and D. H.
Lawrence.

A few years ago Henry Miller was asked to comment on the
sexual revolution. Miller promptly called it "a new tyranny, a
tyranny of the flesh." [3] In place of the Victorian hush-hush attitude toward sex, there is now, according to Miller, an equally
reprehensible mechanical preoccupation with sex. It is all so
puritanical in its concern for constant sex and so clinical and
joyless in its stress on techniques that it all seems to him a
throwback rather than an advance. Miller concluded that his
avant-garde position had been overrun and that he now seemed
more a part of the Establishment than the New Frontier.[4]

The same overreaching has enveloped D. H. Lawrence, except
that in his case he is not around to see or comment on it.
When the film version of *The Fox* recently appeared, it was
indiscriminately bracketed with a number of others sympa-
thetically exploring homosexuality. But anyone who is familiar
with Lawrence in general and with *The Fox* in particular knows
what a distortion this is. Lawrence's novella, in fact, is an unrelenting and at times even hysterical attack on homosexuality as a

relationship which destroys the principle of opposites built into creation. It thus violates sexual separateness which, to Lawrence, was essential to both sexual potency and psychological and political individuality.[5] But perhaps the most dramatic instance of change is the new attitude toward Freud. No longer the savior or revolutionary, he is increasingly being regarded as a bourgeois heterosexual whose Victorian notions of sexuality need either to be drastically modified or totally discarded.[6]

I

In this new literary climate, there do not seem to be any taboos that are valid anymore, no hiding places for even a private hell. The unconscious no longer lurks in the background like a threatening gnome but brassily occupies the center of the stage in open fact. In the new drama of assault the respectful distance between players and audience is no longer respectful or distant. The new "reality" of directness rejects the illusion of clothes and now appears stark naked, with no referents to the past, to God, to anything, except itself. As the private goes public, the private parts become central to the public spectacle. It is as if the unconscious, having been emptied of its more or less normal sexual frustrations, now only has perversions left as the new, escalated norm. Earlier in history when a Rochester or de Sade shrilly extolled the beauties of buggery and flagellation, there was always the comforting sense that here was pathology at work and further that it was at variance with what society, officially at least, could sanction. But today when a Genet, LeRoi Jones, Roth, or Lenny Bruce speak out, the pathology seems to be collective as well as personal. Today the twisted roots of the perverse imagination seem so entangled in and nourished by the equally gnarled roots of a culture that civilization seems to be on trial as the parent of perversion.

Bizarre new heroes, brothers and sisters of Faulkner's Popeye, dominate the literary scene: Genet's Divine, Patchen's Albion Moonlight, Trocchi's Cain, Reage's "O," Nabokov's Humbert Humbert, Terry Southern's and Mason Hoffenberg's Aunt Livia, Vidal's Myra Breckinridge, Roth's Portnoy, *et al.* Collectively, these sexual gargoyles stake out a new gothicism or contemporary version of de Sade's. The cosmos they inhabit is that of science fiction turned inside out; the focus is the exploration not of outer but of inner space. Settings are merely quick props for the real landscape: the geography and geology of the body. Human anatomy is treated as a structure whose plumbing and electrical wiring are to be surgically ferreted out and examined. Indeed, it is striking how many of the perversions actually occur in anatomical or clinical contexts and how often the presiding genius is no longer the psychiatrist but the gynecologist or the urologist.[7] In *Candy*, the feminine Candide is seduced on the hospital floor of her father's room by her uncle; and later a Dr. Johns, an appropriate name for a gynecologist, examines Candy's clitoris while she straddles the commode in a men's room of a local bar. Myra Breckinridge sets Rusty up for her anal revenge in the nurse's examining room of an acting school. In LeRoi Jones's *The Toilet*, a homosexual is brutally beaten in a latrine and left on the floor with wet toilet paper draped over his face. Portnoy's expertise often centers on his father's constipation and his own diarrhea. Divine's scatology is so obsessively urological that he seems to be trying to find the private parts of his private parts and to discover once and for all the connection between urine and sperm. Moreover, whether the situation involves a solitary descent into the center of the human joint or the ins-and-outs of multiple congresses, the details are rendered with the cool neutrality of a clinician or with the same bloodless and uninvolved voices of NASA officials presenting data. It all seems so reasonable and routine, like passing through a tunnel not of darkness but of light, that at best it recalls the classic horror of Kafka's "The Penal Colony" and at worst the flagrant composure of Nazi scientists conducting sexual experiments. Perhaps, the supreme spokesman for the entire futuristic group is Myra Breckinridge. With the cocksureness of an Amazon armed with a dildo instead of a bow and arrow, and with her perfectly shaped silicone breasts projecting the ultimate in Hollywood plastic packaging, Myra-Myron, transvestite, sets out for the new frontier of mid-century gothicism: to live out in real life every single unfulfilled fantasy she has ever had.

How did all this come about and so rapidly? Surely, a few stages in the process must have been skipped or overleaped, for these new writers and works are neither the heirs of Lawrence and Miller nor the exemplars of Freudian sublimation. Indeed, traditional Freudian concepts no longer seem to be able to contain or comprehend what is happening. The tried and tested notion of culture as sublimated sexuality seems tired and bested; and in the hands of Marcuse and Norman O. Brown it has been turned so upside down and inside out that the history of sexuality now has become the history of culture. Even the catch-all notion of a sexual revolution offers false comfort, for it presupposes a revolution limited to sexuality whereas in reality it embraces all of life, society, and art, and lunges forward into a future that is completely discontinuous with the past. And yet for all its dislocations, the emergence of the perverse imagination in mid-century does provide, no matter how feverishly, a moment of historical clarity. Specifically, by its *guiltless* trafficking with and escalating of the unconscious, the perverse imagination compels a reexamination of the entire concept of repression. Perhaps, the geography of the body may serve as an historical metaphor for considering the shifts from spirituality, to sexuality, to perversion.

II

Man's erect stance positioned him alone between heaven and earth and forced upon his consciousness not only a permanent condition of duality, but also an apparently permanent arrangement of that duality. Once man stood up, he set a top over a bottom and thereby established a mortal priority that gave him no peace until he created post-mortal equivalents in a heaven and hell. Much of what we call religion, culture, and philosophy is precisely the expression of this incontestable superiority of mind over matter. In contrast to the rapidity and simplicity with which man's bestiality was disposed of—the same impatience politically characterized the aristocratic attitude toward the masses—man's intellectuality and spirituality generated an apparently inexhaustible source of complexity and variety. The body seemed to exist only to provide the territory for the mind's

dominance. Except for a few like Chaucer, Montaigne, Rabelais
and Shakespeare, whose genius in fact is measurable by its span-
ning of the lofty and the lowly, the unconscious bottom was assumed to be reducible to a drive—powerful, persistent but basically short-lived and singular. But much of what legitimizes
romanticism's claim as the threshold of the modern world was
the recognition not only of man's essential doubleness, but also
of the involving contribution of the bottom in the life of the
mind and heart.

For the first time in history on a broad scale, the repressed was
granted the troubling separateness of a distinct, if muffled, voice.
Dialogues between the upper and lower depths begin to appear
with gothic and revolutionary compulsiveness in both literature
and politics. Blake juxtaposes the crabbed songs of repression
with the celebratory lyrics of liberation. The proverbs not of
heaven but of hell are given to us, whether we want them or
not, and an irrepressible satanic energy proclaims that "Opposition is friendship." Diderot in his pornographic *Bijoux Indiscrets* strikes a new note of equity by having the genitals speak
what clearly the mouth refuses to acknowledge. Traditional
rebels or villians, Prometheus, Faust, Cain, Judas, the Wandering
Jew, even Lucifer himself, are transformed into heroes or at
least objects of rallying sympathy. As the Victorian world expanded through imperialism and travel, the upper and lower
halves of man found new expression in the polarity of northern
and southern climes, and sustained the kind of geographical
morality one finds in Tennyson, Matthew Arnold, and later D. H.
Lawrence. Above all, the recognition of what Dostoevsky called
man's "satanic depths" reached beyond the confines of literature
to embrace society and history as a whole: "The child is glorified
over the man, the peasant over the courtier, the dark man over
the white, the rude ballad over the polished sonnet, the weeper
over the thinker, colony over mother country, the commoner
over the king—nature over culture." [8] Finally, the three great intellectual giants of the last century, each in his own independent
way, clinched the centrality of the underground. Darwin exposed the evolutionary underside of man; Marx probed deeply

into the primitive origins of the family and the state; and Freud documented the personalized repository of the *id*.

To be sure, dispatching all of recorded history in two paragraphs may set a record for monumental oversimplification, but I have set it up quickly and starkly in order to wreck its predictability. The customary way we have categorized all that has happened since Freud is as confirmation. New priorities were quickly assimilated into a reinforced concept of sublimation; and until recently, the processing worked. Thus, it is not difficult to find in the above list of romantic preferences modern echoes, and to update and to extend the list by including such Victorian and modern emphases as the city over the country, women over men, men over machines, the artist over the bourgeois, the individual K. over the state, the internationalism of the Wandering Jew and Odysseus over the national isolationism of Babbit, etc. But suddenly—and here is where the processing broke down—there was no way to predict or to absorb a contemporary situation which perversely put forth not a new face but a nude body.

It is one thing to contemplate the prospect of the child over the adult. That presents a challenge, a not unaccommodating or unnegotiable situation. But it is quite another matter to confront the child *as* adult. That represents a threat, a quite uncompromising situation. A literary parallel may be instructive here. The difference between *Ulysses* and *Finnegans Wake* is the difference between a work which alternately is traditional and experimental but which remains developmental; and a work which anarchistically rejects dualistical straddling or ambiguity as a final position. Perversely, Joyce unleashed a mythological fecundity and protean stylistics that shattered form. Similarly, the earlier prophets of sexuality, Lawrence and Miller, sought through sexual exercises an equality with traditional spiritual exercises and in the process canonized their own saints of sexuality as not inferior to the saints of spirituality. But the perverse imagination, like the protean imagination of *Finnegans Wake*, refused to play the dialectic game of choosing the body over the soul or the soul over the body. Instead, it shattered good form by proclaiming that the body is the soul. Moreover, it went on to reject all charges of abnormality and reductiveness, and to maintain instead that it was the victim of gross historical and psychological distortions which, when understood, would make its extremes eminently normal and even sane.

What distortions? Historically, there were at least three. First, it becomes clear now that even when the suppressed voice was allowed to speak, it was expressed in the language of consciousness. For all its acceptance of the underground, the mind retained its grip on the body and in a sense kept it in its place by speaking for it. The problem persists to this day. When writers like Herbert Gold and critics like Charles Glicksberg and Steven Marcus [9] object to the repetitive and boring depiction of sexuality, they are, once again, identifying the life of the mind with the life of literature and clearly signifying that both are infinitely superior to the wearisome predictability of the body. In other words, sex might be granted importance, even fullness, but never depth or surprise. The problem then is essentially epistemological: the mind is brightened, even electrified, by tension whereas the body moves toward the darkness of its pacification. In addition, consciousness tends to value only a hidden complexity, for it is a probing instrument. But there also can be an outer complexity in which surface is substance. The situation is not unlike that described by Conrad's favorite narrator, Marlow, who at the outset of the *Heart of Darkness* rightly lamented the tendency of many readers to be so anxious to come to the fruit that they ignored the fascinating configurations of the shell. If to the perverse imagination, the shell is the fruit, and if the body's way of knowing is through act not analysis—then can consciousness possibly do justice to that which is its antithesis? The point here is not that consciousness should be contracted to make room for the body—that would be playing the meaningless game of circular extremism—but that its achievements should come not in spite of but because of the body. For example, although William Phillips is right to chastize George P. Elliott and George Steiner for straying beyond literary bounds in their discussions of pornography, Phillips fails to recognize that Elliott and Steiner are being carried against their will by a stream of sexuality that cannot be contained by the dams of consciousness and genital sexuality.[10] In short, the problem of "sex-in-the-head" that Lawrence posed is still very much with us. The most recent example is Gustav Eckstein's new book, *The Body Has a Head.* From the point of view of the perverse imagination, the title should be turned around to remind man that the head has a body.

The second distortion proceeds from the first. The self-conscious imagination never granted equal time and space to its perverse counterpart. Specifically, it never granted to the repressed world the density and complexity associated with matters above ground. The unlived life and unspoken voice were regarded, sadly, as part of the silent sacrifices required of life, society, and success; and shouldering that tragic denial had to be sufficient satisfaction for the repressions seething below. But with the gradual escalation of those suppressions, what suddenly became apparent was that the unlived life was in fact liveable, and no one was struck down by lightning. Even more heady was the gradual emergence of an almost infinite series of unlived lives and unspoken voices. In other words, there is the strong suspicion that the real reason suppression was imposed in the first place was that the complex consciousness feared it might be overwhelmed by the incredible and threatening richness of its own lurking promiscuity. It is with this fear of competition or retaliation that we come upon the most serious distortion of all.

The Freudian concept of repression, for all its gestures to unconscious complexity, rests on the absolute assumption that such suppression is as inevitable as it is benevolent. Thus, ironically, the power granted to multiplicity is impotence. Whatever integrity it enjoyed could only be stillborn; or if it sought to emerge it could do so only in the acceptable disguise of sublimation or as gnarled pathology. But the perverse imagination which shamelessly inhabits and embodies without dilution the underground world *above ground* rejects the principle of singular repression. Instead, it conceives of suppressed sexuality as a series of suppressions: of erotic experimentation leading to promiscuity; or bawdy impulses tyrannically converting all experiences into voluptuous ones; of sadistic sexuality bordering on violence and masturbation; and of sexual perversions ultimately leading to and celebrating incest.[11]

As Eric Bentley rightly noted, "a period which can reasonably be seen as a decadence in relation to what is ending can often be seen quite differently in relation to what is beginning." [12] It is only by questioning reason's dominance over the passions that one can understand why the conventional dialogue between order and chaos is frustrated by the unaccommodating voice of anarchy which rejects both order and chaos as long as they remain alternatives rather than versions of each other. It is only through the historical process of escalated suppression that we come to understand why Portnoy quite rightly cries out that he has not a hidden but a wide-open, explicit Oedipus complex. It is only by acknowledging the pluralistic world of suppression that we can measure the distance between Diderot's challenging acceptance of man's essential doubleness and Gore Vidal's threatening notion of man's essential bisexuality. Indeed, Vidal's notion, though artistically botched, neatly stakes out the range of the change. Bisexuality is essentially a horizontal leveling of traditional vertical hierarchies. What follows is not a playful competition with but a rejection of marriage itself. Bisexuality also normalizes homosexuality, and reaches for futuristic self-reproduction. The children of oneself will be all the unlived fantasies. Finally, it is this reformulated world of suppressions that indicates—and here we come back to literature—why almost all previous and most recent discussions of pornography and obscenity are for the most part useless.

III

The standard critical attitude toward pornography is one of welcomed disdain, for it offers the opportunity to contrast such formalistically and morally loose works with the loftier concerns and structures of serious literature. What I am questioning here is not the condemnation—much pornography is dreadful—but that it was made for the wrong not the right reasons. It already has been noted the extent to which consciousness demanded of the body a kind of linguistic variety and philosophical complexity it could never satisfy in such intellectual terms. Similarly, the misguided attempt to protect "literature" from pornographic contamination, pretty much as those who favor censorship invoke the image of the pure child, has resulted in a liberal breakthrough that ironically lost as much as it gained.

The critics' campaign to separate pornography from literature achieved success and official recognition when the Supreme Court essentially granted what the critics wanted—a literary yardstick of socially redeeming value. But as Joyce and Lawrence were enjoying a respectability which perhaps made them less dangerous, the same criterion created a loophole which "I Am Curious (Yellow)" exploited with perfect cynicism. But even more defeating, the Supreme Court in effect judged sex to be guilty unless a counterbalancing sanction of marriage, society or literature proved it to be innocent or harmless (perhaps the most backhanded compliment to society and culture imaginable). By failing to conceive of sexuality as having a socially redeeming value in its own right, the critical and juridical attitude actually imparted to the pornography of *guilty* sexuality a longer lease on life. Moreover, that sin of complicity was accompanied by an equally serious one of opacity. The refusal of critics to grant pornography at least the status of a sub-literature precluded their awareness of what the pornographic impulse could be in the hands of serious artists.

Most contemporary works of perversion contain many of the standard devices of pornography. Thus, the *Story of O* features all the whips, branding tools, corsets and dungeons associated with sadistic pornography. The difference is that what was secretly guilty in pornography is arrogantly normalized in perversion. Moreover, perverse works attempt what all literature does—to transform the personal pathology of pornography into the collective pathology of art. Specifically, the radical message of the *Story of O* resides in its fusion of the Victorian taboo on sex with the modern taboo on death to create the sensuality of death. Our shock or revulsion to such sadistic nihilism is not wrong or even excessive, but when it is predicated on the demotion of the *Story of O* to a level beneath contempt and literature, then the price we pay for our moral and literary indignation is a blindness to the real nature of the shock—a kinship between cruelty and sexuality that is of a piece with the partnership between pornography and literature. The same obtuseness toward another pornographic impulse has made the critic unresponsive to another kind of perverse literature which is part and parcel of a modern literary mainstream.

Pornography exists in a timeless world of "dream and impossibility where penises never grow tired, vaginas are always ready, cruelty never runs up against obstacles and meekness constantly finds its painful reward." [13] Adolescent? Self-indulgent? True, and those epithets perjoratively pushed rightly characterize the kind of pornography which served as a contrast to the Victorian novel. But critics like Steven Marcus speak of pornography in this century as still performing the same function of making literature look good, as if the sameness of the pornography assures the sameness of the literature. But such a static view ignores the unique fact that a number of significant authors like Henry Miller, Durrell, Genet, Donleavy and Nabokov were published —sometimes first published—by pornographic presses. Moreover, their ascent from ignominy to acceptance is not aberrational but central to the modern literary revival of the picaresque mode. In fact, the picaresque mode could be better termed the pornographic impulse, for aside from more accurately mirroring the modern surface of meandering fluidity, the latter term has the additional advantages of easily converting the rogue on the move to one on the make, and of reflecting the alteration of the hero from one who is steadfast, responsible and scrupulous to one who is an outcast surviving by his wit and cunning. Clearly, the gain of liberalism involved a subversive loss: the critic who severed the branch of pornography from the trunk of literature may not have been aware that he was cutting himself off as well.

IV

I have sought to clear the field of confusing, distortive or questionable obstacles before any meaningful discussion and definition of the perverse imagination is possible. Although we are closer to the goal, the negative clarifying spirit must still be operative, for there are false and true versions of the perverse imagination. Specifically, there are three worrisome entanglements: the first has to do with propaganda; the second with amateurism; and the third with commercialism. So that there is no misunderstanding, my own stand as well as the commitment of this entire volume is that art is infallible. I grant that the problem of artistic form inevitably involves the issue of morality, but I am not concerned with immorality or pathology or even the normalizing of both if either exists apart from the artistry. Frankly I do not feel involved in what the psychiatrists will have to do about revamping Freud or with how the sociologists will respond to the threats to family and marriage, although I recognize that what is going on in art clearly runs through all areas like the geological fault in our civilization. But as a literary critic, it is my job to worry about art, past, present, and future; good, mediocre, and shoddy. And I find there is much to worry about.

The first thing that bothers me is that the sexually liberated and polymorphous are often tyrants of freedom or contemporary versions of Dickens' bullies of humility. They relentlessly harangue us for our hang-ups and bombard us with sex programs or encounter groups. Now sex programs or encounter groups do not bother me but art pressed into the service of propaganda does.[14] So that I do not appear as an aristocratic aesthete inviting either Tolstoy's irreverence or assaults by the new sexual Red Guard, I wish to make it clear that I am not defending the purity but the complexity of art. To the good artist, a man is a man before he is ever a symbol, and existence a flowing puzzle before it is ever a static construct. Total comprehension was never a legitimate aim of art; a character or vision is always in excess or in advance of even the most sensitive formulations. People and reality are complicated in a deep, contradictory way and to force a one-sided sexual happiness on either or both only unleashes the very contraries propagandists are blind to. It provokes the eternal spite of Dostoevsky's underground man who takes perverse pleasure in his diseased liver and even greater pleasure in throwing his pain and decay in the serene faces of the men of the Crystal Palace. All good art is sociology but even the best of sociology is not art.

When D. H. Lawrence made Lord Chatterley impotent as a

result of a war injury and then mercilessly ridiculed him for not making love to his wife, Lawrence was forcing meaning to give way to message. A more flagrant compromising of artistic principles occurs regularly in the works of the sexual utopian Robert Rimmer, whose *The Harrad Experiment* (1965) and *Proposition 31* (1968) read like medieval morality tracts pontificating a new sexual theology. The propagandistic compulsion often compels a reasonably interesting poet to surrender his complex understanding for simplistic romanticism. Thus, Lawrence Lipton's advocacy of the beats leads him to this bit of nonsense: "The violence of the delinquent is usually directed against older people. The beatnik would not commit such acts of violence. He would write a poem about it." [15] Occasionally, the evangelical impulse may arrest creation and result in a work that is stillborn. Such is the case with Norman O. Brown's *Love's Body* which, unlike his earlier and excellent *Life against Death*, is not really a completed work but the working notes for one that evidently will not be written. Then, of course, there are the many efforts of LeRoi Jones and other bitterly disillusioned blacks who conceive of audiences as dart boards or projection screens on which they can hurl artistic abuse and sometimes excrement in some non-cathartic orgy.

Such writers are half-artists and half-programmers. The artist-programmer is, in such instances, a sociological pornographer: both proceed from a preconceived fantasy of what would make them or others happy. Art is treated as a prostitute who does whatever she is told to do. She has no integrity, no contribution of her own to make; she is there just to take orders. But art is no passive slut; she may begin as an invisible or insubstantial partner, but as the artist has an affair with her, she becomes a visible and tangible force resisting his laziness and tasking the fullness and honesty of his vision. Art thus operates on the same principle as reality and good education do: it is not always good for the artist to have his own way. Above all, when the desire for social change masters the impulse toward art, that is a basis for suspecting even the quality of the social aim.

A more formidable prospect than propagandistic art is a new

aesthetics of transience and amateurism. Interwoven in much of contemporary perverse literature and drama is the notion that art should be made spontaneously, of the materials and events of the moment, and then wither away like yesterday's news-papers.[16] Art should actively conspire in its own dissolution, for the perfecting of form and the polishing of style are considered self-aggrandizing or identity-ridden. To strive for permanence is a wilful obstruction to the need for constant renewal; to insist on a diamond finish for what finds its fulfillment in the moment and then dies, is narcissistic preciousness. Traditional art is con-ceived of as Establishment monument-building, a way of guar-anteeing the solidity of its future empire. Clearly, this new aes-thetics of ephemera is actually a sexual aesthetics for it takes its inspiration from what it celebrates, sex and group sex. A sexual relation, so the argument goes, must not be made once and for all time, but must constantly be remade. Similarly, art should not be put together unnaturally of lasting materials but should be made of and by flesh which never claimed immortality for itself. More-over, because this new aesthetics eulogizes the group or the tribe and regards the present as the time of infinity, the traditional em-phasis on the solitary artist seeking immortality is replaced by the emphasis on the tribal ritual of the moment, the collective happening, seeking cosmic oblivion. A spontaneous group per-formance rejects the coordinates of time and space. There is no past, and no future; all time is present. There are no beginnings or endings, only broken circles which need to be made whole. Any place is all places through the tactile immediacy of collective brotherhood.

Unlike the propagandistic impulse which, except for the cur-rent ideology, is not new, this aesthetics represents a radical departure from traditional aesthetics. When Jack Richardson con-fesses that he lacks the critical vocabulary to discuss a per-formance of the Living Theater [17] or when Robert Brustein laments a tendency towards amateurism in the same performing group,[18] both indirectly are confirming the encirclement of tra-ditional singular consciousness by tribal proletarianism. More-over, although there is much that is accurate and vibrant in this new pagan assault on civilized professionalism and expertise, once again what also seems to be involved is not just a misunderstanding of the nature of art, but even more seriously a betrayal of it.

One obvious danger is that the inept may pass off his lack of talent as intentional imperfection and the genuinely talented may not realize all that he is capable of if he stops short of what a finished art can extract from that talent. Then, too, I am not completely convinced that the materials one works with have no bearing on the results. If an artist works with junk or garbage, his work may turn out to just that. But the most serious misunderstanding is the failure to recognize that it is the fitting together, not the materials, which lasts. If parts are capriciously or loosely put together, the sequence of enduring order is jeopardized, for they can just as easily be jumbled out of sequence and made to appear arbitrary rather than inevitable. Form itself is the only real antidote to egotism and vain-glory. The keystone of an arch gathers to itself and returns the strength of the supports so that it is both sustained and sustaining. Similarly, the artist creates and is created by his work. The pressure of form is like wrestling with the angel of death to see if, like Jacob, the artist can extract before the dawn a promise of permanence. To throw off the problem of form is comparable to casting away all things that are fearful of death and thus divesting the wrestling game of its value and terror. Perhaps, there is a need to challenge the cult of the singular or transcendent artist, or more accurately the critics' support of that cult. But to go to the other extreme of uncritically embracing group anonymity or amateurism and to regard everything as beautiful because it is all-together, is to be singularly blind to the group's function as a body of ordered eccentricity. It is to make liberation and competence mutually exclusive. To return to Nature is to return to a cruel mistress; the noble savage was quite often not noble and quite often savage.

Finally, there is the matter of commercialized pornography and perversion. Commercialism is manipulation for profit; the means are forced to serve an end. Because the commercial strategy can never break free of its own pattern of acquisition, it invariably has only one story to tell: a success story. Indeed, all commercialized pornography and perversion transform the drive for success into a drive for sex; what makes Sammy run becomes easily what makes Sammy swing. The cynical notion that everybody has a price tag becomes in the hands of the arch-manipulator, Julius, in Iris Murdock's new *A Fairly Honorable Defeat*, sexual satanism: " 'There is no relationship . . . that cannot be broken. . . .' " Happily, however, for the first time we have a substantial body of serious pornography and perverse literature to help separate the true from the commercial, and thus to provide a basis for defining the perverse imagination.

V

The genuine perverse work of art resists facile tagging because its own rejection of manipulation makes it harder to handle. Thus, its totality is never summed up by four-letter words or sexual gymnastics, the favorite short-cuts of commercialism. Works like *Candy* and *The Valley of the Dolls* are gross and vulgar not because they deal with sexuality or even perversions but because they are cheats—they pass off gilt for gold, technique for emotion. To treat a man or a woman solely as a series of anal, oral and genital orifices which are to be filled, exhausted, emptied or violated is to practice the true pornographer's reduction: to cut the parts off from the whole. But art is not content with a piece of a piece; the hole is not the whole. Perhaps the distinctions will be clearer by briefly comparing *Candy* and *Portnoy's Complaint*.

Both works feature sexual perversions but there the similarities end. The authors of *Candy* are always superior to and safely insulated from what they present by wearing the mantle of parody. Their uninvolvement grants them such manipulative power that one can often hear the typewriter clicking and the chatter of collaboration in the background. But Roth is never aloof or very far removed from Portnoy; in fact, Portnoy regularly threatens and endangers Roth. The four-letter words are not put there opportunistically with one ear cocked for the reader's shock-waves or the ring of the cash register; they are born organically of Portnoy's enormous rage and his determined ferocity to tell the truth, the brutal, dirty truth about himself, without mincing words. Next to Roth, Southern and Hoffenberg seem like two tittering schoolboys playing with the idea of anality and incest and ignorant of the fact that the two are variations of each other. The energy that propels Portnoy along is the hidden and entangled momentum of his own reduction of sex to mutual masturbation. In *Candy* there is no similarly genuine integrity and motivation granted the cast of puppets who jerk and copulate at the whims of its authors. Portnoy thrashes and agonizes over his entire life and seeks in vain to find an answer to a question that is both personal and generational: "How was I so fitted for success and so unfitted for existence?" In *Candy* there are no questions asked or issues raised; we do not have even the consoling complexity of Voltaire's irreverent philosophizing. Above all, *Candy* rests on the assumption that its readers are as sexually starved, preoccupied or bored throughout their *entire* lives as the authors are throughout the *entire* book. But even D. H. Lawrence noted that the birds and bees do not fornicate incessantly. I do not think about sex all the time; the only time I seemed to was when I was an adolescent. If that is the kind of literature that *Candy* is, then it ought to be called that, or by that good old-fashioned scholarly term, *juvenilium*. And conversely, *Portnoy's Complaint* should be described as the mature artistic portrait of an adult chained to his adolescence.

The genuine perverse artist does not provide his readers with instant satisfaction because he knows that to excite a reader thusly binds that reader to the work only for the subsequent excitements it can provide. The good artist places aberration off center but never out of reach. In fact, the characteristic structure progresses from the safety of normalcy to the danger of perversion. In contrast, the phony perverse writer is sloppy and in a hurry. He immediately offers gratification. His work tends to be episodic because his transistions are not really thematic binders but excitement extenders. He promises and sometimes delivers a steady escalation of sensations that are as single-minded and apparently insatiable as those of a population devoted to endless consumption. Often, he gets stuck and must whip himself forward. As a result, every *ersatz* work, regardless of what special dish it is serving up, inevitably involves flagellation. Its charac-

teristic structure is that of a horizontal spiral—a boring, pene-
trating screw that neither goes anywhere nor holds anything
together. Above all, the *ersatz* perverse writer promises to preserve the very schizophrenia or double-level thinking that the
genuine artist seeks to expose or destroy. The lazy and opportunistic artist seeks always to reassure his reader by saying in
effect, "Look, there are all kinds of people—you, of course, are
not one of them—who lead weird sex lives. In fact, you will see
how much healthier you are when you read what is going on in
the valley of the dolls or the East Village, etc." But the genuine
perverse imagination treats aberration as a way of coming to a
new norm. He resists writing a case history; for to do so would
reduce his work to that of a monograph on sexual deviation
and safely insulate the reader. He seeks precisely to make continuous what the inept writer characteristically presents as discontinuous. The strategies the genuine artist may employ may
be infinite, but they always seek to break down the wall that
separates the normal from the wild, the familiar world from that
of dreams. But whatever technique is employed to outflank the
resistance to continuity, the artistic test is whether the work can
contain the strain of such inclusiveness.

The aesthetic stretch of the perverse imagination mirrors its
ideological reach. The perverse imagination courts the danger of
total freedom and, bizarre though it may seem, cherishes the
possibilities of idealism. For Kafka, as it was for Dostoevsky before him, the ideal is justice; but as Ivan Karamazov insists, not
postponed to some vague future or after-life, but here and now.
For the perverse imagination, the ideal is sexual justice. The
typical perverse hero is determined not to leave this world unsatisfied. The very rationale of his existence is: I am yet-to-be-
satisfied; therefore, I exist. To be sure, Myra Breckinridge, because of what she desires, seems "hell-bent for heaven" [19]; but
the ideal is to have heaven here and now, if for no other reason
that there is no heaven anywhere else.

The desire to have all is the desire to be all—to be more than
one identity and one sex—to have more than one partner, job,
country—perhaps, ultimately to have more than one life. According to Vidal, once man "has ceased to be confined to a single

sexual role, to a single person" he can become "free to blend with others, to exchange personalities with both men and women, to play out the most elaborate of dreams in a world where there will be no limit to the spirit's play." Traditionally, such dreams have been dubbed infantile or purist and been treated to a healthy dose of discipline and toilet training. But far from disclaiming infantilism, the perverse imagination cherishes it and regards it as the only true avenue to man's original nature. Typically, infantile cravings, if they ever achieved satisfaction, had to do so through a screen of sublimation and thus had to settle not only for less, but also for what was less pure. But both Freud and the perverse imagination are faithful to man's tyrannical origins: Freud notes that the reason money does not bring happiness is that it is not an infantile wish; the perverse imagination maintains that the reason genital sexuality does not bring satisfaction is that it is a reduction of infantile sexuality. In works of perversion, such original desires are not deflected but emerge with such shocking directness that perhaps for the first time the child's erotic dreams of perfection are emerging in untampered form through adult acts. In other words, the continuity between childhood and adulthood is of a piece with the disconcerting partnership between purity and perversity. Moreover, the almost fanatical fidelity to this Eden of satisfaction is presented with the kind of uncompromising fervor associated with children or saints. The result is a religion of innocence in which children do not so much grow up as grow bigger. What differences appear among perverse works have nothing to do with the idealistic quest which unites them all but with how the ideal is to be realized. I find that the means as well as the literary modes selected tend to fall into two main, although unequal, groups which I have called the hard and the soft.

VI

Plato in the *Symposium* uncharitably describes Orpheus as a harp-playing sissy who was punished by the gods for his "softness" (179D). The full classical polarity emerges in Shakespeare's *Venus and Adonis*. Adonis reveals that the hard hunt is the hunt after the boar; that requires courage, strength and endurance. The soft hunt is the hunt after the rabbit or Venus; that more appropriately takes place in the boudoir than the forest. Heroes are hard and vertical; Casanovas are soft and horizontal. Aesthetic dimensions subsequently enrich the concepts. Thus, Schiller, according to Marcuse, identifies the soft with the sensuous principle and the hard with the "form-impulse": "The former is essentially passive, receptive, the latter, mastering, domineering." [20] Inevitably in this century the duality entered the cultural arena: Alex Comfort associates the hard-center with the scientific and technological and the soft with the artistic and the humanistic.[21] Schmalhausen centers the effort to harmonize the two around sexuality and points to the rather pathetic attempts "to believe at one and the same time in the science and poetry of sex." [22] Finally, in contemporary works of perversion, the hard hunt worships the discipline of control; the soft the discipline of surrender.

The hard form of perversion seeks total gratification in the most direct and vengeful way. The *Story of O* is sustained by the spirit of the Marquis de Sade. The male characters are aggressive, demanding, merciless and god-like; the women dependent, submissive, unprotesting and devoted. The relationship between the two rests on a common bond of humiliation: the desire on the part of the men to dominate and to degrade; the desire on the part of the women to be made into objects of disdain, unworthy sewers of sexuality. Although this concept of men and women is a medieval throw-back, it is justified by the fact that whereas the men cherish the highest ideals of friendship and never betray any homosexual taint, the women are bitchy toward each other and engage in lesbian asides. The enormous energy and planning devoted to creating this separate sadistic organization replete with the most modern conditioning and behavioral techniques are offered as further proof of its broad-based appeal and exoneration.

The desire for total gratification in this hard world takes the form of bending another completely to one's wilful desires. This is essentially the gothic impulse, for as Kenneth Clark's classic study of *The Nude* suggests, the gothic nude unlike that of the

Greek is governed by the total subjugation of all separate parts of the body to the tyranny of the oval.[23] By calling her leading character "O," the anonymous author of that work graphically indicated that the aim was to transform a woman into a series of totally obedient and permanently accessible apertures. The variety as well as the complex uses to which they would be put were in turn dictated by the multiple repressions that needed to be satisfied. But unlike Sade, who often frustrated sex-hungry readers by his long metaphysical digressions and relentless caricature of God as the supreme sadist, the modern heirs are obsessed with religion. To be sure, it is an agony-oriented, distortive religion, but that is precisely the point. O's desires for humiliation are glorified into sexual martyrdom. Her wayward lust needs to be chastized, not by abstinence but by abuse; her sexual orifices are either spited or violated because redemption comes from confirming O as a biblical cesspool. At the end of the novel, her desire to be humiliated gives way to the more basic desire to die. But once again the religious dimension is supportive, for by asking permission of her god-like master to kill herself, O finds her final guiltless exoneration in the modern notion of crucifixion: the permissiveness of suicide.

The essential assumptions of hard perversion are disturbingly clear. The basic one is that the relations between men and women are governed not by love but by power. Children do not have to be taught to take; they have to be taught to share. But according to de Sade to share pleasure is to weaken it; there is never enough available for the insatiable man to do otherwise. The compulsion towards mastery is thus sanctioned by a law of scarcity which mortality imposes. Moreover, what has added fuel to the drive for sexual power is that the traditional outlets of mastery—nature, science, business—no longer require man's hardness or Hemingway's stoicism. The hard machines man has created have made his own aggressiveness obsolescent, except that he has turned that technology exclusively to the private sector. Hard perversion thus has much in common with the genre of the spy story. The scientifically buttressed secret agent is a more powerful figure in bed precisely because his technology supports his sexuality.[24]

The desire for total power is in the final analysis a desire always to be a user of others and never to be used in return. Gore Vidal maintains that during sex each partner, absorbed in his own fantasy, secretly believes he is achieving mastery over the other. The example given is that of a sailor having oral relations with a homosexual. At the moment when the sailor concludes that he is the master of the situation and humiliating the mouth of his partner, the homosexual believes that by extracting from the sailor his power and posterity he is achieving victory over both the sailor and women in general. As Paul Goodman rightly notes, "It is not that the queer boy is not attracted to the girl, but that he begrudges giving her anything." [25] The determination to be a user is backed up by the stronger determination not to be used, just as conversely the desire to be humiliated ultimately becomes the desire to be finally used up—to die. Similarly, the sexual monks of the *Story of O* either spill their seed on the ground or give it in ways or areas that preclude its being used for pleasure or reproduction. Myra Breckinridge, although surgically no longer a man but a woman, never allows her vagina to be used. With her dildo she takes anal revenge on Rusty by proclaiming " 'Now you will find out what it is the girl feels when you play with her.' " The only other sexual encounter she has is when someone takes her from behind.

That the hard impulse should take both a heterosexual form in the *Story of O* and a homosexual form in *Myra Breckinridge* should not be any more surprising than that the creation of the hard machine should simultaneously encourage the continuation of the hard hero and the counter-creation of the soft. It is the same power play, or, as Millet has called it, sexual politics, that makes strange bedfellows of the *Story of O, Myra Breckinridge, Who's Afraid of Virginia Woolf?* and *Cities of Night.* Indeed, what binds all these works together is the common obsession not to make children. The way to be a user and never to be used up is to avoid at all costs the creation of the maximum user, the child. The child as adult is thus able to avoid rivalry and to maintain his narcissistic centrality, just as the hard homosexual's final begrudging triumph over women is to withhold from them their separatist victory of reproduction. The ultimate subversion of hard perversion is not solely the rejection of marriage as contractual servitude, but its replacement by the notion of man or woman (or transvestite) as a self-serving, self-perpetuating self-creation. Whatever paternal or maternal instincts remain are jealously reserved for the permanent taker who moves toward Rochester's wish to be the father of oneself:

> Oh, that I now cou'd by some Chymic Art
> To sperm convert my Vitals and Heart,
> That at one Thrust I might my Soul translate,
> And in the Womb myself regenerate:
> There steep'd in Lust, nine months I would remain
> Then boldly fuck my passage out again.[26]

If the hard form of perversion represents gothicism recast, the soft form represents sentimental fiction revisited. Hard perversion is aggressive and gritty. It is metaphysical because it is vertical, with the difference that because the bottom is on top Satan is God. It is allied to sadistic spy stories because that new world aligns the old vertical theology of power and evil with that of modern bureaucracy and is sufficiently monstrous by virtue of its scientific horrors to accommodate the traditional terrors of gothicism. But the soft form is fluid and horizontal. It takes its inspiration from Gide and Joyce and above all Kafka who essentially redefined original sin as not something one does but that is done to one. Its favorite mood is the passive voice. Stylistically and structurally, it is a flattened world of inundation, of form so rounded and softened as to be without sharp shape. Its prose yearns secretly for its final embodiment as poetry. In fact, in the works of J. P. Donleavy, the hero's movement from cold to warmth is pitched to the prose's being distilled into islands of poetry. The same blurring of the hard world of prose sustains the endlessly reassuring fantasies of Genet. An umbrella of masturbation encloses the soft hero in the womb of self-sufficiency, for the masturbator is all things to himself—both sensation giver and sensation receiver. As Portnoy, taking himself in hand, reminds us, no one can do it as well as one does it to oneself. To be sure, In Genet masturbation is worked up finally to a religious aesthetic.[27] The rhythm of building excitement, crescendo and final sense of flat and endless peace eases Genet's ascension up the cross of the penis to a heaven which is as blissfully absorptive as it is artistically resolved. Unlike the hard form which is joyously hellish, the soft is obliviously paradisical. The assumption of hard perversion is man's original sin; its inevitable legacy is a quest for power. The assumption of soft perversion is man's original goodness; its inevitable legacy is a quest for peace. In films, the hard heroes like James Cagney and Humphrey Bogart fight their way out of Hell's kitchen or from the wrong side of the tracks. The new soft heroes come from the new aristocracy, the affluent middle class, or from a romanticized peasantry; they include "the epicene O'Toole, the distracted Mastroianni, . . . the cheerfully incompetent Belmondo,"[28] the graduates, midnight cowboys and easy riders. The literary list would have to include the softies of Salinger, Joseph Heller, Tennessee Williams, J. P. Donleavy, William Burroughs, John Rechy and lately Philip Roth. The favorite causes of soft perversion are those sustained by indignant identification: what has been done to one has been done in turn to children, homosexuals, Indians, Blacks, Eugene McCarthy (the epitome of the soft politician), Ché Guevara, Black Panthers, and of course now the world of nature. Soft perversion is thus not unlike sentimental fiction in that it embraces the role of the victim and extols the power of passivity. To be sure, it makes a virtue of promiscuity rather than of virtue, but all that means is that the moral has been redefined as the natural, and that the belief in ultimate justice is futuristic rather than otherworldly. Indeed, lest one wrongly conclude that the fantasies of soft perversion are without substance or that its self-indulgence is occasional, one need only recognize the existence already of a substantial counter-culture and, I would suggest, of an equally significant counter-literature.

The perverse imagination is a nexus for accommodating a number of directions of contemporary fiction. We already have noted the extent to which hard perversion embraces under the aegis of gothicism, sadistic heterosexuality and homosexuality, and the genre of the spy story. The soft form is equally comprehensive. Steven Marcus rightly merged utopianism with pornography to suggest a new genre, pornotopia. Taylor Stoehr took him to task for many things, not the least of which was the failure to include science fiction.[29] But the perverse imagination makes them allies not enemies. Specifically, soft perversion is the sexual version of science fiction and utopian impulses. All three genres are sustained by a common image of an hospitable world, by a belief in man's essential goodness, and by the sanction that every impulse that comes from the body is good and natural. To be sure, the goals seem to be different: the perverse imagination seeks personal or group satisfaction; the utopian, collective or world gratification. But the value of the perverse imagination resides precisely in its insistence that such collective quests have failed in the past because the personal has been set at odds with the societal; and further that unless the truth of personal promiscuity be not only admitted, but also incorporated into the utopian plan then it is doomed to the same rich public facade and empty private core that it has set out to replace. Thus, for all its softness, the perverse imagination may have a firmer grip on the real and the ideal (or rather the ideal as the real) than its utopian counterparts, and clearly offers in place of tentative speculation a more uncompromising immediacy. Thus, the characteristic strategy of utopian science fiction is to "invent" and project an ideal race on another planet or in a distant future. But the same reactions of astonishment and disbelief accorded such projected creations appear now in the reactions to perverse literature. Mankind I is not comfortably confronting Martian I but Mankind II.

VII

To sum up, what then is the perverse imagination? It is an artistic temperament engaged in its own dissolution as an artistic temperament. It puts forth a literature which ultimately seeks to go beyond literature. At its best, it rejects propagandistic simplicity, amateuristic capriciousness and commercial manipulation because it recognizes that such self-seeking or coercive ends compromise the need to translate art into culture, utopian fiction into utopian fact. Uncompromisingly idealistic, the ultimate stage, as Paul Goodman suggests, is a new creation story:

> Then be the practical scientist and alter the intolerable to the possible . . . this is the scientific truth. The artistic truth is still larger—the imitation of Paradise. Truth is to make beauty possible.

In other words, what the perverse imagination treasures is what the artist always has stood for with this difference: that what was traditionally an individual achievement becomes a collective possibility. It is thus not accidental in this connection that certain perverse writers, like Pauline Reage and more recently Jean de Berg (*The Image*), use pseudonyms; or where the authors are known, as in *Oh! Calcutta!*, what they have contributed is not. In other words, in seeking to go beyond literature to culture, the perverse imagination favors the kind of anonymity characteristic of pornography or of material stitched together in Homeric fashion at the beginning of recorded history. There is thus about much perverse literature a curious and disarming fusion of the old and the new, the pagan and the sophisticated. It appears to be moving in two directions simultaneously, as if it is a futuristic throwback. Its paradoxical chronology of progressive regression grants it a circular shape in which ends are buried in origins as the child once again becomes the father of the man. What all this signifies is a point in history where man seems embarked on a totally new evolutionary cycle. This second Copernican revolution seems to be undoing the first, for man in mastering the world has forced it to grant back his centrality:

> radical thought must focus on the first and last things, on the alpha and omega. It must push the critical question as far back and as far forward as it will go until both movements meet. In short, radical thought understands the archetypal statement: in the end is the beginning.[30]

And what are the ingredients of this new image? According to the perverse imagination, a central desire is to remain undefined and unfinished. The perverse imagination opposes the finality of the tragic mode by refusing to bring its own art to a definite close; its only end is the rejection of ends. It is constitutionally and artistically opposed to offering the reconciliation of resolution or to terminate its love affair with unlived possibilities and fantasies. As Saul Bellow in *Mr. Sammler's Planet* notes, such

> people want to visit all other states of being in a diffused state of consciousness, not wishing to be any given thing, but instead to become comprehensive, entering and leaving at will. . . .

The enormous stress put upon sexuality and perversion is meant to dramatize the castration of man's wholeness. Historically and psychologically he has been forced to be half a man and lead half a life. The perverse imagination demands instead that the range of the body's secret desires be granted the same span of fulfillment and free play previously reserved for those of the soul. It is thus futile and irrelevant to hurl punitive charges of pornography, obscenity, promiscuity, and even perversity at such demands, for, far from cringing, the perverse imagination neutralizes the sting of such accusations by stripping them of their guilt. There is nothing more infuriating or frustrating than working up an elaborate argument to the fine point of a devastating accusation only to have your adversary thank you for the appellation and march off triumphantly bearing it as a badge of honor. Because the perverse imagination regards inhibition not exhibition as a taboo, and because it rejects the language of consciousness as the inhibitor rather than the exhibitor of the body, the contemporary critic now finds his entire critical vocabulary in jeopardy. Terms like obscenity and pornography buckle in his hands; others like promiscuity and perversity recoil back on him like a spring. It is like watching a chameleon change from harsh black to innocent white at the very moment of diagnosis. Often the final result is the kind of muffled rage or baffled silence one experiences in trying to fumble with a foreign language spoken by a future race that has not had the courtesy to wait for the present one to die.

Another aspect of the perverse imagination which reinforces its stress both on total gratification and anonymity is its concept of identity. Specifically, it has shifted the search for the self to the search for the self's continuity. The traditional question, "Who am I?," is immediately entangled in new qualifiers: "It depends; you mean today?" Identity is not conceived of as a developmental series of ascending planes in which each subsequent stage is a triumphant advancement over its predecessor but as a non-developmental, cumulative continuum. The internal interplay of infant and adult, and the interchangeability of body and mind force the self to abandon its heroic isolation for the collective fluidity of the body which by virtue of its tactile totality sets a new standard of multiplicity for the mind. The supreme enemy of the perverse imagination is thus separatism. Indeed, all that the perverse imagination is against may be suggested by the following catalog of separatist arrangements which it rejects: the separation of one man-one woman (marriage); of men from men and women from women (heterosexuality); of masculine men from feminine women (sexual politics and war); of top from bottom (sublimated sexuality); of black from white (racism); of power from people (bureaucracy). The antidote to marriage, heterosexuality, etc., is a self exploded into a maze of personalities whose full variety is less known than discovered. Everything imagined is possible; everything dreamed is an unlived reality; all life is so daringly tentative and richly discontinuous that perhaps it will finally lead to something so substantially different from the life of the species that the protean self can escape the death of the species.

The perverse imagination thus carries the Faustian quest to the absolute end of immortality. Its horror at the prospect of satisfaction may really be a horror at the prospect of death. And it must be admitted that the frenzied pursuit of pleasure seems joylessly propelled by the fear that castrating death, or its more familiar ally, boredom, may be the one absolutely unalterable repression of all. It is possible, too, that the rejection of so-called normal sexual relations may be based less on their inadequacy as the desire to avoid at all costs a love relationship precisely because it does not last, anymore than life does. A real danger, then, is that the perverse imagination may become as unfeeling and desensitized as the separatist groups it opposes. Then, too, the incontestability of the tragic point of view always has been based on the assumption that man cannot bear, or at least for very long, the burden of happiness, let alone multiple happiness; because he is a despoiler; and even when he is grandiose, his ambitions exceed his mortal allowance. Thus, to Ibsen the desire for success and the desire for successful love are absolutely irreconcilable. And once again it must be acknowledged that the world of the perverse imagination, like that of the pornographic impulse, is never tired. It is never peopled by the infirm or aged; desire never seems to flag, decay seems to have been banished, and no one ever seems to die. The one exception, and it is a serious one, is that in hard perversion there is murder. The ultimate issue of limits, artistic or moral or mortal, thus still looms as an inescapable problem of form.

In many ways, the perverse imagination has yet fully to recognize and to solve its affinity with violence and murder. Its politics is rough and nasty and often betrays a dictatorial inability to negotiate. What it wants, it demands; what it is against, it curses. It is often too flushed with the vigor of the body to have any patience or sympathy with decay. One of the dangers of rejecting all limits and of sanctifying as natural and good every impulse that comes from the body is that soon nothing may be wrong with anything.[31] Indeed, frequently in perverse works there is the secret request to be stopped, for if someone or something does not intervene between the unsatisfied body and its addictive hunger, it will kill another body or itself. In this connection, it is significant that the time span of the *Story of O*, is one year; O, used up, as it were, commits suicide. Perhaps, in a total lifetime one year of sexuality is all one has. But, of course, in contradiction to this notion as well as all the other reservations raised above, the perverse imagination is never that conciliatory.

The perverse imagination instead maintains that all judgments of man's tragic limits proceed from an impoverished notion of potency in the first place. The body has never been allowed to be all that it might be because much of its energy has been spent in being turned against itself. Similarly, even much of the mind's power has been wasted in unnecessary rear-guard acts of repression. Then, too, although the perverse imagination is not unaware that its desire for total gratification runs headlong into its contrary desire never to be satisfied, it squirms free of that contradiction by rejecting the dualistic form in which it is cast. By conceiving of the self not as a singular mortality but as a multiple infinity, the perverse imagination allows the life that has come to its satisfaction to end so that a new one is free to be born. In other words, the legitimate "immortality" the perverse imagination seeks is the refusal to grant premature victories to death by accepting the repression of less life.[32]

The final answer of the perverse imagination then to grim tragedy is bacchanalian comedy. The pressure of a final end is countered with an utopian open-end; its favorite mark of punctuation is the on-going, never-ending dash. Its alliance with utopian science fiction, moreover, offers for the first time since the Industrial Revolution the possibility that the arts need not be opposed or inferior to the sciences, but can stand as equals shaping a new image of man which perhaps is beyond the comprehension of contemporary readers but clearly not beyond the imagination of perverse artists.[33] In the meantime, there is a need for complex sanity and art. In *Hair: The American Tribal-Love Rock Musical*, the Age of Aquarius is defined as a time of greatness or madness. The dilemma of the perverse imagination is that it may mistake its madness for greatness. The dilemma of its critics is that they may mistake its greatness for madness. And if that happens, then there will be little that is genuinely new to the future and little that is memorable to the past; and art and perhaps more will expire in the present between the two extremes.

NOTES

1. Karl Jaspers, "Freedom and Authority," *Diogenes* I (1950), 25–42. According to Jaspers, there can be no freedom without authority

and no authority without freedom. A genuine authority is one that grants freedom; an authentic freedom is one that is responsive to authority.

2. As far as I have been able to determine the first use of the phrase, "The New Morality" as well as that of "the Sexual Revolution" was by Samuel D. Schmalhausen in a prophetic article entitled "The Sexual Revolution" which appeared in *Sex in Civilization,* eds. V. F. Calverton and Samuel D. Schmalhausen (Garden City, 1929). Indeed, Schmalhausen as early as 1929 was aware that the issue is no longer pornography but perversity: "Out of this colossal change in erotic fulfillment from the stability and sociality and morality of procreation to the instability and egocentricity and immorality of recreation springs what we shall have to accept as The New Morality. Abnormality becomes the new normality. The new psychology is a study of pathology and perversion" (p. 401).

3. David Drury, "Sex Goes Public: A Talk with Henry Miller," *Esquire* LXV (May, 1966), 118ff. In this connection, it might be noted that D. H. Lawrence was among the group of students at the University of Nottingham who dubbed themselves "The Pagans."

4. For a less flattering reason for Henry Miller's eclipse, see Kate Millet's "Sexual Politics: Miller, Mailer and Genet," *New American Review No.* 7 (New York, 1969), pp. 3–32.

5. What has happened to Lawrence's mystique is presented sensitively in a recent poem by the Swedish poet, Henry Martinson:

> The hour you waited for, when things would assume soul anew
> And their interiors visited by soul and sensation
> on the day of inward turned sensuality.
>
> But the world was turned outward.
> Only misunderstanding ripened fully.
>
> The new, deep communion you sang never happened.
> The table was spread inside,
> but only a few came
> And only a few could eat.
> The others came out of a curiosity that meant nothing.
>
> Your church within the flesh must close.
> Now it stands abandoned in steel storm
> on the devil's heath of the outward turned.

Times Literary Supplement (September 3, 1966), p. 820. Translated by Morton Seif.

6. See Wayland Young's appendix on Freud in *Eros Denied* (London, 1964), pp. 367–70; and Susan Sontag's overhaul of sublimated sexuality in "The Pornographic Imagination," *Partisan Review* 34 (1967), 181–212; and, of course, Herbert Marcuse's *Eros and Civilization* (Boston, 1955).

7. Preoccupation with the toilet may be pushed back to Swift's excremental vision or placed more recently in this century with the setting of Molly Bloom's soliloquy. But nothing in the past compares with the toiletry of *Candy*, Genet's urological obsessions, Roth's bathroom masturbations and above all LeRoi Jones' *The Toilet* (1964). For a profound analysis of the relationship between excrement and money, see Norman O. Brown's "Filthy Lucre" in *Life Against Death* (New York, 1959), especially pp. 264–6.

8. Leslie Fiedler, *Love and Death in the American Novel* (New York, 1960), p. xxx.

9. Herbert Gold, "The Sexual Stalemate," *Nation* 187 (Nov. 1, 1958), 309–11; Charles Glicksberg, "Sex in Contemporary Literature," *Colorado Quarterly* IX (1961), 277–87; and Steven Marcus, "Pornotopia," *Encounter* XXVII (April, 1966), ii, 9–18.

10. "Writing about Sex," *Partisan Review* 34 (February 1967), 552–63.

11. The only critics to reflect in a single work the enormous diversity and complexity of sexual expression are again Wayland Young and Susan Sontag. Not accidentally, Young and Sontag involve their discussions of perverse pornography with a reevaluation of Freud. The only psychologist who treats the entire subject not as some curious deviation but as a new norm is Samuel D. Schmalhausen. In addition to calling for a new "psychology of incest," which has not been heeded, Schmalhausen maintained that "Promiscuity is in the nature of things the fundamental reality" (p. 391). He elaborated:

> The psychoanalytic doctrine of the polymorphous perverse nature of the libido of the child is based on a series of important observations indicating the youngling's amoral willingness to experiment with its own body auto-erotically, to play with the bodies of boy friends or girl friends, as the occasion permits and provokes, to toy with the sexuality of cats and dogs and cows and horses (if the sexual milieu allows it), to try out a repertory of erotic stimulation that is surprising when first candidly confronted by the make believe mind of the adult

mentor. The fact remains that children (Nature and God consenting) are promiscuous and polygamous and innocently libidinous. The innocent little darlings! (373).

12. "The Naked American," *New Republic* 161 (August 9, 1969), 31.

13. Richard Gilman, "There's a Wave of Pornography . . . ," *New York Times Magazine* (Sept. 8, 1968), 76.

14. See John Thompson's "Pornography and Propaganda," *Commentary* 48 (August, 1969), 54–7.

15. *The Holy Barbarians* (New York, 1959), p. 139.

16. There is an increasing tendency for some contemporary writers less daringly to approach the topicality and perishability of journalism and television. This goes beyond the techniques of the pioneering John Dos Passos to include the fictionalized documentaries of Truman Capote and the "human interest" essays of James Baldwin and Norman Mailer.

17. Jack Richardson, "Groping towards Freedom: The Living Theater," *Commentary* 47 (May, 1969), 81.

18. Robert Brustein, "The Living Theater Revisited," *New York Review of Books* XII (Feb. 13, 1969), 25–7.

19. Schmalhausen, p. 417.

20. *Eros and Civilization* (New York, 1955), p. 170.

21. *Darwin and the Naked Lady* (New York, 1962), p. 103.

22. Schmalhausen, pp. 377–8.

23. *The Nude: A Study of Ideal Form* (Garden City, 1959), p. 126.

24. The new sexual technology is already graphically before us in the sex machines of Tomi Ungerer's *Fornicon* (New York: Rhinoceros Press, 1970). The title itself suggests the scientific streamlining of new products, and the characters who employ the elaborate machines of masturbating satisfaction are regularly described by critics as a "race of people," as if they were discussing a strange group from another planet.

25. *Five Years* (New York, 1966), p. 7.

26. *Sodom or the Quintessence of Debauchery* (Hollywood, 1966), p. xliv.

27. Alex Comfort maintains that

Orgasm is the most intense human aesthetic experience. . . . In fact, rather than argue for art as an expression of aim-inhibited sexuality, we might find it profitable to consider how far sexual experience can be a form of art. . . . The Indians so regarded it; I strongly suspect that in our culture it is about to become one, and that it may prove superior to others in discharging much of the activity which goes into the typically individualistic art we know (p. 108).

28. Gore Vidal, *Myra Breckinridge* (New York, 1968), p. 13.

29. "Pornography, Masturbation, and the Novel," *Salmagundi* 2 (Winter, 1967–1968), 28–56.

30. Ihab Hassan, "Silence, Revolution, and Consciousness," *The Massachusetts Review* XXXVI (Summer, 1969), 469.

31. Schmalhausen states "the great Freud has helped to solve the moral problem: we shall need an even greater Freud to help solve the immoral problem" (p. 381). But it probably will not work that way, for what was "soluble" by one man was a problem of singularity; solutions now cannot proceed from the top down but must come from the bottom across. In short, the problem of multiplicity will have to be answered with multiple solutions.

32. Ihab Hassan puts it succinctly: "Man shares the experience of life with all animals, but he stands alone in the consciousness of death. Death presumes a sense of identity. The awareness of self is therefore an awareness of mortality. But the self desires immortality, and thus plays havoc with creation" (467).

33. It is, I think, just that Schmalhausen has the last word of summation:

> We confront a new world. In that new world certain novel sexual problems exist challenging our subtlest powers of analysis and comprehension. How to extract a certain psychiatric sanity and serenity from so much bright chaotic material is the really important problem for the new type of educator. If we simply accept two bold facts—the inadequacies of traditional marriage and the quite inevitable spread of the theory and practice of experimentalism in intimate behaviors—we are fairly well equipped to understand, sympathetically, why the newer freedom in love and marriage must not only appear to be, but actually must be, crude, unbeautiful, raw. Life, in so deep a crisis of change and readjustment, squirms and tortures its way into novel forms that may, when in a state of happier equilibrium and internal affirmation, prove to be lovely and most acceptable.
>
> The stink in a chemical laboratory is not a very effective argument against the wonder and utility of science.
>
> Love is a strange subtle coalescence of wonder and disgust. The beauty of love is the triumph of adoration over nausea. Mother love illustrates keenly this truth. The newer freedom must go through its birth pangs that are anything but beautiful and delay awhile in disgusting swaddling clothes (which intense compassion and psychiatric

affection can accept) until freedom in sex and love creates an individuality of its own, a fine model of spontaneity, infinitely superior
to the formularized affections of the preexperimental days. Freedom,
in the perilous chemical laboratory of life, may disastrously blow up
the living universe: we cannot be blind to that anarchic possibility.
Freedom may re-assort the chemicals of desire and produce such
marvels as life has never yet known. . . . *Qui vivra, verra* (402).

THE PAST

It was round the most secret organs of body and soul that the effort to pervert body and soul went on. The two great sins were fornication and idolatry, and they were in some sense the same sin.

Charles Williams. *Witchcraft*.

There are but two commandments in the new sexology: Mate and Sublimate! If it be our Darwinian doom to mate, and our Freudian doom to sublimate, what wonder we are all psychoneurotics?

Samuel D. Schmalhausen. "The Sexual Revolution."

"There is nothing," writes de Sade, "that can set bounds to licentiousness. . . . The best way of enlarging and multiplying one's desires is to try to limit them." Nothing can set bounds to licentiousness . . . or rather, generally speaking, there is nothing that can conquer violence.

Georges Bataille. *Death and Sensuality*.

IHAB HASSAN

SADE: PRISONER OF CONSCIOUSNESS

He chose the imaginary.
Simone de Beauvoir

It is given to certain authors to reveal the darkness in our dreams and thus to make of history prophecy. These are not always the authors who stand highest in our esteem. They possess an extreme gift, and life blights them for their excess. Their road skirts the palace of wisdom, and their eyes behold a pile of ashes. They see only what they have already, what they have terribly seen—such is their autism. But their blindness points the way. Mysteriously, they expend themselves in the avant-garde of literature.

The Marquis de Sade is one of these authors. He was a scoundrel and a libertine; they also said he was mad. He may have been worse things though his biographers doubt it. The authorities—of the French Monarchy, Republic, Terror, Consulate, First Empire and Restoration—put him under lock and key for nearly thirty years. He comes back to us now as a cliche of language, a force in our erotic and political behavior; he

comes back as a writer and even as a thinker. He writes monot-
onously and thinks, on the whole, equivocally; his profound
duplicity delights, and finally confutes him. Yet we seek him out,
behind the walls of Vincennes, the Bastille, Charenton, between
the cheap yellow covers of pornography, because something in
his monstrous fantasy continues to betray us to ourselves, because
his judgment haunts our civilization.

.   .   .   .

Paradox and duplicity riddle Sade's ideas as well as his life.
His ideas are not seminal, but they have the partial truth of
excess, the power of release. They constitute a dubious paradigm
of consciousness. We perceive the outlines of that consciousness
as we move from his exoteric to his esoteric works, from his
avowed to his underground publications. The movement, regardless of chronology, is toward total terror.

Sade's public stance is that of a novelist. In an astute essay,
"Idée sur les romans" (1800), he sketches the history of the
genre, paying particular tribute to the "masculine" novels of
Richardson and Fielding, and declaring his admiration for Gothic
fiction, especially *The Monk* of M. G. Lewis, that black fruit of
European history. He also gives us his theory of fiction. The
theory puts forth in respectable guise—Sade strenuously dis-
claims the authorship of *Justine*—his outrageous theory of life.
Man has always been subject to two weaknesses, Sade argues:
prayer and love; these are weaknesses that the novelist must
exploit. The first inspires hope mixed with terror; the second
inspires tenderness; and both combine to sustain the interest of
fiction. Terror and tenderness, however, create the greatest
interest when virtue appears in constant jeopardy; had "the
immortal" Richardson ended *Clarissa* with a conversion of Love-
lace and a happy marriage between the seducer and the seduced,
no reader would have shed "delicious tears."

Sade speaks for the novelist and pretends to explore the business of fiction. He asks that the full ambiguity of man's nature
be recognized; he rejects the sentimental and didactic rhetoric
that dominate the novel. But we insult Sade's intelligence when
we take him at his word. His concern is neither art nor nature

but dreamful liberty. He found that liberty in evil. The mono-plot requires villainy to remain in ascendance till the parodic resolution. In his original "Preface" to *Contes et Fabliaux,* written about 1787, he makes this pronouncement:

> The basis of nearly all tales and nearly all novels is a young woman, loved by a man who is akin to her, and crossed in her love by a rival whom she dislikes. If this rival triumphs, the heroine, they say, is extremely unfortunate. . . .
>
> This, then, is what has decided us to add an extra touch, more than age and ugliness, to the rival who crosses the heroine's loves. We have given him a tinge of vice or of libertinism to alarm truly the girls he tries to seduce. . . .

With droll duplicity, Sade concludes: "One has been able to lift a small corner of the veil and to say to man: this is what you have become, mend your ways for you are repulsive." The formula applies rigidly to *Contes et Fabliaux,* and applies, with minor variations, to *Les Crimes de l'Amour* which Sade originally intended as part of his *Contes.*

But hypocrisy becomes a luxury that Sade can less and less afford. *Dialogue Between a Priest and a Dying Man,* written in 1782, states his "morality" more explicitly. God, according to Sade, is a superfluous hypothesis; and the Redeemer of Christianity is "the most vulgar of tricksters and the most arrant of all imposters." The Marquis glibly invokes cultural and religious relativism to bolster the arguments of his dying man. The only constant is Nature, and Nature is indifferent to what men call vice or virtue. It is simply a process of death and regeneration in which nothing is ever lost. Men are part of Nature and subject to instinctual necessity; they have no freedom to choose. "We are the pawns of an irresistible force, and never for an instant is it within our power to do anything but make the best of our lot and forge ahead along the path that has been traced for us." The dying man ends by persuading the priest; and, needless to say, both join in an orgy with six women kept on hand for the funeral occasion.

The personal argument is hidden. Sade attacks God in the

name of Nature. The idea of Christian Divinity repels him
because it rests on piety and tradition, and it often serves the
advantage of corrupt men. But the true cause of his revolt
against Deity is double: he needs the erotic release of transgression against authority—in blasphemy, in desecration—and he
resents any power that might qualify the omnipotence of the
Self. These twin motifs, still implicit in the *Dialogue,* pervade
his tales of sexual terror. As for Nature, it is itself Sade's largest
fantasy, existing only to give substance to his wishes. Since
fantasy admits all contradictions, he can claim that crime is both
a necessity of Nature and the only freedom in it.

Crime, at any rate, is merely one aspect of libertinage, the
politics of human freedom. This is the lesson of *Philosophy in
the Bedroom* (1795). The book is a manifesto ringing as loud
as Marx's: "Voluptuaries of all ages, of every sex, it's to you only
that I offer this work. . . . It is only by sacrificing everything
to the senses' pleasure that . . . this poor creature who goes
under the name of Man, may be able to sow a smattering of
roses atop the thorny path of life." It is also a catechism of
libertinage relieved, with deadly regularity, by practice orgies
and computerized perversions. Like all Sade's works, the book
is repetitious. But it is also grotesquely comic in parts, a parodic
novel of manners which insists on the complaisancies of the
drawing room, the schoolroom, and the bedroom.

The assertion of Dolmancé throughout the seven dialogues is
hard to miss; in the pursuit of pleasure, everything is permitted.
Dolmancé is therefore consistent when he says of man: "Victim
he is, without doubt, when he bends before the blows of ill
fortune; but criminal, never." Crime presupposes the existence
of others. Since each one of us is alone and for himself in the
world, cruelty to others is, from one's own point of view, a matter
of profound indifference—unless it can be made a source of
orgasm. But the benefits of cruelty are not exhausted in orgasm,
Dolmancé insists; cruelty is also "the energy in a man civilization
has not yet altogether corrupted: therefore it is a *virtue,* not a
vice." (Italics mine.) Sade revives the terms which he has raged
to obliterate. This does not prevent his heroine from learning
her lesson too well. When her mother arrives to rescue her from

the orgy, Eugenie helps to torture her viciously, and in a perverse reenactment of Oedipal fantasy, plays the sexual role of a man, Eugenie's own father: "Come, dear lovely Mamma, come, let me serve you as a husband."

In the middle of his fifth dialogue, Sade inserts his famous revolutionary appeal, "Yet Another Effort, Frenchmen, If You Would Become Republicans." After speaking as a libertine, he now chooses to speak as a libertarian; the two, Sade pretends, are twin aspects of the free man. His sophistry as moralist, sociologist, and legislator reaches new heights. His conclusion is predictable: "In pointing out . . . the nullity, the indifference of an infinite number of actions our ancestors, seduced by a false religion, beheld as criminal, I reduce our labor to very little. Let us create few laws, but let them be good. . . ." The libertarian makes an honorable plea which conceals the motive of the libertine; the latter offers a rationalization of the Sadian temper which further conceals a motive Sade himself did not perceive.

That motive is Manichean. Virtue and Vice are locked in eternal combat, though Vice seems to hold the upper hand. Sade poses as a naturalist who lives beyond good and evil. Yet his constant use of such terms as "degrade," "deprave," "debauch," and "pervert" indicates that his world is anything but morally neutral. It is a world in which transgression is real and sacrilege dear. "Oh, Satan!" Dolmancé cries, "one and unique god of my soul, inspire thou in me something yet more, present further perversions to my smoking heart, and then shalt thou see how I shall plunge myself into them all." And later he adds: "I never sleep so soundly as when I have . . . sufficiently befouled myself with what our fools call crimes." Can we wonder that he, like all Sade's villains, constantly applies religious imagery to sexual functions? Furthermore, Sade's world is one in which Nature must remain sterile. Copulation thrives, procreation never. He abhors the womb, and therefore sodomy, heterosexual and homosexual sodomy, rules all desire; he offers not the Lord's way but the Devil's. Though Dolmancé speaks reverently of lifting the veil off the mysteries of Nature, as a libertine he can only assault her, he can only impose his will, his fantasy, on life. The libertine is thus shown to be, at bottom, a desecrator of mysteries. Finally the world of Sade is a prison of consciousness. The power of Vice and Virtue, the vitality of Nature, vanish in the dungeon of the Self. In the moment of orgasm, the Sadian Self seeks desperately to become something other than itself. Yet it cannot; it ends by incarcerating the world with itself. As a despot in its dungeon, the Self cannot tolerate pleasure in anyone else. It induces pain in order to assimilate others to its unique existence. Sade topples the vast republic of Freudian instincts, and the practical democracy of the Dionysian orgy. Instead, the Marquis establishes not a bedroom aristocracy but a solipsist's paradise.

Justine: Or Good Conduct Well Chastised (1791), the most cherished of Sade's works, is a sly parody of picaresque, Gothic, and sentimental fiction. (The book enjoyed an early popularity, went through six printings, and led to the arrest of both author and publisher in 1801.) It pushes the fantasies of Sade one step farther toward outrage without altering their content; it merely varies the format by accretion of horrors. The dedication to Marie-Constance Quesnet states the novel's claim to originally thus:

> But throughout to present Vice triumphant and Virtue a victim of its sacrifices, to exhibit a wretched creature wandering from one misery to the next; the toy of villainy; the target of debauch; exposed to the most barbarous, the most monstrous caprices . . . briefly, to employ the boldest scenes, the most energetic brush strokes, with the sole object of obtaining from all this one of the sublimest parables ever penned for human edification; now, such were . . . to seek to reach one's destination by a road not much traveled heretofore.

One can feel Sade's rising frenzy as he contemplates the misfortunes of the heroine of his dreams. And one can also feel his naive relish of deception in presenting the "traitorous brilliancies of crime" as a warning to his readers. With the former, Sade manages to indulge his sadistic taste; with the latter, he gratifies his need for culpability. Thus *Justine* brings to its author a double satisfaction: living out an erotic fantasy and then perpetrating it on humanity.

Nothing Justine ever does is too good to escape terrible chastisement, and no chastisement is too terrible to corrupt her goodness. It is a world of eternal fixity. The assaults on her alternate between the sexual and the intellectual; the latter are meant to explain or justify the former, Sade sees no inconsistency in his absolute tyrants who choose to expound their views at great length to abject victims. God, Nature, Society, Sex, and Crime are exhaustingly treated. Here and there, the author introduces a bizarre new idea. Coeur-de-fer, head of a robber gang, undertakes to refute Rousseau's doctrine of the Social Contract by arguing that it benefits only the middle class; the powerful and the deprived risk only to lose by it. Coeur-de-fer opts, therefore, for perpetual strife, radical anarchy. Another villain, the pederast Bressac, announces: "The primary and most beautiful of Nature's qualities is motion, which agitates her at all times, but this motion is simply a perpetual consequence of crimes. . . ." The coprophagous monk, Clément, explains his habit by invoking the imagination:

Extraordinary, you declare, that things decayed, noisome, and filthy are able to produce upon our senses the irritation essential to precipitate their complete delirium . . . realize, Therese, that objects have no value for us save that which our imagination imparts to them. . . . The human imagination is a faculty of man's mind whereupon, through the senses' agency, objects are painted, whereby they are modified, and wherein, next, ideas become formed, all in reason of the initial glimpsing of those external objects. . . . To like what others like proves organic conformity, but demonstrates nothing in favor of the beloved object. . . . It is in the mother's womb that there are fashioned the organs which must render us susceptible of such-and-such a fantasy . . . once tastes are formed nothing in the world can destroy them.

This opinion is echoed by the formidable counterfeiter, Roland—
his tastes lean toward necrophilia—when he proclaims that the
libertine's mind is stirred not by a woman's beauty but by the
species of crime he commits against her. All the ideas of Sade
tend toward creating an absolute moral vacuum in the world,
which he then proceeds to fill with his overweening consciousness.

The special effect of *Justine* derives precisely from its two
correlative fantasies: the omnipotence of the Sadian tyrant-
villain and the abjectness of his victim-heroine. The characters
move in a veritable fortress that reality can never breach. In
that fortress, they reign supreme; their actions defy all logic, all
predictions, defy time and history, and attain, each, the status of
a superlative. The dream of sexual abundance, which Steven
Marcus has shown to be a characteristic of pornography,
expresses here a transcendent will.

The consummation of the Sadian will is in death; the limits of
an omnipotent consciousness are murder and suicide. We should
not be surprised, therefore, if the villains of *Justine* serve Thanatos
reverently. The gargantuan glutton with a child's penis, Count
de Gernande, reaches his climax only when his wife is bled
before his eyes. Roland keeps an effigy of death in a coffin in his
necropolis within the bowels of the earth. He employs the noose
ecstatically on his victims, and employs it even on himself.
Surely no power is more absolute than in the act of annihilating
a human consciousness, unless it were in the act of creating
another, which Sade finds intolerable. The ultimate revenge of
man, who can neither kill god nor can, like god, create, is to kill
his creatures. This is why, in the end, Sade must arbitrarily kill
off his own fictional creations. Justine, who has survived all
hazards and finally earned her peace, is suddenly transfixed by
a thunderbolt as she stands idly in her room. The bolt goes
through her breast, heart, and belly. Thus the Marquis succeeds
where all his villains have failed: he murders Justine.

The escalation of terror continues in *The 120 Days of Sodom*
(1785); the orgy is now openly conceived as a massacre.
Sade completed only one of the four parts of this work; the
other sections remain in the form of notes and catalogues. No

ideas mar the onanistic intentions of this book. Such exclamations as "Oh, incredible refinement of libertinage!" recur in order to seduce the author more than his readers. "And now, friend reader, you must prepare your heart and ready your mind for the most impure tale that has ever been told since our world was born, a book the likes of which are met with neither amongst the ancients nor amongst us moderns." Sade, the pornographer, speaks out frankly, speaks even truly, but even as a pornographer, he speaks mainly to pleasure himself.

This is why the form of *The 120 Days* is reflexive; it can only mirror, or rather echo, itself. The four master libertines listen to four historians enumerate the 150 Simple, 150 Complex, 150 Criminal, and 150 Murderous Passions, which they then put into practice. Thus story and action echo back and forth to advantage; for as Sade says: "It is commonly accepted amongst thoroughbred libertines that the sensations communicated by the organs of hearing are the most flattering and those whose impressions are the liveliest. . . ." The historians, in fact, serve their masters as Sade the author serves the man. The words we read turn back upon themselves; their form, repudiating an audience, becomes an antiform.

The pattern of the work justifies the rubric of antiform in another sense: it is purely arithmetical. With demented ingenuity, Sade reduces his fantasy to an equation. There are four master libertines, four wives who are their daughters, four woman historians, four duennas, eight fuckers, eight young girls, eight young boys, and six female cooks and scullery maids. The book is divided into four parts; the orgy lasts 17 weeks, or 120 days. All the arrangements of this mathematical menage are specified meticulously, the number of wines and dishes, the number of lashes for each punishment. The statutes which govern the progress of the orgy are as clear as they are inflexible; the schedule for the whole period is fixed. From a total of 46 characters, precisely 30 are massacred and 16 permitted to return to Paris. "Under no circumstances deviate from this plan," Sade enjoins himself in his notes, "everything has been worked out, the entirety several times reexamined with the greatest care and thoroughness." Number and ratio, we see, rule the form of this game directed by an autoerotic computer. In this Sade prefigures the parodic constructions of Beckett.

But the work is not only abstract, it is also hermetic. Nothing, absolutely nothing, must penetrate the Fortress of Silling where the action takes place, except the mind. That castle, situated somewhere on an impossible peak in the Black Forest, is impregnable because it lies within the skull. "Ah, it is not readily to be imagined how much voluptuousness, lust, fierce joy are flattered by those sureties, or what is meant when one is able to say to oneself: 'I am alone here, I am at the world's end, withheld from every gaze, here no one can reach me, there is no creature that can come nigh where I am; no limits, hence no barriers. I am free,'" Sade writes. It is a curious freedom. In the real world, money and status define the power of the four master libertines. But at Silling, where there are no guards or jailers, 42 people submit unconditionally to the will of four. Why? Sade wills it so.

Occasionally, the Sadian Self rises to metaphysical rebellion. Curval, for instance, cries: "Ah, how many times, by God, have I not longed to be able to assail the sun, snatch it out of the universe, make a general darkness, or use that star to burn the world!" This is spoken in the demonic vein of Ahab. We also learn of certain libertines who poison the rivers and streams, and strive to annihilate a province. But these apocalyptic postures are always furtive, and their motive is less philosophic than sexual. Were Sade truly to recognize the rebellious imperatives of the Self, he would never tolerate four libertines to coexist on the same level: there would be only one. A society of omnipotent beings can be chartered only in pornographic fiction.

The Sadian Self, I have said, finds its consummation in death, and this is nowhere more obvious than in the apocalypse of *The 120 Days* where the final authority rests with Thanatos. At Silling, entropy is dominant, and annihilation the ultimate goal. Denial of others reaches a climax not in the affirmation but in the denial of self. "What can be more disturbing," George Bataille asks, "than the prospect of selfishness becoming the will to perish in the furnace lit by selfishness?" We see at last the sad equation of Sade: man is orgasm, and orgasm is death. Prisoner of his consciousness, he tries to escape through the language of macabre onanism. His visions mortify, desiccate the body, and open in the flesh an abyss wherein consciousness is swallowed. The Sadian Self, seeking desperately to become another, finds release only in death. "It was not murder that fulfilled Sade's erotic nature; it was literature," Simone de Beauvoir keenly observes. His heroes speak on indefatigably, and their words adapt terror to human history. Thus Sade makes his way into the domain of letters; his dungeon opens on the present. Apollinaire and Breton, Heine and Lely, Blanchot and Camus have made him our familiar.

We see Sade, almost, as the first avant-gardist, the daemon of Romanticism and of Gothic fiction, a surrealist before our time, and a herald of anti-literature. We imagine him as a precursor to Darwin, Freud, and Nietzsche, and as a forerunner of the anarchists, Max Stirner and Bakunin. We feel his genius in Dachau, Belsen, and Auschwitz, and in all apocalyptic politics. We accept him, at the same time, as an apostle of pornotopia, a child of the Enlightenment, and an example of metaphysical rebellion. This is all to say that we still struggle to see Sade clearly through his outrageous myth. Yet there is no doubt that his spirit moves in our culture, and defines, more than an aspect of pathology, a crucial element of our consciousness.

The element is easiest to discern in the domain of letters. Sainte-Beuve believed that Sade's great influence in the nineteenth century was as clandestine as Byron's was overt. In *The Romantic Agony,* Mario Praz sets out to redress the balance. He shows that the Divine Marquis casts his shadow on the *roman noir,* the *roman feuilleton,* the *roman charogne,* the *roman frénétique* of the period, inspires the satanism, vampirism, lycanthropy, incest, necrophilia, and cannibalism of various Romantic works, and breathes a perverse, new life into that major Richardsonian theme, the persecution of a virtuous maiden. Chateaubriand, Petrus Borel, Eugene Sue, Lautreamont, Baudelaire, and even Flaubert, in France alone, are haunted by the specter of the Marquis. In America, England, and Germany, the erotic sensibility honors him secretly in the Gothic romance, the tale of terror, and the *Liebestod.*

But Sade's contribution to literary history does not exhaust itself in romantic decadence. It depends, rather, on his effort to supplant the sentimental novel, and to give Gothic fiction new authority. During his own lifetime, the morality of the bourgeois novel spent itself; revolutionary thought demanded new values. Sade calls hell to the rescue, thinking thus to redeem the reality of fiction. He even assumes a larger task which he never quite realizes: the creation of the modern novel. The Gothic genre that Sade seeks to regenerate, Fiedler has shown in *Love and Death in the American Novel,* is by its nature parricidal, opposed to the authority of Church and State, and to all middle class pieties. It is a voice from the dungeon keep, from the unconscious, breaking all the primal taboos of civilization, hollow with guilt, frenzied with marvelous imaginings. And it tells the improbable tale of the diabolic male hero, pursuing Woman and desecrating her at every opportunity. In its deepest conception, the Gothic novel touches the rebellious motives of avant-garde literature, foreshadows its spiritual isolation, and announces its death wish. In this, if in nothing else, the Marquis is, Kafka once said, "the veritable patron of the modern age."

Sade also presages anti-literature. The Surrealists, we know, claimed him after Apollinaire published a selection of his works in 1909. Their claim, however, does not recognize the peculiarly modern problem of his language. The life of pure eroticism and the life of pure violence are equally silent. Their excesses stand outside of reason and speech; their culmination in death is mute. Yet Sade speaks volubly. As Bataille notes, "A paradox underlies his behaviour. De Sade speaks, but he is the mouthpiece of a silent life, of utter and inevitable speechless solitude." Language is forced to cheat in order to express annihilation, and in doing so it cheats itself. An icy awareness persists where no awareness can subsist; every whiplash is counted. The style of total terror becomes numbers, subject to obsessive additions, variations, repetitions, permutations. The style takes us out of the field of terror, expressing merely the rationalized will to violence in terms of an algebra of coitus. The style moves toward the field of nonsense.

Sade's language is further silenced by his solipsistic attitude. With whom can this author communicate? In whose ears does his speech ring? Sade stands alone as subject; all others vanish into objects of his pleasures. There is no question of genuine response. Sade's words are intelligible only as a masturbatory fantasy, taking the form of conversations between tyrant and victim. In these stylized dialogues, the characters are forced to contradict their logical destiny, immutable silence and solitude, in order to provide their author with his sexual entertainment. "The enactment of the erotic scene interested him more than the actual experience," Simone de Beauvoir says. True: Sade's language serves him as a mirror, reflecting lewd dreams.

Certainly, the language is not intended to convey fact or truth. It is rather an organ of deceit, about which Dolmancé says:

> Without hesitation I say I know of nothing more necessary in life; one certain truth shall prove its indispensability: everyone employs it. . . . Let us behold it as the key to every grace, every favor, all reputation, all riches, and by means of the keen pleasure of acting villainously, let us placate the little twinge our conscience feels at having manufactured dupes.

Language as deceit reminds us of the anti-languages of propaganda in our own century. We have now seen the extremes: for Herr Goebbels, all official speech is truth; for William Burroughs, all speech is lying. Sade confirms the current revulsion against language by making mendacity his policy. When shall we believe him? His words remain as equivocal as those of the Cretan who declares all Cretans liars. Sade's language subverts itself, and suffers from the bad faith he shows toward his inexistent readers.

The very form of Sade's work qualifies for the term anti-literature. The conventions of Gothic fiction, the picaresque novel, the novel of manners, the philosophical dialogue, and utopian pornography make their perfunctory appearance in that work. But the function of form as control or realization of a human impulse is denied, for Sade's impulses defy all satisfaction. Steven Marcus argues: "The ideal pornographic novel . . . would go on forever. . . . If it has no ending in the sense of completion or gratification, then it can have no form. . . . We see here one more reason for the opposition of pornography to literature." It is really a question of difference rather than opposition; pornography is a kind of anti-literature. In this as in other respects, Sade outshines the common pornographer. His works are almost wholly independent of time, place, and person, and their autistic purpose is single. Without full comprehension of his role in Western thought, Sade thus may be the first to wrench the imagination free from history, to invert the will of art, and to set language against itself.

He may also be the first to limn the modern consciousness, see the void around it. He wants to restore man to Nature; he recognizes in man the dominion of instinctual forces. He perceives, with a rigor akin to Freudian determinism, the bizarre equivalences of mind and body, fantasy and flesh, in the pursuit of love. He has an intuition of the primal horde, the taboo against incest, the Oedipal drama we re-enact continually with our fathers and mothers, brothers and sisters. He knows that dreams extend the meaning of our waking life, and employs them in his stories accordingly. Above all, Sade complicates for us, in a tragic and irrevocable way, the image of life-giving Eros by revealing the long shadow Thanatos casts upon it. He understands that violence is a condition of vitality, and that Nature revels in destruction; he brings the Enlightenment to an end. Yet he never loses the sense that love always lurks where death rules. As Brigid Brophy puts it: "The unitive purpose of Eros is never wholly defeated, because in Sade's conception the torturer and victim tend towards what Simone de Beauvoir calls a genuine couple. Sade is aware that the torturer's real crime will be not simply to inflict pain but to seduce and corrupt the victim into being his accomplice and wanting pain to be inflicted. The relation comes close to being a game. . . ." This is the game that may become the apocalypse of our time.

In the end, however, Sade limits his relevance to us because he demands to be taken only on his own terms. The Sadian Self permits no encounter, no negotiation. It solves the problem of evil by converting all pain, whether inflicted or received, into a source of personal pleasure. Sade can therefore experience orgasm when he hears that he has been burned in effigy. He can even look forward to the posthumous joy of being one of "those perverse writers whose corruption is so dangerous, so active, that their single aim is, by causing their appalling doctrines to be printed, to immortalize the sum of their crimes after their own lives are at an end; they themselves can do no more, but their accursed writings will instigate the commission of crimes, and they carry this sweet idea with them to their graves. . . ." This is the perfect crime which perpetuates itself even when the agent has ceased to act: the crime of the imagination.

The imagination of Sade is inflamed by crime because all its energies are committed to transgression. Vice defies Virtue; against God stands the Devil. But this Manicheanism is superficial. Sade denies God vehemently, and ends by identifying himself with Omnipotence. The dialectic of transgression moves toward infinity. As Blanchot perceives: "the conception of an infernal God is but a way station of the dialectic according to which Sade's superman, after having denied man in the guise of God, next advances to meet God and will in turn deny him in the name of Nature, in order finally to deny Nature by identifying it with the spirit of negation." The true spirit of the Sadian Self is priapic and continuous denial. This leads it finally to deny itself by invoking a void which may engulf even its own omnipotence. The consciousness of Sade, raised to the highest level, is anti-consciousness as his work is anti-literature. The mind and the language, caught in revulsion, seek release from their own forms into a silence commensurate with outrageous vision. They fail to attain release, and in their failure lay bare the destructive element within our world.

JOSEPH BENTLEY

SATIRE AND THE RHETORIC OF SADISM

You may, if you are an old-fashioned schoolmaster, wish to consider yourself full of universal benevolence, and at the same time derive great pleasure from caning boys. In order to reconcile these two desires you have to persuade yourself that caning boys has a reformatory influence. If a psychiatrist tells you that it has no such influence . . . you will fly into a rage and accuse him of being coldly intellectual.

Bertrand Russell

I

Dr. Samuel Johnson's definition of satire seems both precise and unsatisfying. Satire, he says, is a kind of work which "censures wickedness and folly," and holds them up to ridicule. The definition must be called precise, for its emphasis on the moral and intellectual function of satire is true to the practice and stated purpose of virtually every major satirist from Aristophanes to Aldous Huxley. Over and over, through the history of the art of literary violence, the high moral claim is made. *"Difficile est*

57

saturam non scribere," says Juvenal; for the world seems so
steeped in depravity that any spontaneous overflowing of powerful feelings must be, for the honest man, an overflowing of powerful feelings of moral disgust. In Ben Jonson's *Every Man out of
his Humour* the feeling gives rise to ferocious moral cruelty:

> my soul
> Was never ground into such oily colours,
> To flatter Vice, and daub iniquity:
> But (with an armed and resolved hand)
> I'll strip the ragged follies of the time
> Naked as at their birth: . . .
> . . . and with a whip of steel
> Print wounding lashes in their iron ribs.

And Aldous Huxley proclaims his work to be the inflicting of
"retributive pain to shock the stupid and wicked truthhaters"
into an acceptance of reality. The historical record speaks for
itself.

Despite the record, however, there are serious problems with
the definition. A closer look at the satirists who have issued
justifications of their art on moral grounds suggests that they
were speaking in response to the heavy disapproval of society
and, perhaps, to their own sense of the questionable moral
validity of their cankered muse. Also, the entire concept of
motive has become so complicated in our own time by psychol-
ogies of one kind or another that we must automatically suspect
any simplistic formula based on it. What follows in this essay is
a series of notes on the possibility that moral motives are not
essential to satire and that, as a result, satire can take the form
of pure sadistic aggression. The problems are immense and the
conclusions will be largely inconclusive, but an airing of some
of the implications of satire's relationship to sadism might clear
the air for further investigation. If satire is a mode of social
violence it must be related to other modes of violence, both
reputable and disreputable. Militant morality, purification, pe-
nology, disciplinarianism, flagellation, sadism, masochism—all of
these terms refer to violence as a means to some desired end,

either to the elimination of evil and stupidity in society or to the gaining of some personal satisfaction. In addition to a concern for violence as violence, we must consider its form and structure; depending on its context and manipulation the inflicting of pain can cause such diverse responses as laughter, fear, disgust, sexual passion, self-righteousness, and religious awe. The problem is fundamentally this: what is the relation between violence as a means to personal satisfaction and violence as a means to moral improvement? The answer must be sought in the areas of structure, context, and motive.

For an initial working concept I propose the principle of motivational duality. In the post-Freudian period moralists, among others, cannot be credited with simple, single-minded motives. We are likely to uphold the axiom that all actions are motivated, in the last analysis (and sometimes even in the first analysis), by egocentrism, greed, sublimated infantile eroticism, or by any of the other manifestations of the essential *amour-propre*. As a result it is often difficult not to smile at the moralists, the reformers, the disciplinarians, the other pretenders to selflessness, and assure ourselves that they are either deluded or fraudulent. This view, obviously based on the idea that man seldom understands his "real" motives and that the hidden ulterior motive forms the common ground of all activity, leads us to the general concept of the unavoidable and necessary hypocrisy of the human race. Further, if we accept the cogent arguments of the psychologists that the self is organized upon multiple levels (Freud's tripartite diagram of the mind, for example), we will conclude that noble motives are very often ignoble (or *id*noble) motives in disguise. The final implication of the principle is that all acts of reformatory violence, religious, moral, legal and literary, spring from "sadistic" impulses and are but rationalized ways of justifying one's pursuit of the atavistic pleasure of inflicting pain.

I have used as an epigraph Lord Russell's commentary on the sadistic pedagogue in *Human Society in Ethics and Politics* because there is a sense in which satire is the literary equivalent of the harsh disciplinarian. Instead of caning aberrant boys, satire applies the birch to an aberrant society; it is a literature which really tries to censure the wicked and the foolish. But like the benevolent schoolmaster, the satirist perhaps gets more pleasure from the caning than from whatever virtue may result. Like most terms which stand for a frame of mind and a related behavioral patern, sadism is virtually impossible to define precisely. Krafft-Ebing, whose *Psychopathia Sexualis* was the first taxonomic treatise on aberrant sexual behavior after Sade's *120 Journées de Sodome,* defined sadism as "sexual emotion associated with the wish to inflict pain and use violence." Later, Havelock Ellis in his *Studies in the Psychopathology of Sex* discarded this term, along with its obverse, masochism, and subsumed both under the term "algolagnia." Using broader terms to suit a broader frame of reference, we can arrive at this working definition: sadism is the desire to gain satisfaction, sexual or otherwise, from direct participation in the discomforts of others. Geoffrey Gorer, in *The Life and Ideas of the Marquis de Sade,* broadens the terms of sadism to include a constructive as well as a destructive side. The trouble with such an overly broad definition will be clear when we try to label as sadists such people as engineers, sculptors, and plastic surgeons.

Significantly, this definition implies that sadism must include not only the shadowy psychopaths of the case histories but also the militant reformers, the Torquemadas of history. If Torquemada was in his professional guise a vicious beast, we must realize that he was probably not aware of his beastliness; no doubt he sincerely believed himself to be fulfilling God's purpose. In a similar fashion the sophisticated satirist dwells primarily on the virtue which his mockery serves; when he does consider the pain and violence of his pronouncements he considers them justified, because, after all, someone must take on the task of chastising the wicked and the foolish. Outer directed violence is the common denominator of reformers and sadists. A character like Sade's Saint-Fond will outrage his victim in a purely gratuitous stroke of violence, and at the same time, by means of the collective fear his act engenders, outrage the entirety of his audience. In like manner, the reformer chooses his victim and proceeds to outrage him; but the introduction of a new element into the process—the element of social justification—alters the final response. This time society identifies, not with the victim, who is wicked or foolish, but with the reformer himself. Society's reaction to this moral violence is that "it served him right." Thus, we can postulate that the acts of the sadist do not differ from the acts of the reformer; it is the motivational context of the act which preconditions its effects, not the act itself. To shift the categories somewhat with a simple analogy, we can observe that a surgeon in the operating room may inflict the same wound as the madman in a dark alley. The acts (as acts) are identical, but their motives and results differ so widely that we have difficulty in interpreting their relationship. Kenneth Burke's very useful distinction between "scene" and "act" is particularly helpful here. We must explore the nature of the "scene" in order to understand the "act" which springs from it. In satire and sadism "scenes" differ while "acts" coincide.

To get a clearer picture of the relationship between "justified" satire and "unjustified" sadism, we must carry several steps further our analysis of the architecture of violence. Sade's extant writings provide the most convenient literary account of gratuitous violence, so a brief analysis of his ideas will clarify the forms, motives, and contexts of sadism. Sade's dominating premise seems to be a direct cosmic extension of the dogma of original sin. The difference in Sade's conception is that original sin is the essence not only of man but also of the entire universe —God, of course, not excepted. *"Le mal,"* he writes in *Juliette,* *"est necessaire a l'organisation vicieuse de ce triste univers. Dieu est très vindicatif, méchant, injuste."* Nature, in his opinion, creates only to destroy, and murder is the primal law of the universe. Murderers are therefore the only pious and law-abiding men. Not only is original sin extended to the cosmos and dignified as *"l'essence d'être";* it also becomes an inverted virtue. Vice becomes virtuous and virtue (in addition to being abysmally foolish) becomes vicious; and, as all of Sade's heroes proclaim, this vice-virtue gives the highest of all possible pleasures. *"Oh! quelle action voluptueuse que de la destruction . . . je n'en connais pas qui chatouille plus délicieusement; il n'est pas d'extase semblable à celle que l'on goûte en se livrant à cette divine infamie."*

An exhaustive catalogue of the possible forms of this divine
infamy would be tedious as well as unprintable. But, as Sade's
biographer Maurice Heine has pointed out, Sade's analytical
descriptions of irregularities are objectionable now only because
of his common monosyllabic diction; because, in other words, he
chose not to disguise his meaning in a nonconnotative vocabulary. It is possible now to consider these aberrations in the open,
with the understanding of course that the effects described depend in large part on the semantic reverberations of the taboo
words. These aberrations fall roughly into two categories: acts of
covert and overt violence. The first category includes such relatively nonviolent acts as pederasty, fellatio, coprophagia, and
several more specific forms of scatophilia. These acts do not involve physical destruction but are valued nevertheless for the
social and religious horror which they inspire. In the border
territory between the covert and the overt acts, we find such
practices as necrophilia (which is covert violence when it is only
scatophilically ghoulish, overt when it involves murder), several
varieties of blasphemy (the Black Mass, consisting of *"faire des
horreurs avec des hosties,"* vandalism, setting nunneries afire, and
ritualistic cannibalism), and larceny (especially when the victim
is a pauper with starving children). In acts of covert violence the
sadistic effect is often heightened by the unwillingness of one
of the participants. When we move into the category of overt
physical violence we find an extraordinary series of painful
practices ranging from flagellation and gratuitous imprisonment
to starvation, vampirism, arson, and the most imaginative
methods of individual torture as well as the most elaborate
genocidal conspiracies. The corrupt financier Saint-Fond in
Juliette, after becoming bored with poisoning drinking fountains,
inaugurates a plan to corner the farm products market to gain
the power to amuse himself by starving half the people in France.
These more ambitious criminal acts are usually compounded
with the simple aberration to produce the worst (or best) possible
effect.

Sadistic acts should also be understood in relation to the types
of victims assaulted. At first glance the acts seem to fall into four
conventional categories: crimes against individual men, crimes

against society, crimes against nature, and crimes against God. But a closer examination of Sade's random outrages tends to destroy the categories. Since Sade espoused a kind of passionate atheism, the last category, crimes against God, actually consists of crimes against a pious society. And since he admitted the absolute impossibility of outraging nature—nature being the ultimate outrage in itself—the third category is also a way of committing crimes against a society that believes piously in the sanctity of God's natural world. Obviously, the violence directed toward the individual is but another example of social violence, because the victims are never victimized for some personal motive like revenge, jealousy or robbery; they are victimized only because they are human beings capable of responding to pain. Sadistic violence I would therefore describe as social violence—a way, perhaps, of punishing the race for presuming to exist. One suspects that Sade's only real victims were the good people who were scandalized and horrified by what he so meticulously displayed. The divine infamy is but another kind of social infamy.

It would seem that this categorizing of sadism is incomplete without a notice of spiritual or psychological sadism. Although the more refined exponents of sadism, like Richardson, Hugo, Flaubert, Swinburne, and most emphatically, the Wagner of the *Liebestod*, dwelled on a subjective, more metaphysical violence, Sade himself could never focus on anything less (or more) than the flesh. In his *romans noirs* we encounter an opaque world of mere matter, a world in which the characters—especially the victims—are reduced to the status of instruments for provoking the divine ecstasy of destruction. It is true that much is made of the moral will of characters like Justine, and that their unshakable virtue highly qualifies them to be forced into criminal action; but the point is that the pain administered to such characters is always entirely physical, never spiritual. Further, Sade frequently goes so far in reducing all sensation to physiological phenomena that he loses sight of divine wickedness in his descent toward simple chemistry. Take, for example, this passage justifying murder: *"Et voilà donc ce que c'est que le meurtre; un peu de matière désorganisée, quelques changements dans les combinaisons, quelques molécules rompues et replongées dans le creuset de la nature qui les rendra dans quelques jours sous une autre forme à la terre; et où donc est le mal à cela?"* Clearly, Sade's episodes and arguments always work out to be socially and physiologically outrageous, not spiritually violent.

The formula of sadism can now be stated as follows: humanity is distorted by being deprived of all its uniquely human attributes; mind, soul, spirit, and intellect are abandoned and man remains as a purely physical structure in the crucible of its own raw, animal force. Sadistic action constitutes a mortification of the flesh in the face of the brute reality that flesh is all that exists. Preoccupation with vile flesh in all of its malodorous animality is thus the sadistic constant upon which an intricate structure of violence is based. Reduction to flesh is the rhetoric of sadism.

II

Satire employs the same central rhetorical maneuver. Even a casual glance at the history of this genre will show that scatological reductionism is its most frequent technique. Aristophanes creates a carnival of obscenity, Chaucer laughs at the libidinous misadventures of the human race, and Rabelais lectures cheerfully on dung, tripes, and codpieces; Voltaire catalogues the terrors of the flesh with superficial good humor, Sterne finds comedy in castration, and Smollett evokes a world of falling chamber pots. The medieval moralists warn in extravagant terms of the horrors of concupiscence; for example, consider Aldous Huxley's translation of Bishop Odo of Cluny's attempt to discourage adultery by insisting on the physiological nastiness of women:

> If men could see beneath the skin . . . then the sight of a woman would be nauseous unto them. All that beauty consists but in phlegm and blood and humours and gall. If a man consider that which is hidden within the nose, the throat, and the belly, he will find filth everywhere; and if we cannot bring ourselves, even with the tips of our fingers, to touch such phlegm or dung, wherefore do we desire to embrace this bag of filth itself?

The twentieth century is of course also concerned with the concept of man the *saccus stercorus*. Perhaps the most extreme physiological *tour de force* in contemporary satire is Nathanael West's *The Dream Life of Balso Snell*, whose entire action takes place inside the intestines of the Trojan Horse. In this striking microcosm of civilization Balso encounters, among others, a man who imagines himself to be Christ and tries to crucify himself with thumbtacks and an equally devout person who has made a study of St. Puce, a flea who lived in the armpit of Christ and wrote the apocryphal *Geography of our Lord*. Aldous Huxley's satiric novels provide more subtle but equally powerful examples of ironic reduction to flesh. In *Point Counter Point* we experience the spirituality of a Bach suite in totally physical terms:

> The vibrating air rattled Lord Edward's membrana tympani; the interlocked malleus, incus, and stirrup bones were set in motion, so as to agitate the membrane of the oval window and raise an infinitesimal storm in the fluid of the labyrinth. The hairy endings of the auditory nerve shuddered like weeds in a rough sea; a vast number of obscure miracles were performed in the brain, and Lord Edward ecstatically whispered, "Bach!"

And again in the same novel spirituality is reduced:

> The cell in her belly had multiplied itself and become a worm; the worm had become a fish, the fish was turning into the foetus of a mammal. . . . Fifteen years hence a boy would be confirmed. Enormous in his robes, like a full-rigged ship, the Bishop will say: "Do you here in the presence of God, and of this congregation, renew the solemn promise and vow that was made in your name at your baptism?" And the ex-fish would answer with passionate conviction, "I do!"

The examples could be multiplied indefinitely. Man is never allowed to forget his vile flesh. The insistent voice of the satirist continues to proclaim, usually with great good humor and gusto, that beauty and order are illusions fig-leafing the stark reality of flesh.

Swift is the satirist who comes most readily to mind when considering scatological reductionism in literature. In one of his letters to Stella he sets the keynote to his work: "The Queen," he writes, "is well, but I fear she will be no long liver; for I am told she has sometime the gout in her bowels (I hate the word bowels)." He of course did not restrict his hatred to the mere word; he applied it with full force to the things in themselves, as well as to the entire associated physiological cluster. One finishes *Gulliver's Travels* with the impression that the worst thing about the Yahoos was not their lack of morals but the fact that they were so distressingly physical. And Swift's poetic treatment of women surpasses his prose treatment of the Yahoos. For example, savor this passage from "The Lady's Dressing Room":

> And first a dirty smock appeared,
> Beneath the armpits well besmeared . . .
> But oh! it turned poor Stephen's bowels,
> When he beheld and smelt the towels,
> Begummed, besmattered, and begrimed,
> With dirt and sweat and earwax grimed.

Later the rhapsody of disgust continues:

> His foul imagination links
> Each dame he sees with all her stinks;
> And if unsavory odours fly,
> Conceives a lady standing by.

And in "Cassinus and Peter" the poet ends each stanza with the despairing refrain:

> Oh, Caelia, Caelia, Caelia sh—!

Perhaps further quotation from Swift's verse on women would be too dreary. Suffice it to say that Swift could not escape his constant vision of the *saccus stercorus* and thus could not forgive man—and especially woman—for being human.

This type of scatological reductionism is, as we have shown, a form of antisocial violence, the essential antisocial maneuver of the Marquis de Sade. While Sade evoked the pyrotechnics of evil in fleshly terms, Swift used the fleshly terms to point out the shortcomings of the institutions, customs, attitudes, and states of mind to which he objected. To put it another way, Sade employed scatology for its own sake while Swift aimed it against his and his society's enemies. In *A Modest Proposal,* for a perfect example, we see the reduction to matter carried to its logical extreme: man becomes in every sense a commodity. There are cannibalistic scenes in Sade's novels—notably in *Juliette*—which eventually become more tiresome than emetic; but the cannibalism of *A Modest Proposal* produces a far more shocking effect, an effect which does not come from a contemplation of cannibalism as such, but rather, from the way in which it is strategically manipulated. Swift masquerades as a social type, puts on the identity of the average, sincere, rational Englishman, and from there proceeds to the corporeal reduction. Thus, he implies that the average, sincere, rational Englishman is at the same time a howling savage. The resulting situation is rather like what would happen if I pretended to be a madman while impersonating my worst enemy. The strategy is immensely effective; the enemy has no defense.

Now the critical point is this: an elaborate stratagem for reducing an enemy to mere flesh can be forced into a moral framework when the enemy is political corruption, ignorance, foppery, hypocrisy, pedantry, or something similar; the satirist, regardless of his subrational motives, really does censure what his class considers wickedness and folly. The wicked and the foolish deserve to be punished by having their inglorious animality put on display. Here only the putative enemies of the people are implicated, not the people as a whole; hence the violence is social instead of antisocial. But when the object of the satire includes the mass of society, or when, even, society cannot possibly avoid being involved in some more specific violence, then the satiric effect becomes, clearly, an antisocial one. And the satirist cannot claim to be offering constructive criticism in such a case—especially when the wickedness and folly consist of something so inescapable as possessing bowels and other such dismal realities.

This kind of object expansion takes place frequently in satire. It occurs most memorably in the final book of *Gulliver's Travels,* where the victims have become, not simply politicians, bigots, and pedants, but the entire human race, and worse, the human race offends the satirist's nose more than his moral principles. In the well-known passage near the end of *Gulliver's Travels* we encounter a description of Gulliver's traumatic re-entry into society:

> My wife and family received me with great surprise and joy, because they concluded me certainly dead; but I must freely confess the sight of them fills me only with hatred, disgust and contempt, and the more by reflecting on the near alliance I had with one of them. . . . And when I began to consider that by copulating with one of the Yahoo species I had become a parent of more, it struck me with the utmost shame, confusion and horror.
>
> As soon as I entered the house, my wife took me in her arms and kissed me, at which, having not been used to the touch of that odious animal for so many years, I fell in a swoon for almost an hour. At the time I am writing it is five years since my last return to England: during the first year I could not endure my wife or children in my presence, the very smell of them was intolerable, much less could I suffer them to eat in the same room. To this hour they dare not presume to touch my bread, or drink out of the same cup, neither was I able to let one of them take me by the hand.

The only trouble with human society, in short, is that it consists of human beings.

Some critics will of course object to this emphasis on scatological reductionism in Swift; and many Swift scholars will not endure any derogation of the master. One critic argues (and quite convincingly) that the Houyhnhnms represent man's better, rational side, while the Yahoos represent only the lower half of the human personality. And Norman O. Brown, in a brilliant chapter of *Life Against Death* on Swift's "Excremental Vision," demonstrates that Swift's satire is a working out in detail of his own psychoanalytic theory of repression and sublimation. Within the limitations of my present concern I do not object to these interpretations, except to point out that they do not explain away the reductionistic and misanthropic element in the book. The scatological facts remain—however rationalized they may become, and however much they are put into the mouths of Gulliver and other satiric personae. The book ends with humanity in a state of conspicuous vileness, and for Gulliver, as well as for all of us, the final message is this: You shall know the truth and the truth shall make you sick.

III

So far we have seen how the rhetoric of sadism corresponds to the rhetoric of satire, how, in other words, the method of both consists of flesh emphasis as a means of outraging all or part of society. The sadist aspires to an absolute of evil, and the satirist usually persuades himself that he is a moralist; and both, as a matter of paradoxical fact, employ the same technique. On the other hand, the differences between the two are obvious enough to assure us that they are in some way not identical. Voltaire's *Candide*, say, and Sade's *Aline et Valcour* are in many ways strikingly similar: both are picaresque, both catalogue an endless variety of atrocities, both contain utopian elements, and both take a dim view of man's prospects. The difference is that we laugh at *Candide* and are horrified by *Aline et Valcour*. If the action patterns of both are so similar, why are our reactions to them so dissimilar?

A final answer to this question would be a final answer to the perplexing problems of the nature of laughter, for laughter clearly distinguishes satire from sadism. Though final answers to such questions are unusual, we must, however, consider some speculations on the nature of laughter in order to come closer to seeing the satiric elements of sadism as well as the sadistic elements of satire. What is laughter? And why do we laugh at some kinds of violence and weep at others? Why, also, is *ordure* at times hilarious (as in *Roderick Random*), satiric (as in *Gul-*

liver's Travels), cheerful (as in *Gargantua*), and repulsive (as in
Justine)? And where, above all, does it acquire its serpent-like
fascination? Swift, again, gives us the most striking example of
this paradoxical, almost oxymoronic, coexistence of repulsion and
attraction. He hated bowels and, at the same time, bowels constituted the central comic aspect of his life work. In such a situation laughter must be something more than it appears on the
surface to be.

Baudelaire's essay *L'Essence de rire* provides us with a useful
insight. Laughter, he proclaims, is "one of the more obvious
marks of the satanic in man"; it is also a "damnable element born
of a diabolic parentage." In the course of the essay we discover
that the diabolic parentage is none other than nature red in
tooth and claw. "The being who wished to multiply His creatures
in His own image did not give to them the teeth of the lion—but
laughter is man's way of biting." The comic impulse is thus profoundly atavistic, a more genteel manifestation of the growl and
snarl. (Consider, also, in this context the semanticist's differen-
tiation between "snarl-words" and "purr-words.") Laughter, in
brief, is the civilized way of growling. And what is it, specifically,
which causes the refined and unferocious modern man to burst
forth in his uncontrollable growl-laugh? The answer is simple:
laughter is caused by a revelation of superiority. When a man is
confronted by a scene which somehow, on some obscure psychic
level, convinces him of his superiority, he expresses his satisfaction at this triumph in much the same way that the beast in the
forest roars over his fallen prey. "Pride and aberration!" cries the
indignant Baudelaire. It is a mark of madness:

> Now it is a notorious fact that patients in a madhouse are
> all of them suffering from the idea, developed beyond the
> normal, of their own superiority. I know of scarcely any
> lunatics who are marked by humility. It should be noted
> that laughter is one of the most common symptoms of
> madness.

Since we are here dealing with psychological man, that is,
with man the irrational animal, we must expect the motive force

of laughter to consist of contradictory ideas. Laughter, therefore, is a sign of weakness, an inferiority basking in the momentary illusion of superiority. "Indeed," writes Baudelaire, pursuing this obverse corollary of the impulse:

Indeed, what more obvious sign of debility can there be than the nervous convulsion, the involuntary spasm, comparable to a sneeze, provoked by somebody else's misfortune? . . . What spectacle can be more deplorable than that of weakness rejoicing at weakness? But there is still worse to come. The misfortune in question is sometimes of a very inferior kind, something wholly physical. Let me take as an example one of the most ordinary occurrences of daily life. What is there so pleasing in the sight of somebody slipping on the ice, falling down in the street, or tripping over a curbstone, that the face of his brother in Christ should immediately contract in a most immoderate fashion, and all its muscles come suddenly into play like a clock striking, or a spring-toy bobbing? The poor devil will, at the very least, have broken a limb or been bruised. All the same, laughter has burst forth from the spectator, sudden and irresistible. Should one probe deeply enough, it is pretty certain that there will be found in the mental attitude of the one who laughs, a certain unconscious sense of pride.

Even though it must be readily admitted that there are probably many kinds of laughter, and that this description cannot begin to account for all of them, we must accept the partial validity of Baudelaire's commentary. Laughter is frequently a manifestation of the will to power, an expression of power over one's environment and a reaffirmation of one's value in contrast to the suddenly depleted value of some competing entity. Clearly, the easiest way to feel intelligent is to dwell upon foolishness; and, also clearly, foolishness is invariably laughable. Now we must emphasize that only this special type of superiority revelation, superiority as antithesis to an incongruous inferiority, causes laughter. When we are praised, flattered, or complimented in some way, we are pleased or embarrassed, but do not laugh. We

laugh only when our worth contrasts with the unworth of another. Hence Baudelaire's insistence on the "satanic" or "sadistic"
essence of laughter.

In terms of this concept of laughter, we can draw together the
diverse threads of this consideration of the relationship between
satire and sadism. Baudelairean laughter is clearly satiric laughter, and satire is inevitably an example of the so-called satanic
element. Inevitably so; for satire is a linguistic structure designed
to point out as forcefully as possible the inferiority of certain
chosen objects in a social context, a structure designed, in other
words, to root out, display, or even create, things which by their
wickedness, foolishness, dirtiness or abnormality will cause in
the onlooker the illusion of superiority. The resulting spasm of
laughter acts as an emotional cathartic by purging the ego of its
frequently disturbing awareness of inadequacy.

An important implication emerging from this concept is that
wit, rather than moral purpose, is the primary difference between
satiric and sadistic acts. Wit, in the sense of comic cleverness as
well as in the sense of formal artistic complexity, is crucial, perhaps even essential, to satire, while, as we have pointed out,
moral function frequently disappears in a satiric holocaust of
values. In terms of Freud's ideas in *Wit and Its Relation to the
Unconscious,* we can see that wit can function as a medium
through which forbidden, criminal material can be transmitted to
the social world and be enjoyed. Like sublimation, it is a kind
of safety valve for the pressure built up by repressed antisocial
material. To put it another way, wit is, like dream symbolism, a
way of having one's cake and eating it too; a way of retaining
the patterns of civilized behavior while also enjoying the forbidden areas beneath the rational social consciousness. Sadism,
by contrast, must avoid wit as well as moral purpose, and achieve
its quality of pure outrageousness by going directly to the id;
thus violating the mandates of the censoring superego.

Another aspect of this fusion of Baudelairean laughter and
violence is that it helps to elucidate the connection between
primitive rituals and the beginnings of comedy and satire. Corn-
ford's theory, in the *Origins of Attic Comedy,* that comedy was
a later development of phallic songs and immolation rituals, is

enforced by these elements which are common to modern satire and the ritualistic structure of violence. The victim of the satirist is in a very real sense a scapegoat—the individual whose degradation is intended to have a purifying or cathartic result. (Since the Cambridge anthropologists recognize two basic types of scapegoats—the noble or heroic victim as opposed to the pharmakos, the ignoble victim—we can see how the former is the archetypal tragic hero, while the latter is the archetypal butt of satire and the comedy of violence. The sacrifice of the hero, to put it another way, is a reverential appeasement of gods, while the degradation of the *pharmakos* is a symbolic casting out of devils.) Satire, then, casts out devils and, in doing so, convinces the spectator of his virtue. But then, having served society by purging of it its awareness of personal inadequacy, satire frequently performs a psychological double reverse by suddenly expanding its field of fire to include all of humanity and thus negates its socialized function.

An interesting sidelight here is the putative connection between early phallic rituals, witch cults, the Black Mass, and sadistic literature. Sadism is probably a sophisticated outgrowth from medieval witch cults, and medieval witch cults probably are underground survivals of pagan Dionysian rituals. Thus, sadism might well stem from the same source in western culture as satire. Regardless of sources, however, they certainly employ the same techniques for the same psychic purposes. The sadist achieves his goal by distorting his victims, that is, by reducing them to the level of nonhuman organisms or chemical structures. In satire the victim is distorted in the same manner; he is presented in such a way as to make his entire identity conceivable only in nonhuman terms. Swift's Yahoo, for example, is a distortion of the race to make it appear (almost surrealistically) as a being with bowels, genitalia, armpits, appetites—and nothing more. Since the satirist reduces the victim by excluding mind, and since the sadist manipulation follows the same formula, we must conclude that, on the unrationalized level, both in action and in method, satire is sadistic.

GEOFFREY GORER

THE PORNOGRAPHY OF DEATH

"Birth, and copulation, and death.
That's all the facts when you come to brass tacks;
Birth, and copulation, and death."
T. S. Eliot, *Sweeney Agonistes* (1932)

Pornography is, no doubt, the opposite face, the shadow, of prudery, whereas obscenity is an aspect of seemliness. No society has been recorded which has not its rules of seemliness, of words or actions which arouse discomfort and embarrassment in some contexts, though they are essential in others. The people before whom one must maintain a watchful seemliness vary from society to society: all people of the opposite sex, or all juniors, or all elders, or one's parents-in-law, or one's social superiors or inferiors, or one's grandchildren have been selected in different societies as groups in whose presence the employment of certain words or the performance of certain actions would be considered offensive; and then these words or actions become charged with effect. There is a tendency for these words and actions to be related to sex and excretion, but this is neither necessary nor universal; according to Malinowski, the Trobrianders surround eating with as much shame as excretion; and in other societies personal names or aspects of ritual come under the same taboos.

Rules of seemliness are apparently universal; and the non-observance of these rules, or anecdotes which involve the breaking of the rules, provoke that peculiar type of laughter which seems identical the world over; however little one may know about a strange society, however little one may know about the functions of laughter in that society (and these can be very various) one can immediately tell when people are laughing at an obscene joke. The topper of the joke may be "And then he ate the whole meal in front of them!", or "She used her husband's name in the presence of his mother!", but the laughter is the same; the taboos of seemliness have been broken and the result is hilarious. Typically, such laughter is confined to one-sex groups and is more general with the young, just entering into the complexities of adult life.

Obscenity then is a universal, an aspect of man and woman living in society; everywhere and at all times there are words and actions which, when misplaced, can produce shock, social embarrassment and laughter. Pornography on the other hand, the description of tabooed activities to produce hallucination or delusion, seems to be a very much rarer phenomenon. It probably can only arise in literate societies, and we certainly have no records of it for non-literate ones; for whereas the enjoyment of obscenity is predominantly social, the enjoyment of pornography is predominantly private. The fantasies from which pornography derives could of course be generated in any society; but it seems doubtful whether they would ever be communicated without the intermediary of literacy.

The one possible exception to this generalization is the use of plastic arts without any letterpress. I have never felt quite certain that the three-dimentional *poses plastiques* on so many Hindu temples (notably the "Black Pagoda" at Konarak) have really the highfalutin Worship of the Life Force or Glorification of the Creative Aspect of Sex which their apologists claim for them; many of them seem to me very like "feelthy" pictures, despite the skill with which they are executed. There are too the erotic woodcuts of Japan; but quite a lot of evidence suggests that these are thought of as laughter-provoking (i.e., obscene) by the Japanese themselves. We have no knowledge of the functions of the Peruvian pottery.

As far as my knowledge goes, the only Asian society which had a long-standing tradition of pornographic literature is China; and, it would appear, social life under the Manchus was surrounded by much the same haze of prudery as distinguished the nineteenth century in much of Europe and the Americas, even though the emphasis fell rather differently; women's deformed feet seem to have been the greatest focus of peeking and sniggering, rather than their ankles or the cleft between their breasts; but by and large life in Manchu China seems to have been nearly as full of "unmentionables" as life in Victoria's heyday.

Pornography would appear to be a concomitant of prudery, and usually the periods of the greatest production of pornography have also been the periods of the most rampant prudery. In contrast to obscenity, which is chiefly defined by situation, prudery is defined by subject; some aspect of human experience is treated as inherently shameful or abhorrent, so that it can never be discussed or referred to openly, and experience of it tends to be clandestine and accompanied by feelings of guilt and unworthiness. The unmentionable aspect of experience then tends to become a subject for much private fantasy, more or less realistic, fantasy charged with pleasurable guilt or guilty pleasure; and those whose power of fantasy is weak, or whose demand is insatiable, constitute a market for the printed fantasies of the pornographer.

Traditionally, and in the lexicographic meaning of the term, pornography has been concerned with sexuality. For the greater part of the last two hundred years copulation and (at least in the mid-Victorian decades) birth were the "unmentionables" of the triad of basic human experiences which "are all the facts when you come to brass tacks," around which so much private fantasy and semi-clandestine pornography were erected. During most of this period death was no mystery, except in the sense that death is always a mystery. Children were encouraged to think about death, their own deaths and the edifying or cautionary death-beds of others. It can have been a rare individual who, in the 19th century with its high mortality, had not witnessed at least one actual dying, as well as paying their respect to "beautiful corpses"; funerals were the occasion of the greatest display for working class, middle class, and aristocrat. The cemetery was the centre of every old-established village, and they were prominent in most towns. It was fairly late in the 19th century when the execution of criminals ceased to be a public holiday as well as a public warning. Mr. Fairchild had no difficulty in finding a suitably garnished gibbet for his moral lesson.

In the 20th century, however, there seems to have been an unremarked shift in prudery; whereas copulation has become more and more "mentionable," particularly in the Anglo-Saxon societies, death has become more and more "unmentionable" as a natural process. I cannot recollect a novel or play of the last twenty years or so which has a "death-bed scene" in it, describing in any detail the death "from natural causes" of a major character; this topic was a set piece for most of the eminent Victorian and Edwardian writers, evoking their finest prose and their most elaborate technical effects to produce the greatest amount of pathos or edification.

One of the reasons, I imagine, for this plethora of death-bed scenes—apart from their intrinsic emotional and religious content—was that it was one of the relatively few experiences that an author could be fairly sure would have been shared by the vast majority of his readers. Questioning my old acquaintances, I cannot find one over the age of sixty who did not witness the agony of at least one near relative; I do not think I know a single person under the age of thirty who has had a similar experience. Of course my acquaintance is neither very extensive nor particularly representative; but in this instance I do think it is typical of the change of attitude and "exposure."

The natural processes of corruption and decay have become disgusting, as disgusting as the natural processes of birth and copulation were a century ago; preoccupation about such processes is (or was) morbid and unhealthy, to be discouraged in all and punished in the young. Our great-grandparents were told that babies were found under gooseberry bushes or cabbages; our children are likely to be told that those who have passed on (fie! on the gross Anglo-Saxon monosyllable) are changed into flowers, or lie at rest in lovely gardens. The ugly facts are relentlessly hidden; the art of the embalmers is an art of complete denial.

It seems possible to trace a connection between the shift of taboos and the shift in religious beliefs. In the 19th century most of the inhabitants of Protestant countries seem to have subscribed to the Pauline beliefs in the sinfulness of the body and the certainty of the afterlife. "So also is the resurrection of the dead. It is sown in corruption; it is raised in incorruption: it is sown in dishonour; it is raised in glory." It was possible to insist on the corruption of the dead body, and the dishonour of its begetting, while there was a living belief in the incorruption and the glory of the immoral part. But in England, at any rate, belief in the future life as taught in Christian doctrine is very uncommon today even in the minority who make church-going or prayer a consistent part of their lives; and without some such belief natural death and physical decomposition have become too horrible to contemplate or to discuss. It seems symptomatic that the contemporary sect of Christian Science should deny the fact of physical death, even to the extent (so it is said) of refusing to allow the word to be printed in the Christian Science Monitor.

During the last half-century public health measures and improved preventive medicine have made natural death among the younger members of the population much more uncommon than it had been in earlier periods, so that a death in the family, save in the fullness of time, became a relatively uncommon incident in home life; and, simultaneously, violent death increased in a manner unparalleled in human history. Wars and revolutions, concentration camps and gang feuds were the most publicized of the causes for these violent deaths; but the diffusion of the automobile, with its constant and unnoticed toll of fatal accidents, may well have been most influential in bringing the possibility of violent death into the expectations of law-abiding people in time of peace. While natural death became more and more smothered in prudery, violent death has played an ever growing part in the fantasies offered to mass audience—detective stories, thrillers, Westerns, war stories, spy stories, science fiction, and eventually horror comics.

There seem to be a number of parallels between the fantasies which titillate our curiosity about the mystery of sex, and those which titillate our curiosity about the mystery of death. In both types of fantasy, the emotions which are typically concomitant of the acts—love or grief—are paid little or no attention, while the sensations are enhanced as much as a customary poverty of language permits. If martial intercourse be considered the natural expression of sex for most of humanity most of the time, then "natural sex" plays as little role as "natural death" (the ham-fisted attempts of D. H. Lawrence and Jules Romains to describe "natural sex" realistically but high-mindedly prove the rule). Neither type of fantasy can have any real development, for once the protagonist has done something, he or she must proceed to do something else, with or to somebody else, more refined, more complicated, or more sensational than what had occurred before. This somebody else is not a person; it is either a set of genitals, with or without secondary sexual characteristics, or a body, perhaps capable of suffering pain as well as death. Since most languages are relatively poor in words or constructions to express intense pleasure or intense pain, the written portions of both types of fantasy abound in onomatopoeic conglomerations of letters meant to evoke the sighs, gasps, groans, screams, and rattles concomitant to the described actions. Both types of fantasy rely heavily on adjective and simile. Both types of fantasy are completely unrealistic, since they ignore all physical, social, or legal limitations, and both types have complete hallucination of the reader or viewer as their object.

There seems little question that the instinct of those censorious busybodies preoccupied with other people's morals was correct when they linked the pornography of death with the pornography of sex. This, however, seems to be the only thing which has been correct in their deductions or attempted actions. There is no valid evidence to suggest that either type of pornography is an incitement to action; rather are they substitute gratifications. The belief that such hallucinatory works would incite their readers to copy the actions depicted would seem to be indirect homage to the late Oscar Wilde, who described such a process in *The Portrait of Dorian Gray;* I know of no authenticated parallels in real life, though investigators and magistrates with bees in their bonnets can usually persuade juvenile delinquents to admit to exposure to whatever medium of mass communication they are choosing to make a scapegoat.

Despite some gifted precursors, such as Andréa de Nerciat or Edgar Allan Poe, most works in both pornographies are aesthetically objectionable; but it is questionable whether, from the purely aesthetic point of view, there is much more to be said for the greater part of the more anodyne fare provided by contemporary mass media of communication. Psychological Utopians tend to condemn substitute gratifications as such, at least where copulation is involved; they have so far been chary in dealing with death.

Nevertheless, people have to come to terms with the basic facts of birth, copulation and death, and somehow accept their implications; if social prudery prevents this being done in an open and dignified fashion, then it will be done surreptitiously. If we dislike the modern pornography of death, then we must give back to death—natural death—its parade and publicity, readmit grief and mourning. If we make death unmentionable in polite society—"not before the children"—we almost ensure the continuation of the "horror comic." No censorship has ever been really effective.

WAYLAND YOUNG

IN DESPITE OF CHRISTENDOM

With much misgiving, I have rather arbitrarily set the erotic
books and pictures which have arisen within Christendom into
five categories, and shall attempt to order the material accordingly. The categories overlap; many works show the characteristics of two or more of these categories. The works I mention
below are only the most interesting ones, whether because they
are good of their kind, or because they are the works of writers
or artists who interest us for other reasons.

The five categories are the comic, the perverse, the haptic-
convulsive, the all-out pornographic, and the celebratory.* In
my judgment, that is also an ascending order of interest.

1. THE COMIC

These are not primarily works of erotic content at all, but ones
which use the erotic as a vehicle for satire, or for jokes which

* (Not discussed fully in this excerpt.)

seek to please simply by associating one thing with some other, unexpected, thing. The comic-erotic is primarily an eighteenth-century form; it took up, consciously or not, a strand present in the Greco-Roman culture. Examples are Voltaire's *Pucelle d'Orleans,* Diderot's *Les Bijoux Indiscrets* and, in the visual field, the print called *Hogarth's Cottage.*

In the *Pucelle d'Orleans,* Voltaire uses the following formula in narrative heroic couplets: take the history of Joan of Arc and her times and retell it so that whenever anything boring and historical, and especially a battle, is about to take place, they all stop and copulate instead. It is certainly very funny, not because of its sexual content but because of the unsuitability of everything, and because of Voltaire's familiar naive delight in the bumps and grinds of divine intervention; St. Denis is forever floating about on a cloud and exclaiming in a shocked way at the goings-on. There are excellent lines in it: for instance, the description of the Biblical heroine Judith as *"galante et homicide."* And there is one idea which gives the full force of Voltaire's atheism in a way that nothing in *Candide* does; it is that the Apostles chose Judas by lot to do what they were all agreed had to be done. Very many eighteenth-century editions.

Diderot's novel, *Les Bijoux Indiscrets,* has been translated as "The Indiscreet Toys." The toys are the woman's cunts, and they and indiscreet because they talk. It is a pseudo-Oriental hodge-podge, in which encyclopedist notions, day-to-day theatrical and musical criticism, Africa, Sultans, and "Brama" are all mixed up. The hero, a prince, obtains from a Sultan a magic ring which will make any girl's cunt prattle about what it has been up to recently. The narrative framework is provided by the thirty trials the prince makes of his ring before finally daring to try it on his own girl friend, who turns out to have been chaste all along. It is full of an exuberant and mercurial wit; though sometimes quite specific, it is not often very lascivious in effect. Here is the first appearance of the ring. "The Sultan leveled his ring at her. A loud burst of laughter, which seized Alcina at some comical saying of her husband, was suddenly cut short by the operation of the ring; and immediately a murmuring noise was

heard under her petticoats." (An indiscretion.) ". . . all the
ladies grew pale, looked at each other in deep silence, and grew
vastly serious . . . lest the conversation should grow warm and
become general."

The print "Hogarth's Cottage" shows a boathouse standing in
a wood, reflected in a calm lake, while the sun sets between two
hills like the Langdale Pikes. This is a visual pun. The boathouse
is a cunt, the hills breasts, and the sun the chin of a woman
between whose legs we are standing.

As far as I know, the comic-erotic form did not exist in Christendom much before the eighteenth century—Rabelais was not
an erotic writer, but a digestive-excretory one—and did not
endure long after. This is not to say there is no wit and humor
in erotic works which are not primarily comic in intention.

2. THE PERVERSE [1]

The perverse tradition in erotic art rests on the need of the writer
or artist to make, and the reader or beholder to receive, descriptions and depictions of whatever sexual oddity it is that controls
their desires.

There is a very great bulk of sadistic books and pictures. . . .
A conspicuous modern sadistic novel is Guillaume Apollinaire's
Les Onze Milles Vierges, ou Les Amours du'un Hospodar. It
is concocted from his own reading in the tradition, efficiently
enough, and contains some horrible impalements, and so forth.
The same reasons which prevent the sadist from coming into a
workable relationship with his environment also prevent the
sadistic artist from achieving anything very much. There is per-

---

[1] The fact that I use the word perverse here and not the currently
more favored deviant or deviate implies not a moral judgment or a
social attitude, but linguistic caution. Perverse means "turned across";
deviant means "going off the way." I cannot see that the former is any
ruder than the latter. Colored people and developing nations change
their designation every so often, or have it changed for them; in the
hope that justice and humanity can be introduced by synonym. What
would come after deviant? Paragyrist?

haps something to be learned from Leonor Fini's illustrations to Sade's *Justine;* it does not seem likely that one could go much further along the road of being pretty about pain and death.

Each kink has its literature. For pederasty, the first work is probably the best; this is the *Alcibiade Fanciullo a Scuola* attributed to Ferrante Pallavincino, who was born in 1616 and lived his short life as a political journalist in Venice. He incurred the wrath, as they say, of the papal family of Barberini, who sent someone to him pretending to be a messenger from Cardinal Richelieu. This man told the unworldly and exalted Pallavincino that Richelieu had invited him to go to Paris as his official historian. They set off together, and at Avignon Pallavincino was arrested, kept twenty months in prison, and then beheaded. He was twenty-eight.

The Boy Alcibiades at School was posthumously published in 1652. (Reissue, Paris, 1862.) In it the schoolmaster describes to the boy the pleasures of buggery, working up from double entendre of a most philosophical nature to open description, and at the end they get down to it. Pallavincino promised "more lasciviousness" in the second volume but it was never written. The style is heavy and soft, and has a certain complex majesty. His world is the private one of carefully cultivated feeling, based on Platonic philosophy and the equation of the body personal with the body cosmic; it is full of a gentle gravity which transcends the special limitation of the object of desire, and it is also quite without the terrified guilt or the jumpy awareness of hostile pressure which, understandably enough, disfigures so much later homosexual writing.

The doyen of incest writing was the eighteenth-century French novelist Restif de la Bretonne. He was a crazy individualist full of quite private beliefs and values, who thought Sade wasn't nice enough to women, and set out to put the matter right with a series of enormous novels in which he praised incest instead of cruelty. Not all of them are now locked up; in France they are fairly easy to come by. One of them, *Monsieur Nicolas,* was translated into English and published by Havelock Ellis.

Restif de la Bretonne was a shoe fetishist, by his own account, from the age of four, and calculated that he had had 217 daughters by the time he was sixty. This was because he believed that all chance encounters should result in offspring; he was never quite clear whether he had a corresponding number of sons; he was not interested in sons. The daughters he used to meet again by chance, recognize them by the voluptuous turn of their legs and feet and "by the thermometer of his heart" and start all over again. His biographer [2] has noticed that the only people he called "monster" were his wife, his son-in-law and Sade. He discovered his bent as a writer through an early compulsion to write about how his balls were feeling on the parapets of bridges over the Seine; his novels run to 194 volumes. His *Anti-Justine,* which he wrote specifically to show up the brutality of Sade, starts with the hero laying half a dozen of his sisters in quick succession, and then gets down to the serious business of life, which is father-daughter incest. There is in fact no brutality in his novels, but there is a great deal of shoe-smelling. The incest is used as a *sause piquante;* the forbiddenness heightens the thrill.

A notable modern novel written out of a perverse compulsion is *Trois Filles de leur Mère* by Pierre Louys. A few hundred copies of this, in facsimile of the manuscript, were published posthumously in 1929. It narrates the adventures of a young man who finds he has taken lodgings next to a family of Italian whores who specialize in buggery; the three daughters have been trained for this work by their mother. The fantasy is deviant enough; incest, general nymphomania, little girls of ten, and so on, and it tails off in a senseless repetition which shows the obsessive character of the impulse to write it, and which Louys, who was a considerable writer of narrative and dialogue, would no doubt have cut if he had been writing for publication. But there is one character in it, Charlotte, the eldest daughter, who is real and touching, and the dialogue throughout is also real; that is to say it is as sharp and true and respectful of human motive as the dialogue in the overtly published novels which we usually judge to be considerable. There is a real eloquence in this girl's part (it is almost like a play, all talk). She hates everybody and everything for what has been done to her, which

[2] See C. R. Dawes, *Restif de la Bretonne,* London, 1946.

is every horror, and loves only her own finger. She knows the whole world can't be wrong in its values, and she alone right, but she can't see what the world holds right, is blind to it and knows her blindness, and therefore holds herself in contempt. This is one of the largest and most real presentations of the whore-character in European fiction.

3. THE HAPTIC-CONVULSIVE

The writers and artists in the tradition of perversity are bound in a peculiar lock with their own compulsion; those in the much larger tradition of the haptic-convulsive are bound in the same lock with sexuality itself. They are mastered by it, at the mercy of that in them which cannot leave it alone. To use the word perversion for the former category and not for the present one is perhaps illogical; one should use it for both or neither. I put into the category of haptic-convulsive all those books and pictures which make one think: "Poor fellow; he had to." The hallmarks are a mixture of horror and delight, and a brute emphasis on the mechanical and the local, on the organs themselves, the details.

At this point it becomes hard to distinguish the categories; there is a three-dimensional continuum between this one and the next two. The statements "this is horrid but fascinating" (haptic-convulsive), "I am giving you your money's worth" (all-out pornographic) and "this is beautiful and real" (celebratory) can coexist up to a certain point in a picture, and can succeed each other very swiftly in the same written work.

I believe the first book of purely or mainly erotic content to be published in Christian Europe was the *Hermaphrodite* of Antonio Beccadelli, written in about 1426, and this is haptic-convulsive. The Latin text was reissued in 1892 with a French translation by Isidore Liseux, the copious and scholarly French publisher of erotica and the general literature of love. Beccadelli, who wrote under the name of Panormita, the man from Palermo, was one of the first generation of Italian Latinists who later got called humanists and were found to have brought about the Renaissance. At that time, the Italian writers had hardly gone beyond imitations of this or that Latin original. Beccadelli's model was Martial, and to a lesser extent the "fescennine songs" of antiquity, little bawdy rhymes which were so called either because they abounded in the Tuscan town of Fescennia or, which is perhaps more likely, because they fulfilled the same function in words that the fascinum, or phallic charm, fulfilled in the realm of magical objects.

Beccadelli was an excellent imitator; his verses run very smoothly and sweetly and sometimes have a musical melancholy which would have endeared them to nineteenth-century school-masters if they had not been surrounded by such filth, as they would have found it, and if Beccadelli had been born fifteen hundred years earlier.[3] He was in the mainstream of humanist learning; the hermaphrodite of the title is an emblem of that hobbyhorse of humanist philosophy, the reconciliation of oppo-sites, and the arrangement of the book takes up the allusion. The first half is prick, the second half cunt. The poems were dedi-cated and sent to Cosimo de' Medici, and there is one addressed to Battista Alberti asking him, because he is a good scholar and a good friend, what Beccadelli should do because his girl is so demanding that he is quite exhausted, and then, suddenly, because she stinks so. Like Martial himself, which presumably was what endeared Martial to him, he was half fascinated and half disgusted by women and fucking. He is full of jokes and melancholy, now savage and sparkling, now meltingly sad. He is also much concerned with buggery. How, he keeps asking, can anyone who has once discovered the joy of buggery ever revert to that dreary business, fucking? On the whole, the impression he makes is one of grappling with a new idea—that the Roman writers could be adapted to contemporary life—and making only a fairly good go of it. He was born in Palermo in 1394, worked in the universities of Siena and Bologna, where he loved the loves he writes about, and died in Naples at the age of eighty.

Pietro Aretino, the greatest erotic writer in Christendom, who comes in my last and best category, the celebratory, had two

[3] E.G., *Morte sua lugent cantus lugentque choreae, Flet Venus, et moesto corpore moderet Amor.*

pupils who tried to handle the erotic, and succeeded enough to
be locked up ever since, but not enough to be read with any
pleasure. Lorenzo Veniero wrote a couple of long poems:
Zaffetta, which consists mainly of abuse of a girl who wouldn't
open her bedroom door to him, and *La Puttana Errante,* the
Wandering Whore. This rather famous narrative poem is a convulsive declaration of horror and fascination, and is very different from Aretino's cool understanding of prostitution. For 380
eight-line stanzas the whore wanders around the cities of Italy,
usually being welcomed in triumph because her fame had preceded her, the fame of being able to cope with more and bigger
clients than any other whore in the world. Veniero cannot come
to terms with the fact that a whore is promiscuous, he keeps
repeating in horror this one fact that she has a great many men.
He is also delighted by the fact that she is old and smelly.
Aretino dignified this stuff by writing an introductory sonnet
for it.

The other pupil was Niccolo Franco, who turned against
Aretino. He wrote a cycle of a hundred ninety-five sonnets, which
he put into the mouth of a wooden figure of Priapus in a garden.
This Priapus passes his days lamenting how wet he gets, explain-
ing to any girls who happen to pass by what a good fertility god
he is (all they have to do is climb up on him), insulting Aretino
as a bugger, and damply impugning clerical morals. There is an
occasional flash of gloomy fun.

> Buggera il Papa, e tutti i suoi prelati,
> Con ogni altra persona religiosa. . . .[4]

But what really held Franco up was the fact that his old
master Aretino praised buggery and, he assures us, practiced it.
When he had finished with the Priapus sonnets, he wrote a hundred and nineteen more devoted exclusively to this fact. Later
in life he was imprisoned for heresy, and was finally hanged as a
result of the posthumous reinstatement of a certain Cardinal

---

4   The Pope buggers, and so do all his cardinals,
         And so do all the other clerics. . . .

Carafa, to whose downfall he had contributed in the first place.

Continuing to leapfrog chronologically through the vast collections of the haptic-convulsive: Rowlandson. Rowlandson was the most copious draftsman in the English erotic tradition, and largely determined the way it went. There are mountains of his erotic tradition and drawings in many different collections, and I imagine they cannot be hard to come by on the open market. He had tremendous dash and openhandedness, but the enormous output is obsessive. He was clearly as much repelled as pleased, though always fascinated, by the fact that men and women, incredible creatures, do this amazing thing. The men are usually caricatured, and sometimes both men and women are, and these are painful to see. Dirty old men figure a great deal, paying to peer up the cunt of a whore, gawking at a nude model, etc., etc. Often music comes in: a military band, a string quartet all frigging away as they play. When the satire is not simply at the expense of fucking itself, it sometimes comes off rather well. There is one on the perennial theme of loose behavior in the park, where smart couples walk up and down in their Sunday best, but these are not people, they are pricks in various stages of erection and dejection. There is one of an over-virile Latin waiter carrying a tray on his prick.

Very occasionally he breaks through the barrier of his laughing horror and comes into a sort of peace and grace. The best of these are a handful of prints in the series called *Pretty Little Games,* and one of the two called *Jolly Gypsies,* which is his shot at the Golden Age myth.

Fragonard belongs here; his erotic pictures are strangely disappointing. He seems not to have been able to carry over his grace and balance into this field; everything comes out wrong. Clothes are rolled up and peered under, girls play with little dogs, and again and again naked virgins clutch pillows in their sleep, which is not really so much what girls do as what men like to think of them doing. Somehow his heart is not in it; he seems to have been working from a part of himself, the haptic-convulsive part, which might never have come to the actuality of canvas at all if it had not been for the fashion of the society he lived in. The effect is one of uncertainty.

Other good painters tried and failed to achieve something in the erotic; Turner (little booklets of washy water colors, obscurely voyeurish), Millet (soggy chalk drawings of lovers in fields), Degas (who could not give a whore a tenth of the attention he gave a dancer; illustrations to an edition of Lucian's *Dialogues*).

At the time of the Decadence, the draftsmen snatched and leered. Beardsley (illustrations to the *Lysistrata* and other books); effete and solipsistic, a hard struggle to get an authentic *frisson*. Franz von Bayros (many illustrated books); hectic wasted forms —the literary clichés show through the images—tiny pretty Lesbians, girl with rhino horn, girl with elephant trunk; sometimes an offhand badness in the drawing, betraying contempt for the consumer. The decorator of the Sezession movement in Vienna, Gustav Klimt (illustrations to Lucian); through the keyhole, communicating a panting lust. Bony people. None of these was an inconsiderable draftsman, but none was master of his material.

As archetypes of the haptic-convulsive, let us take one illustrator and one writer, Francois Bouchot (1800–1842), in a book of illustrations called *Diabolico-Foutromanie* (Diabolico-Fuckomania) carried to the farthest possible extent the feeling that fucking is a base and animal affair by simply putting animals' heads—bears and goats and pigs—on human bodies. Possible connection with witchcraft.

The literary archetype is the English Victorian pornographer Edward Sellon. His many novels are the gratification of impotent dreams; dreams of absolute power, of absolute indulgence, in castles not of this world, with girls not of this world. At crucial moments his characters say Erghhh! and Ughhh! like characters in a contemporary comic.

The makers and consumers of the haptic-convulsive fail only by partiality. Everybody has erotic fantasies, most also have erotic realities. These people could grasp nothing bigger than their dreams, and them they bottled and sold. It is the bottle which offends, not the dream; since the proper use for dreams is to flow and mix into the whole knowledge and feeling which makes a man.

This localization of perception in the arts and of feeling in life is itself an exclusion mechanism. In that it excludes the rest of the person, or the scene, or the life, it is simply the obverse of prudery. Pornography inflates what prudery has first excluded. In this sense, prudery makes pornography.

4. THE ALL-OUT PORNOGRAPHIC

This category differs from the former, the haptic-convulsive, in that the writer or artist does it not because he has to but because he wants to. (Of course he may "have to" from the financial point of view, but he is not emotionally compelled to.) He is in command of his material, has decided that he will turn to this particular form, and proceeds to do the reader proud. It shades off on the one hand into the former category when undigested dreams and compulsions come to the surface, and into the next category, the celebratory, when it rises above arbitrary specialization and becomes a valid synthesis of perception and execution, in other words, when it lapses into art. The hallmarks of the all-out pornographic are thus a sane but capricious gusto, a determination that the consumer shall have his money's worth, and an impression that the purpose of the whole operation is to provide male consumers with something to masturbate over.

The literature is once again enormous; but here I will discuss only a few books.

The form was only half-fledged in the Renaissance; perhaps Aretino's *Ragionamenti*, of which more below, came nearest to it, but that book is full of social and political observations, and could not qualify as "all-out." The book which first developed the form and which largely determined its future development right down to the latest paperback was the *Satyra Sotadica* of Nicholas Chorier.

It would be interesting to give a short biography of the father of Western pornography, but almost nothing is known about Chorier. He was a provincial worthy and historian of the Dauphine. *Satyra Sotadica* was first published about 1660, that is, about the time when the prose novel as a whole first made its appearance in Europe. It claimed to be the work of a national Spanish court lady called Aloysia Sigea, translated into Latin by a real, but recently dead, Flemish scholar called Meursius. There have been numerous editions in French since 1680.

It consists of dialogues among girls with Latin names, and repeatedly harks back to classical times as the golden age of fucking, from which the moderns have fallen off. The dialogue form was presumably chosen on the precedent of Aretino, and before him Lucian. The manner is rather heavy and boring; there is something stodgy and pedantic about it, quite unlike the vernacular fire and sparkle of Aretino. But it is an epochal work in the sense that it is the first book (I think) which contains nothing but sex from start to finish. It contains just about everything that two or more people can do in bed, and runs through the stages, which are followed in almost all later works of all-out pornography, from simple fucking through buggery and homosexuality, different forms of "contact" to use the jargon of modern sexology, orgies, flagellation, and incest. There is nothing else and, within the demarcated field, nothing is left out. It is the first work of rigid specialization, and thousands of later works have done no more than ring the changes on it.

Though the literature of this category in English is substantial, it is less so than in the preceding one, and less interesting than the literature of this category in French and Italian. The first English book is on all counts still the best; this is *Fanny Hill,* by John Cleland, first published in two volumes in 1748–49, expurgated edition, 1750, and since reissued very many times, sometimes under the original title, *The Memoirs of a Woman of Pleasure.* It is not a purely pornographic work, only about eighty per cent so. That is to say, Fanny's background is sketched in, she falls in love, she needs money to live on, her lovers have careers and positions which we are told about, even if shortly, and in the end she marries the man of her choice. But with those small intermissions, it follows pretty closely the pattern laid down by Chorier; you get a bit of everything, and lots of most things.

Cleland had a most remarkable prose style. He set himself the task of avoiding coarse words, that is, all those words which I argued should not be avoided. This drove him to extremes of flowery periphrasis; I have already quoted "his inestimable bulse of ladies' jewels." Here are some more, taken at random: "his plenipotentiary instrument," "a just concert of springy heaves," "what delicious manuals of love devotion" (breasts), "the prodigious effect the progressions of this delightful energy wrought in this delicious girl," "the baronet led the extasy, which she critically joined in," "refrain who could from such provoking enticements to it in reach?" "sometimes he took his hands from the semi-globes of her bosom and transferred the pressure of them to those larger ones, the present subjects of his soft blockade."

There are some ambitiously illustrated eighteenth-century editions of Fanny Hill. Some of the early illustrators tackled the job without too much fuss and guilt, but none of them was a good draftsman.

Cleland's devious and florid style, presumably because he was the only English "pornographic" writer of any interest at all, and was consequently so often republished, has affected English pornography right down to the present. A striking recent example is *Lust*,[5] by Count Palmiro Vicarion, a pseudonym which conceals, strangely, one of the tersest and most colloquial of our younger poets. Examples: ". . . she tried to avoid my outstretched arms and advance clamour calling for satisfaction in similar regions." "The most malleable zones of my unique masculine effects," "circumlocuting their buttocks in a unified and widening orbit."

Mirabeau wrote pornographic novels, and they are a very good example of this category; one gets a clear impression of a man who could do plenty of other things, doing this simply because he has chosen to. *Erotica Biblion* adduces texts from the classics to prove that the Romans fucked too. *Ma Conversion* is a first person account of the life of a gigolo, avid for *tartufferies*, for the license behind the pious facade. There is a startling picture of an American woman with "brownish red breasts, as hard as marble." The book contains the first appearance known to me of the overt notice to the reader of its own purpose which later became commonplace in pornographic novels: *"Eh bien, lis, dévore, et branle-toi."*[6] A lot of it is written almost in note form,

---

[5] Paris, Olympia Press, 1959.
[6] "And now, read, devour, masturbate."

suggesting a hurry to get the damn thing over and done with. The following paragraph from *Ma Conversion* will give an idea of the style of a great deal of the inferior *lecture galante* of eighteenth-century France.

> Tout favorisait mes feuz; la beauté du jour, dont les rayons, amollis par une gaze diaphane . . . .[7]
> "Arrête, témeraire!" s'écrie la tendre Julie. "Cher amant, Dieu . . . je . . . je meurs," et la parole expire sur ses lèvres de roses. L'heure somme à Cythere; l'Amour a secoué son flambeau dans les airs; je vole sur ses ailes, je combats, les cieux s'ouvrent . . . j'ai vaincu . . . O Venus! couvre-nous de la ceinture des Graces! etc., etc.[8]

Another book of Mirabeau's, *Le Rideau se Lève, ou L'Education de Laure*, is a more carefully written affair. He cunningly starts off with a father-daughter incest and then reveals that he was not her father at all. But she continues to call him Papa, so you get it both ways, the forbidden thrill without the forbidden reality. It goes on through a lot of meticulous, cheerful, rather monotonous "pornography," until he suddenly changes the plan, kills off most of the characters with declines brought on by over-indulgence, sends the remainder into a convent, and gets down to a long exposition of sexual morality, which, he says, ought to be tougher for women than for men.

The Manual of Classical Erotology of Friederich Karl Forberg appeared in many different languages throughout the nineteenth and into the twentieth century. Forberg, who wrote in the late eighteenth century, was the inventor and most wholehearted exponent of pornography as "science." The ostensible idea is that such things will leave the serious and scholarly unmoved,

---

[7] "Everything favored my ardor; the beauty of the day, whose rays, softened by diaphanous drapes . . . ."

[8] "'Hold, rash one!' cried the tender Julie. 'My dear love . . . Oh God . . . I . . . I am dying!' and the words expired on her rosy lips. The hour has struck in Cythera; Love has brandished his torch on high; I fly upon wings; I do battle: the heavens open . . . I have won . . . Oh Venus, cover us with the girdle of the Graces!" etc., etc.

and only inflame the depraved. His *Manual* is a collation of all the "sexy bits" from the classical writers, from which he derived a tabulation of everything that two or more people can do in bed. The upshot comes by another route very close to the "nothing-but" narrative form invented by Chorier.

Fuseli did a number of erotic drawings: they are more often in his open and decorative manner than his Gothic one. In quite a number the man, the "I" of the wish-fulfillment, is being seen to by several girls at once, like a patient surrounded by nurses.

After the works of Sade, perhaps the most famous erotic novel in the French language is *Gamiani*, attributed to Alfred de Musset. It went through forty-one editions before 1930. A preface claims that the author wrote it in answer to a challenge that he could not write an effective erotic novel without using "coarse" words. He does in fact avoid the short ordinary words, and does so with very much less fuss than Cleland in his parallel attempt in English. The action of *Gamiani* is largely Lesbian; the name, which comes from the surname of the heroine, an Italian countess, is to suggest the word *gamahucher*. The style is not bad, in a frenetic and exclamatory way. A young man plans to seduce the mysterious countess, hides himself in a cupboard, and finds that he is the witness of a Lesbian affair. So he comes out and joins in. Most of the book is taken up by the ensuing triangle, and later on there is a dog and a monkey as well. It belongs squarely to the romantic tradition in that love and death go together. There is a scene where Gamiani climbs onto the erection of a just-hanged man (Félicien Rops in his illustration changes this to a crucified one) and it ends when the two Lesbians take poison and experience orgasm and death simultaneously. Gamiani's last words are: "I still had to know whether in the torture of poison, in the agony of another woman mixed with my own, there was a satisfaction of the senses . . . It is frightful, do you hear? I die in the rage of pleasure." Romanticism in a nutshell.

· · · · · · · · ·

To sum up this section: fucking is not automatically exempt from art. The nature neither of fucking nor of art demands that the two should be kept apart, that the eye of art should be averted from this subject matter alone of all subject matters. When we find a culture in which this exemption is the rule, and we in Europe and America live in such a culture, the exemption teaches us nothing about either love or art, it only teaches us about the culture. It teaches us that our culture holds fucking to be either too disgraceful or too holy to be included in art, and, which is another way of saying the same thing, holds art to be too feeble to include fucking. That there should nevertheless be a trade in erotic art, whether good or bad by the usual canons of judgment, tells us no more than that, though European or American, we are still human. Human beings are fucking animals and art-making animals. That the trade of erotic art should be a clandestine one, with artificially high prices, subject to legal penalties, tells us that whatever else our culture may be, it is not an integrated one.

It is a feeble, blind, and tense culture that withdraws its vision, which is art, from anything. When that from which art is withdrawn is that which continues life, and therefore culture, the culture wills its own extinction. When we call sex a "blind force" we are saying that we will not look at tomorrow. We deny ourselves. We deny our children, casting them off from the chain of existence which justifies us and defines them, by denying their origin. And we have externalized the denial, the withdrawal, the exclusion, through our favorite medium: technology. We have built weapons which threaten to do in the flesh what our taboo does in the spirit, to discontinue human life, and with it our culture. How could we not? It was possible. Will a thing long enough, and you find the means to do it. Meanwhile black and brown and yellow peoples, without Christianity and its attendant technology, stand amazed and slowly understand that the final message of the Christian and post-Christian West, from the Urals to the Pacific coast, is despair, is severance, is an ending, is No.

.   .   .   .

Christian and post-Christian and Communist culture is a eunuch; pornography is his severed balls; thermonuclear weapons are his staff of office. If there is anything sadder than a eunuch it is his balls; if there is anything more deadly than impotence it is murder.

We imagine that women feel and fuck like men, we imagine that the ancients fucked more than we do, and that foreigners and animals still do. That which we deny and distrust in ourselves, we have to place somewhere. We know well enough that there is sex, lots of it, going on, but it can't be us who are doing it. We take the sexuality that is in us and we extrude it from ourselves and constitute it as an autonomous balloon. But action means agent; who shall be agent? Anybody will do: animals, foreigners, ancients, women. "Please sir," we say to the jealous God who still lives so strongly in us, "it wasn't us. It was them."

But it wasn't them; it was us. And only when we face the fact that it was us can we go on to face the more interesting facts, so unbearable before we have faced them, so obvious after, that nobody blames us, and that the pleasure comes from the pleasure, not from breaking a taboo.

THE PRESENT

Repressiveness is perhaps the more vigorously maintained the more unnecessary it becomes.

Herbert Marcuse. *Eros and Civilization.*

I doubt whether the kind of cold promiscuity current in youthful circles today is much more satisfactory than the restraints it has replaced. It is as much an expression of the consciousness's hatred for instinct and the body as was puritanism—puritanism inside out. . . . the essential thing is the restraint without which, it seems to me, there can be no passion or love, only a cold lasciviousness.

Aldous Huxley. *Letters.*

In the immediate present, there is no perfection, no consummation, nothing finished. The strands are all flying, quivering, intermingling into the web, the waters are shaking the moon. . . . The living plasm vibrates unspeakably, it inhales the future, it exhales the past. . . .

D. H. Lawrence. *Poetry of the Present.*

RICHARD SCHECHNER

PORNOGRAPHY AND THE
NEW EXPRESSION

The first question is, Why such a fuss? Sex has been with us since
the start, and art nearly that long. They have always been intertwined, sometimes openly and graphically, and more recently,
in a variety of covert ways. Every society has sought to regulate
both sexuality and artistic expression, and to a degree, each has
succeeded. Freedom, so called, is nothing other than an agreement on what to suppress. It becomes a social issue only when
opinion diverges. But it is always an artistic issue because the
artistic impulse—to play, expose, and invent—is deeply opposed
to the state's urge to conserve and control. We are terribly
bothered today because our regulatory systems, our behavior,
our expressions, and our tastes are neither harmonious nor static.
The problem cuts deep and involves tensions between perception
and conception, expression and repression, civilization and its
discontented masses. We have always been encouraged to make
love and war; but to make love instead of war undercuts the

social structure at an intolerably basic level. Such mad fantasies have usually been relegated to religions, where they are neutralized by the Church Militant.

Everyone knows the new expression, but no one knows what to do about it: the "Now" movements among Negroes, students, New Leftists, and artists; "God is dead" theology, existential man, automation, electric circuitry, and ontological insecurity; suburban and campus sex (paired and grouped), *Playboy* "sophistication," film nudity. The symptoms of change, exploration, explosion, and implosion are so clear and self-contradictory that one is at a loss to organize them coherently. One wonders if rational discussion suits these phenomena at all. Good is mixed with bad, but standards are so variable that few people can agree on what is good or bad. Previously easy distinctions between the arts and between art and life have blurred. Ann Halprin's dancers act, John Cage's music is visual, and the USCO Group's paintings perform. The synesthesia Utopians dreamed of is upon us with disarming repercussions. One need not accept Yeats's happy dread to understand him:

> Things fall apart; the center cannot hold;
> Mere anarchy is loosed upon the world.

It is not the first time.

In *Understanding Media*, Marshall McLuhan suggests that our literary, individualized culture is being tribalized. By that he means that "commitment and participation" are replacing "point of view" as the criteria for evaluating experience. He credits electric circuitry and the media flowing from it—TV, computers, stereo, telephone, telegraph, and so forth—for the "implosive" revolution which has converted the world, in Buckminster Fuller's phrase, into a "global village." McLuhan urges us to disregard the messages sent by these media; his compelling slogan is "the medium is the message." As the storing and exchange of information become the major human activity, the quality and intensity of life change. The sequential organization of perceptions that is the basis for a literary view of the world yields to a multifocused, many-faceted participation in the world. Things no longer come to us one after another, as on the printed page, the assembly line, or in logical thought. They arrive at once, helter-skelter, as a set of organically interrelated phenomena, like a traffic circle or a problem in topological mathematics. One can certainly connect McLuhan's observations with Freud and Einstein. Psychoanalysis and the General Theory of Relativity are both "in depth" grasps of experienced reality. Neither Freud nor Einstein was as interested in mapping as in exploring laws of transformation and relation. As these complicated and sophisticated ideas percolate through our culture, the result is a rejection of classical abstraction (understanding experience by reducing it to other terms) and an urge to "get with it"—to exist inside a situation.

In America, nothing has accelerated this change in context more than TV. According to McLuhan, the TV image is "cool." The tiny dots which are the picture do not provide us with all the information necessary to make figures out of the sensory material. We must participate in the image, constructing out of its thousands of dots the contours of the picture. McLuhan argues that this high degree of participation in making the TV image involves our tactile, rather than our visual, sense; "The TV image in fostering a passion for depth involvement in every aspect of experience . . . is, above all, an extension of the sense of touch, which involves maximal interplay of all the senses." We don't so much "watch" TV as "do" TV. A child who receives his perceptual training in front of the video tube is one who is anxious to participate in the world. As he matures, he will not make the usual distinctions between life and art, politics and poetics. The specializations of the industrial world—essentially an eighteenth- and nineteenth-century world—are replaced by the generalized electric circuit. And rather than be aghast at Berkeley rebels who mess in the administration of the multi-versity, or civil rights marchers who occupy private property, we should recognize that these crossovers from learning to doing and from "mine and yours" to "ours" are the natural consequences of a world in which there is less and less distinction between categories that once formed the very basis of our grasp of reality. In McLuhan's words:

Perhaps it is not very contradictory that when a medium becomes a means of depth experience the old categories of "classical" and "popular" or of "highbrow" and "lowbrow" no longer obtain.

TV affects our perceptions in still another way. TV offers instant, dramatic, and illogical change. The popular idea of "turning on" refers to more than marijuana or LSD: it is an approach to living that takes its metaphorical cue from TV. The inert tube which is consciousness can be switched into any one of many channels, and these channels can be easily intermixed. And consciousness can do what TV can't—play several experiences simultaneously. The classic rule "each in its own place" now reads "everything in any place."

If one can see the brutal dogs on the streets of Selma and drink Budweiser at home in the same instant, then one can go to Selma and participate personally in someone else's drama, making it one's own, while at home others are watching you and drinking beer. Not only are we able to construct conceptual wholes from perceptual fragments, but we are able to move into the center of what we have made. Traditional lags and gaps are healed. Instant communication leads to rapid transportation, both internally and externally. The age-old dream of no wait between impulse and act is today's reality.

However, the freedom thus achieved is largely illusory. More body conscious, certainly more socially aware than preceding generations, we discover, nonetheless, that the real gaps and lags are built into the human being. Each element of free activity and expression becomes, automatically, an awesome test of our ability to make use of it. A tension is quickly established between a possible and inviting mobility and a stubborn, inborn immobility. Despite TV, and every other prompt and aid, most people sit at home watching someone else's drama. But the awareness that it is possible to go to Selma, or around the corner, or deep inside oneself, is very unsettling.

I think it is from this tension between opportunity and inborn stubbornness—the unique psychic configuration of each individual —that the new expression, including pornography, emerges. A real space has opened up between what we are permitted, even encouraged, to do and what we are. The attempts to fill this space fall as much to fantasy as to real projects. Like the patient on the couch who when told by his analyst to say whatever comes into his head finds he can't say anything, we, as a society and as individuals, fall back into silence or fantasy. Instead of participating, we flee from real involvement and consume, as we go, *The Story of O* and the *Playboy* "philosophy."

Loosed by an image-happy society, a giant bulk of submerged material has surfaced. New work that could not find a commercial sponsor ten years ago is now sought by publishers, film-makers, and stage producers. And classic work long suppressed is now openly sold. We are beginning to understand the difference between masturbatory and celebratory sex; and it may not be long before phallic art becomes as openly popular in our culture as it was in Golden-Age Greece. The attention given sadomasochistic work is both a compensation for the long suppression and an indication that we are far from comfortable with our new liberality.

George Steiner, in an article in *Encounter,* deplored our interest in Sade and his cohorts, both past and present. Steiner suggested a causal link between literary sadism and its horrible actuality in Nazi Germany. However, Steiner, like so many others, confuses two symptoms for a symptom and its cause. The spate of sadistic writing in pre-Hitler Germany was not a cause of the Gestapo, but an indication that such impulses were there. The iron discipline of the Nazis translated these impulses into facts. Suppressing the literature would have had no effect on the underlying causes of both literature and Nazism. In fact, the literature probably served for a time as a safety valve. Our own pornography is to be condemned because it takes a cheap and totally athletic view of sexual experience. But one ought to look at such pornography the way Freud looked at dirty jokes:

What these jokes whisper may be said aloud: that the wishes and desires of men have a right to make themselves acceptable alongside of exacting and ruthless morality. And in our days it has been said in forceful and stirring sentences that this morality is only a selfish regulation laid down by the few who are rich and powerful and who can satisfy their wishes at any time without any postponement. So long as the art of healing has not gone further in making our life safe and so long as social arrangements do no more to make it more enjoyable, so long will it be impossible to stifle the voice within us that rebels against the demands of morality.

The answer is not suppression, but the elimination of that "ruthless morality" which drives people to desperate satisfaction. Pornography—and I include in this category everything from dirty pictures to *The Story of O*—is not a release from inhibitions, but a function of them. Surely we should not, as we have done, outlaw these repressive mechanisms. But neither should we admire them as examples of free expression. They are nothing other than the means by which repressive consciousness keeps a restless psyche in tow. And Freud is accurate when he suggests that our consciousness is repressive because of conditioning made necessary by a social order concerned primarily with productivity. Pornography, whether open or underground, is an important weapon in the arsenal of social control. It does not, as Steiner suggests, lead to activity; its tendency is the opposite. The challenge that electric circuitry presents to this control is real. An expressive society would have need for neither pornography nor oppressive controls. Replacing them would be celebratory sexual art and expression; the phallic dances of the Greeks, the promiscuity of Elizabethan England.

The submerged material now available falls into two classes: stuff that uses words once thought obscene; works that show scenes that once were taboo. Although related, the distinction between verbal and scenic expression is a crucial index. For a long time the community's efforts were concentrated against those naughty "Anglo-Saxon" words. This nineteenth-century fight (which continues today in many backwaters) was one of propriety, of "decency" in its social sense. The images which these words conjured up were simply not to be thought, certainly not to be expressed. This was the result of a sexual segregation in which women were property to be used but not exposed to their uses. Once females became something other than chattel, the verbal taboos were soon to go. Not entirely, of course; the producers of the film version of Edward Albee's *Who's Afraid of Virginia Woolf?* had to buck industry pressure to cut the dirty words. As for the plot, no one cared.

But propriety and decency as understood a generation ago (the "dirty little secret" D. H. Lawrence abhorred) are no longer the major issue. We now see things in scenic terms: scope rather than point, and relation rather than incident, form our opinions. And it is the divergent attitudes toward scenic sexuality that I find most interesting. There is a heirarchy in our tolerance, and this seems to say a good deal about us and our art.

Literature is the most free, filmic representation next, and stage presentation last. One can tell everything in a novel, and the writer need have no fear about how graphic his description might be. One can suggest the same things in a film, but one rarely sees anything more than sexual foreplay and a pair of naked bodies afterward. The "bold" orgasm scene in *A Stranger Knocks* was of course a fraud. Even the twilight nudie and sex films are timid, concentrating on voyeurism. On stage one dare do nothing more than kiss. A seemingly strange variation is that one can buy records which appear to be accurate simulations (or realities?) of the sounds of lovemaking. And the texts of many popular songs are so obviously coital that one wonders how they get on the radio and are sold openly to pre-teens. The fact is that our sexuality is still understood as something visual. The ear is attuned only to catch the "dirty" words; any recorded sentence without them, no matter how suggestive, simply slips by.

The same visual hierarchy applies to nudity. A novelist can describe naked people with as much detail as his words can muster. In films one can show a naked female (but not all of her: the genitals are off limits). On stage, except in specialized nightclub strip shows, nudity is taboo. Last fall I saw *Poor Bitos* at the Theater of the Living Arts in Philadelphia. It was an excellent production. In one scene, a character had a breast exposed. The lobby talk—as one might expect—centered on that passing detail. But this same audience (including me) would go home and read *The Story of O* and *Candy* or see *Les Liaisons Dangereuses* at the movies without a second thought.

This hierarchy of tolerance seems related both to the degree and kind of involvement expected of the reader and viewer. The reader selects his own style of reading; he can put the book down, pick it up, go fast or slow. He is always alone, in a one-to-one relationship to the author. He need tell no one how he felt, or if he felt. The reading experience is therefore the paradigm of secret pleasure; it is an organic relation to an inanimate object. That there are few taboos here is no surprise.

The movie-and-theater-goer is part of a group. But the most important fact about this group is not its largest unit—the entire audience—but its nuclear units—the "families" of viewers. Book reviewers are sent one copy of the book; film and theater reviewers are always given two tickets. It is assumed that the film and stage experience is one which we naturally share with a few others who are emotionally close to us. Many of these nuclear groups make up a single audience; and the relationship of performers to audience is not one-to-one—as is usually supposed—but performers to small groups to larger, inclusive groups. Why don't we go to the movies and theater as individuals? Why does it seem natural to insulate ourselves from the whole audience by means of the nuclear group?

The scenic experience is more explosive and empathetic than reading. The energies generated by a film or play, and the rhythms vibrating between performers and audience *in toto,* are counterbalanced by the restraints inherent in the nuclear group. As a whole audience we are encouraged to participate in the performance; as a part of the "family" we are warned against complete participation. A compromise emerges as a rigid set of audience conventions: applause, laughter, tears, and coughs are all the physical responses permitted. But in a tribal performance, the family, like the individual, is drawn into the larger group; active and total participation is not infrequent. This participation is often orgiastic—a frenzied communally sanctioned release from strict authority.

In our culture we bring the family with us to the movies or theater, and even our wildest dramas, say *Lear* and *The Balcony,* are essentially reassuring as we produce them. Were we to go to the movies or theater as individuals, surrendering the protective envelope of the family, our drama would rapidly become sexualized and orgiastic. A play like Peter Weiss's *Marat/Sade,* as it was produced by the Royal Shakespeare Company, is moving in this direction. But scenic taboos continue in the theater (less in film) because letting go would be too dangerous: the performance which has traditionally included actors and audience would soon become, as in a tribal dance, one unified activity.

There are some reasons, too, why theater has more taboos than film. The movie-goer has no control over the rhythm of what he sees. The projector runs on its predetermined schedule. The viewer has to adjust his perceptual rhythm to what he is seeing, and he is constantly reminded that the film is an abstraction. Even as he is engaged by the pictures, he is disengaged by the form of the film and its steady, mechanical unfolding. Filmmakers turn this to their advantage, using montage, camera angle, and distance to make the perceptual "reality" of film other than the reality of life. But each effort to make the film less abstract is drawn from the abstract nature of filming: a set of machines that permit editing and dozens of other techniques. And because film art is more abstract than theater, it is also more sexually permissive. No matter how torrid the love scene, we never feel concerned for the actor. The masterful thing about film is that the actor vanishes into the character, and the character is always (at least perceptually) a fiction, an abstraction.

The unique thing about theater, of course, is that the actors are *there.* They never vanish into their characters. Like the Christian God who is three-in-one, every actor is two-in-one. It is this double existence that gives him his authenticity as actor. His role in our theater is not very different from that of his primitive counterpart, who is at once dancer and god. Little overt sexuality is permitted on stage because the audience knows that what happens to the character also happens to the actor. One can understand why physical violence is feigned on stage: there are obligations to tomorrow's performance. But why not have nudity and lovemaking? It cannot simply be that human sexual response is an undependable mechanism. The Greeks, who accepted both sexuality and nudity in public life, maintained a strict decorum in their tragedies. It is that stage performance is always on the verge of tumbling from art back into life. Overt and graphic sexuality would destroy the aesthetic fabric of any performance. How then did Aristophanes manage the love pranks of *Lysistrata?* Aristophanic drama is farce and celebration in a combination that we have lost touch with. Filled with regard for the family, schooled in Renaissance humanism, we are not up to the phallic play of Aristophanes. And it is only within a framework of celebration that sexuality can be both graphic and aesthetic.

Celebratory theater is returning to our culture in some Happenings. Many of these events are designed to obliterate distinctions between life and art. Once performers are no longer concerned about maintaining their double identities, and audiences accept the invitation to participate in the performance, almost anything can happen. Carolee Schneemann describes her goals in *Meat Joy* this way:

My kinetic theatre provides for an intensification of all faculties simultaneously . . . a mobile, tactile event into which the eye leads the body. . . . I assume that senses crave sources of maximum information . . . *Meat Joy*, a shifting vision now, relating Artaud, McClure, and French Butcher Shops . . . acting and viewing space interchanged. I see several girls whose gestures develop from a tactile, bodily relationship to individual men and to a mass of meat slices.

Meat Joy is an orgiastic Happening linking butcher's beef and women with the phallic meat. Nude or nearly nude bodies are painted, intertwined, and frolicked with. At once intimate and impersonal, it typifies that strange combination of participation and irony that marks much of the new theater. In some Happenings it is difficult to say whether one is attending a performance or a party. Even in more formal works, orgiastic and celebratory material is included within disciplined frameworks, giving the effect of a performance mosaic, some parts of which are expansive and inclusive while others resemble traditional theater.

Contemporary theater, in fact, has been affected by the new

expression. Jack Gelber's *The Connection*, Kenneth H. Brown's *The Brig*, and Megan Terry's *Viet Rock* are probably the three most important new American plays of the last ten years. (I would add Robert Lowell's *Benito Cereno* to that list—and Lowell's theme, if not his style, is related to my discussion.) Maintaining the scenic taboos, these three plays nevertheless engulf our consciousness, blurring the usual distinctions between performance and reality, audience and stage. Far from being Pirandellian exercises, these plays move in the opposite direction. Pirandello wished to pose insoluble problems: he was the intellectual par excellence. Gelber, Brown, and Terry work rather to make their solutions so unavoidable that they fold the audience into the play. Thus, junk is everywhere, white lines are for crossing, and this ruthless war is our open-eyed choice. The productions of *The Connection, The Brig,* and *Viet Rock*—the first two plays done by the Living Theater and the last by the Open Theater, the successor to the Living Theater in New York—cannot be separated from the plays: the act of writing is so joined to the act of doing that the two become one. The "writer" no longer exists in such a scheme; the craft of making a play becomes a participatory game which involves all the artists and technicians of the theater and the audience.

Surely Happenings, and some of off-Broadway theater, are not art, if judged by traditional criteria. The strategies of Berkeley students and Negro marchers are not traditional modes of academic behavior or political maneuver in the United States. But the Free Speech Movement, the civil rights movement, and new directions in the performing arts are related. They are all participating forms which value involvement more than "style." This demand for "getting with it" links all the varieties of the new expression.

In *Marat/Sade,* the Marquis speaks of the "revolution of the flesh," which, he says, "will make all your other revolutions seem like prison mutinies." This atavistic, cohesive, and participatory revolution is the new expression. The upheaval has barely begun, and if it ever truly gets moving, we may wish we were safe with Sade in his asylum. The new expression seems pornographic and obscene only when it threatens our sexual taboos. That this is frequent is an index of how much both old and new have invested in sexuality. The least interesting part of the new expression is its literature. At best, publication of new, sexy titles and the reissuing of classics are efforts to keep up with change. But Maurice Girodias is hardly Dionysus, and the boldest text is tame in the World of Murray the K. The new expression is a public event, a dramatic shift in scene and context. That is what makes it so disquieting. A society which has been indoors, repressive, and individually protestant is becoming outdoors, expressive, and tribally catholic. And we are never quite certain whether the noise we hear is authentic or merely one more role added to our endless repertory. When authentic, the new expression rejects the sequential logic of print for the simultaneous tumult of experience. We are beginning to see that to "make love, not war" is to go to war against most of what our culture asks of us. The decision in that conflict is not yet clear.

ROBERT BRUSTEIN

THE THIRD THEATER REVISITED

In the middle Sixties I wrote an essay saluting a new theater
that was just beginning to evolve in opposition to the existing
theater on Broadway and in the culture centers. At the time, the
"third theater," as I called it, was a fringe movement whose
continued survival was as problematical as its anti-war position
was unpopular, so it was with considerable surprise that I
watched it, soon after, begin to take a position of power in the
theater. This development paralleled a failure of nerve among
the middle classes, as the forces of conventional culture seemed
to grow guilty and weak before the culture of the young, and
the American avant-garde, for the first time in its history, became
the glass of fashion and the mold of form. What was once considered special and arcane—the exclusive concern of an alienated,
argumentative, intensely serious elite—was now accessible,
through television and the popular magazines; vogues in women's
fashions followed hard upon, and sometimes even influenced,

115

vogues in modern painting; underground movies became box office bonanzas, and Andy Warhol's factory was making him a millionaire.

The narrowing of the traditional distance between serious and mass-middle culture was accompanied, in the "third theater," by a growing callowness, sloppiness, and arrogance which made me suspicious of it. Indeed I developed much the same ambivalence toward the anti-war and black power movements as they have changed from noble acts of non-violent resistance by highly serious individuals to disruptive and histrionic acts by infantile "revolutionaries." For just as the frustrations over the endless conflict in Vietnam and the unresolved dilemmas of the black people have given a vaguely totalitarian coloration to certain cadres of the Left, so the success of the third theater, which reflects these frustrations, has tended to sanctify its failings and conventionalize its virtues. What once seemed daring and original now often seems tiresome and familiar; stereotyped political assertions, encouraged by their easy acceptance, have replaced instinctive, individual dissent; and the complex moral and metaphysical issues of great art are being obliterated by a simple-minded nihilism.

Does this suggest that I am ready to repudiate my earlier assumptions? Only in so far as I must repudiate all theater movements that begin to take an ideological direction. While the new theater as a whole has taken a wrong turn, however, there are still many young American Playwrights with the gifts to blast this theater out of its formulas. Jean-Claude van Itallie, Sam Shepard, Charles Dizenzo, Ronald Ribman, Leo Rutman are a few of them. Similarly, while I overvalued *Viet Rock* in my relief to discover a play that mentioned the Vietnam war at all, I still regard *America Hurrah, Dynamite Tonite,* and *Macbird!* as works of real imagination and originality, and will continue to defend these plays against hostile critics who attack what is genuine in the new theater movement along with what is spurious. On the other hand, it is becoming increasingly clear, now that the new theater has begun to rigidify, that it may be as great a danger to dramatic art as the old theater. It already embodies similar defects. Its anti-intellectualism, its sensationalism, its sexual obsessiveness, its massacre of language, its noisy attention-getting mechanisms, its indifference to artistry, craft, or skill, its violence, and, above all, its mindless tributes to Love and Togetherness (now in the form of "group gropes" and "love zaps") are not adversary demands upon the American character but rather the very qualities that have continually degraded us, the very qualities that have kept us laggard and philistine in the theater throughout the past three decades.

It is ironic that these qualities, already so conspicuous in the commercial theater, should be offered as expressions of a new sensibility—even more ironic that one should find them in the work of the Living Theater upon its return after an exile of four years. Initiating a tour designed to revolutionize not only the stage but the various university and civic centers that it visited, the Living Theater proved, upon its very first appearance, to have changed its style in a manner similar to the changes in the new theater. Indeed, it soon became clear that it was the original source of many off-off-Broadway conventions. Having eked out a precarious existence for seventeen years as an embattled minority troupe dedicated to the great classic and contemporary European works as well as to the more experimental American plays, the Living Theater returned to America with a fierce antagonism to all dramatic texts that could not somehow be translated into its special anarchistic program. The members of the company had developed an almost symbiotic unity in their years of traveling together over the European continent. The company had become a self-generating, self-perpetuating organism whose existence was more important than any work it performed; and it was inflamed with a sense of mission that was less theatrical or even political than religious and evangelical.

These changes were reflected physically as well. Julian Beck's features now contained an ascetic calm usually associated with Hindu gurus and Confucian monks, while his wife, Judith Malina, had taken on the look of an unprotected street urchin, her eyes sometimes ablaze with fervor, sometimes limpid with compassion for all martyrs, not excluding herself. The Becks— as well as the entire company—had developed an extraordinary physical integrity that gave at once the most immediate, and the most lasting, impression one had of them. Dressed like gypsies, hippies, and nomads in clothing from every quarter of the earth, the men sometimes indistinguishable from the women, and even the children beaded, bangled, and longhaired, they moved with a beauty that testified to an inward grace, as well as to months of arduous training in breathing and the body.

Unfortunately, the Living Theater had little of substance to contribute beyond its athleticism and its exotic style of life. Although two of the four works presented on this tour (*The Mysteries* and *Frankenstein*) showed original techniques, they did not fulfill their initial promise largely because they lacked a gifted playwright to conceive them intelligently. It was disconcerting to discover that the Becks no longer seemed interested in coherent theatrical productions. What obsessed them now was their missionary program; they were more eager to convert their audiences, through whatever means, to their special brand of revolutionary politics. In production after production, the company demonstrated its remarkable capacity to manipulate minds. Playing upon the general sense of emptiness in a world where even individual salvation seems far too complicated, the Living Theater proselytized among the young in the manner of hip evangelists, encouraging each spectator to make his decision for love, freedom, and anarchy. The most depressing thing of all was how easily university students, and even some of their teachers, responded to the baldest of slogans and the most simplistic interpretations of reality.

After *The Mysteries*, a series of process exercises which for me was the most interesting and least pretentious of its offerings, the Living Theater proceeded to demonstrate in *Antigone* (a version of the story which reduced it to a melodramatic confrontation between political evil and oppressed good), in *Frankenstein* (a Camp horror tale with Radio City Music Hall prestidigitation techniques about how civilization turns man into monster), and particularly in the audience-participation epic, *Paradise Now*, that it had virtually abandoned its interest in creating serious drama. It was now clear that the Becks' previous efforts to examine the boundaries separating art from life (in some pre-exile productions as *The Connection* and *Tonight We Improvise*) had been expanded into a full-scale assault upon any separation whatever between the spectator and the stage. Audiences were invited over the footlights to join some performer while other performers wandered through the house; actors whined plaintively about their inability to travel without a passport, live without money, smoke marijuana, or take their clothes off, after which they stripped to loin cloths and bikinis; students peeled down, upon this encouragement, to jockey shorts; mass love-zaps and petting parties were organized on stage among couples of various sexes and sexual dispositions; and after the endless, loveless, sexless groping was finally over, everyone was exhorted to leave the theater and convert the police to anarchism, to storm the jails and free the prisoners, to stop the war and ban the bomb, to take over the streets in the name of the people—and, then, to disperse quietly lest any of this end (as it did one night in New Haven) with somebody in jail for disturbing the peace.

Needless to say, unfulfillable demands of this kind were extremely irresponsible, given the impressionable nature of young audiences; they were also extremely meretricious, since the Living Theater invariably took refuge in its theatrical function whenever things threatened to get out of hand. For all its emphasis on reality, the company never quite managed to escape from its performance; for all its emphasis on spontaneity and accident, it still followed an almost fixed pattern which ended the same way every evening. To extend a theatrical action into the audience is not to annihilate the performance, it is to annihilate the audience—everyone becomes a performer, the seats become part of the stage. This paradox was not lost on Jean Genet, whose play, *The Balcony*, was based on his understanding that since revolution is dedicated to the destruction of artifice, its greatest enemy is playacting. But it was a paradox from which the Living Theater was never able to escape. And when the Becks appeared recently on the Merv Griffin show, outlining their political theories between a series of nightclub acts, they only dramatized further their imprisonment in show biz—in Genet's image, they were still in the brothel.

What was finally most disturbing about the Living Theater

was the content of the ideology it was marketing under the name of anarchism. In spite of all the invitations to participate in free theater, it was constraint and control that remained most conspicuous. No spectator was ever allowed to violate the pattern of manipulated consent. At Yale, we saw a female student launch into a passionate denunciation of the Living Theater, only to be hustled offstage by a group of performers who embraced her into silence—unbuttoning her blouse, feeling her legs, and shutting her mouth with kisses. Another student, beginning an impersonation of Ed Sullivan while navigating around the interlocked bodies on the stage, was prevented from introducing a note of satire into the evening by an actor who drowned him out with an imitation of the Kennedy assassination. The company, particularly vulnerable to ridicule because of its lack of humor, allowed no alien laughter ever to penetrate its relentless solemnity, self-righteousness, and self-importance.

Love and brotherhood were continually on the lips of the actors, but no actors in my experience have bristled with so much aggression or more successfully galvanized the aggression of the spectator. As for love and brotherhood, all one saw was herd love and brotherhood among the anonymous. It was, finally, not a vision of human freedom that one took away from *Paradise Now* but vague, disturbing memories of the youth rallies in Hitler's Nuremberg. The return of the Living Theater described a full circle in so far as the company had now taken on the very authoritarian qualities it had once denounced, the very repressiveness that had driven it from the country four years before.

The unprecedented success of the Living Theater with the radical young—and with those who follow the radical young— was, however, of momentous significance because it indicated precisely what these audiences were now demanding of the stage. For these impatient generations, with their inability to sustain frustration for a moment, it was the opportunity for participation that proved most attractive. The passive role of spectator had become insufficient. Now theatrical production had to satisfy the thirst for an elusive, often spurious "relevance" and convince its audiences that they were helping to enact an episode in history. The Living Theater promised the theatricalization of campus revolts, confrontations, and occupations—the theatricalization of those numerous quasi-revolutionary gestures by which students are persuading themselves today that they are having a significant impact on their times. That these gestures are aimed not against the Pentagon or the napalm-producing factories, but rather against the university itself (for all its faults, still one of the last outposts of civilization and humane values) only indicates that the desire for effectiveness somewhere far transcends the desire for effective change.[1] But it also indicates that with the day of protest upon us, the conditions necessary for the creation of great art may very well be over, at least for a time. As one gifted acting student told me when he withdrew from Yale: "I don't give a shit about art. I want to create events."

For myself, I regard this development with mingled feelings, mostly sad ones. This extraordinary generation, upon whom so much praise and attention have been lavished, cannot help but inspire feelings of respect—but my respect is becoming mixed with great apprehension. At once so vital and idealistic, and so childish, irrational, and overindulged, the radical young are questioning the very roots of our civilization, but what they would substitute, apart from continuous improvisation and an ethics of expedience, is far from known. The silent and conservative students of the Fifties are no more, thank heavens; they have gone off to join the system and consolidate its errors. But some of the demonic students of the Sixties may very well, in their impatience for change, destroy what is valuable in our culture along with what is despicable—destroying even the valuable things their contemporaries have helped to create. While the theater, along with popular music, has benefited enormously from an infusion of young energy that has transformed our way of seeing and hearing, the more radical theater is less an advance

---

[1] This is not to say that some of the more extreme revolutionists are not preparing, at least in their fantasies, for assaults on the Pentagon. My sixteen-year-old stepson met a girl the other day who was practicing jujitsu in preparation for encounters with the U.S. Army. "Can you throw a tank?" he asked.

than a throwback. With this theater, we have returned to the Thirties, watching the same abuse of truths that do not serve political ends, the same contempt for writers who do not try to change their times, the same monolithic modes of thought, the same assaults on any expression that is not a form of consent. The "theater of commitment," which had just begun to shake itself free from dependence on narrow ideology, is again becoming a theater of naked slogans and raw emotionalism, and death knells are once more being heard for the works of Western civilization.

These works will, I hope, survive—they are certainly among the few things worth preserving. But they will survive only through renewed efforts at conservation, and this means renewed efforts of intelligence and will. The threatening apocalypse is something for which many of us must share the blame. By radically questioning the prevailing humanism, we helped to start violent engines in motion which may end in pushing everything we value over the precipice. Secure in our powerlessness, and certain that thought would never lead to action, we let our minds play upon questionable possibilities, never suspecting that those possibilities might soon be upon us, more swiftly and more irrevocably than we could dream. These were errors of judgment —but there were those who made less forgivable errors of power. Seeking a Mosaic role, they led these hungry generations to a violent view from Pisgah that could have no creative issue. Guilt-ridden, indecisive, flaccid, hating authority and enamored of influence, they surrendered principles they had once affirmed, accepting again what was so hateful in the past. In a time when intelligence is needed more than ever before, they encouraged a form of intellectual decomposition, becoming fellow travelers of a movement they could never hope to join, which would, in time, proceed to swallow them up.

We honor the young because without them there is no future. But there will surely be no future either unless the more extreme of our young can cease from trying to annihilate the past. With our civilization tottering, the temptation is strong to release our hold on reality and credit the most fantastic flights of absurdity simply because they signify change. But the more radical inventions of the new generation are nothing if they proceed from the same violent and mindless sources that originally brought our civilization to this terrifying juncture. We fail the future when we surrender what we know and value for the sake of fashion and influence, and we fail the theater when we countenance the rejection of language, form, and accomplishment in favor of an easy culture. The third theater I once described contains, in Synge's words, "reality and joy"—which is to say it synthesizes the principle of work and of pleasure, discipline and imagination, form and process, reflection and improvisation, age and youth. It is a theater that spans the generation—a theater, in other words, that has yet to appear in this country of divided spirits.

GORE VIDAL

NOTES ON PORNOGRAPHY

The man and the woman make love; attain climax; fall separate.
Then she whispers, "I'll tell you who I was thinking of if you'll
tell me who you were thinking of." Like most sex jokes, the
origins of this pleasant exchange are obscure. But whatever the
source, it seldom fails to evoke a certain awful recognition, since
few lovers are willing to admit that in the sexual act to create or
maintain excitement they may need some mental image as
erotic supplement to the body in attendance. One perverse contemporary maintains that when he is with A he thinks of B and
when he is with B he thinks of A; each attracts him only to the
degree that he is able simultaneously to evoke the image of the
other. Also, for those who find the classic positions of "mature"
lovemaking unsatisfactory yet dare not distress the beloved with
odd requests, sexual fantasy becomes inevitable and the shy
lover soon finds himself imposing mentally all sorts of wild images
upon his unsuspecting partner, who may also be relying on an

inner theater of the mind to keep things going; in which case, those popular writers who deplore "our lack of communication today" may have a point. Ritual and magic also have their devotees. In one of Kingsley Amis's fictions, a man mentally conjugates Latin verbs in order to delay orgasm as he waits chivalrously for his partner's predictably slow response. While another considerate lover (nonfictional) can only reduce tempo by thinking of a large loaf of sliced white bread, manufactured by Bond.

Sexual fantasy is as old as civilization (as opposed to as old as the race), and one of its outward and visible signs is pornographic literature, an entirely middle-class phenomenon, since we are assured by many investigators (Kinsey, Pomeroy, *et al.*) that the lower orders seldom rely upon sexual fantasy for extra-stimulus. As soon as possible, the uneducated man goes for the real thing. Consequently he seldom masturbates, but when he does he thinks, we are told, of nothing at all. This may be the last meaningful class distinction in the West. Nevertheless, the sex-in-the-head middle classes that D. H. Lawrence so despised are not the way they are because they want deliberately to be cerebral and anti-life; rather they are innocent victims of necessity and tribal law. For economic reasons they must delay marriage as long as possible. For tribal reasons they are taught that sex outside marriage is wrong. Consequently the man whose first contact with a woman occurs when he is twenty will have spent, ideally, the sexually most vigorous period of his life masturbating. Not unnaturally, in order to make that solitary act meaningful, the theater of his mind early becomes a Dionysian festival, and should he be a resourceful dramatist he may find actual lovemaking disappointing when he finally gets to it, as Bernard Shaw did. One wonders whether Shaw would have been a dramatist at all if he had first made love to a girl at fourteen, as nature intended, instead of at twenty-nine, as class required. Here, incidentally, is a whole new line of literary-psychological inquiry suitable for the master's degree: "Characteristics of the Onanist as Dramatist." Late coupling and prolonged chastity certainly help explain much of the rich dottiness of those Victorians whose peculiar habits planted thick many a quiet churchyard with Rose La Touches.

Until recently, pornography was a small cottage industry among the grinding mills of literature. But now that sex has taken the place of most other games (how many young people today learn bridge?), creating and packaging pornography has become big business, and though the high courts of the new American Empire cannot be said to be very happy about this state of affairs, they tend to agree that freedom of expression is as essential to our national life as freedom of meaningful political action is not. Also, despite our governors' paternalistic bias, there are signs that they are becoming less intolerant in sexual matters. This would be a good thing if one did not suspect that they may regard sex as our bread and circuses, a means of keeping us off the political streets, and in bed out of mischief. If this is so, we may yet observe President Johnson in his mad search for consensus settling for the consensual.

Among the publishers of pornography ("merchants of smut," as they say at the FBI), Maurice Girodias is uniquely eminent. For one thing, he is a second-generation peddler of dirty books (or "d.b.s.," as they call them on Eighth Avenue). In the 1930's his English father, Jack Kahane, founded the Obelisk Press in Paris. Among Kahane's authors were Anais Nin, Lawrence Durrell, Cyril Connolly, and of course Henry Miller, whose books have been underground favorites for what seems like a century. Kahane died in 1939 and his son, Maurice Girodias (he took his mother's name for reasons not given), continued Kahane's brave work. After the war, Girodias sold Henry Miller in vast quantities to easily stimulated GIs. He also revived *Fanny Hill*. He published books in French. He prospered. Then the Terror began. Visionary dictatorships, whether of a single man or of the proletariat, tend to disapprove of irregular sex. Being profoundly immoral in public matters, dictators compensate by insisting upon what they think to be a rigorous morality in private affairs. General de Gaulle's private morality appears to be registered in his wife's name. In 1946 Girodias was prosecuted for publishing Henry Miller. It was France's first prosecution for obscenity since

the trial of *Madame Bovary* in 1844. Happily, the world's writers
rallied to Miller's defense, and since men of letters are taken
solemnly in France, the government dropped its charges.

In a preface to the recently published *The Olympia Reader*,
Girodias discusses his business arrangements at length; and
though none of us is as candid about money as he is about sex,
Girodias does admit that he lost his firm not as a result of legal
persecution but through incompetence, a revelation that gives him
avant-garde status in the new pornography of money. Girodias
next founded the Olympia Press, devoted to the creation of pornography, both hard and soft core. His adventures as a merchant
of smut make a most beguiling story. All sorts of writers, good
and bad, were set to work turning out books, often written to
order. He would think up a title (e.g., *With Open Mouth*) and
advertise it; if there was sufficient response, he would then commission someone to write a book to go with the title. Most of his
writers used pseudonyms. Terry Southern and Mason Hoffenberg
wrote *Candy* under the name of Maxwell Kenton. Christopher
Logue wrote *Lust* under the name of Count Palmiro Vicarion,
while Alex Trocchi, as Miss Frances Lengel, wrote *Helen and
Desire*. Girodias also published Samuel Beckett's *Watt*, Vladimir
Nabokov's *Lolita*, and J. P. Donleavy's *The Ginger Man*; perversely, the last three authors chose not to use pseudonyms.

Reading of these happy years, one recalls a similar situation just
after the Second World War when a number of New York writers
were commissioned at so many cents a page to write pornographic
stories for a United States Senator. The solon, as they say in
smutland, never actually met the writers but through a go-
between he guided their stories: a bit more flagellation here, a
touch of necrophilia there. . . . The subsequent nervous break-
down of one of the Senator's pornographers, now a celebrated
poet, was attributed to the strain of not knowing which of the
ninety-six Senators he was writing for.

In 1958 the Fourth French Republic banned twenty-five of
Girodias's books, among them *Lolita*. Girodias promptly sued the
Ministry of the Interior and, amazingly, won. Unfortunately, five
months later, the Great General saw fit to resume the grandeur
of France. De Gaulle was back; and so was Madame de Gaulle.

The Minister of the Interior appealed the now defunct Fourth Republic's decision and was upheld. Since then, censorship has been the rule in France. One by one Girodias's books, regardless of merit, have been banned. Inevitably, André Malraux was appealed to and, inevitably, he responded with that elevated double-talk which has been a characteristic of what one suspects will be a short-lived Republic. Girodias is currently in the United States, where he expects to flourish. Ever since our Puritan republic became a gaudy empire, pornography has been a big business for the simple reason that when freedom of expression is joined with the freedom to make a lot of money, the dream of those whose bloody footprints made vivid the snows of Valley Forge is close to fulfillment and that happiness which our Constitution commands us to pursue at hand.

The Olympia Reader is a collection of passages from various books published by Maurice Girodias since 1953. Reading it straight through is a curiously disjointed experience, like sitting through a program of movie trailers. As literature, most of the selections are junk, despite the presence of such celebrated contemporary figures as Nabokov, Genet, and Queneau; and of the illustrious dead, Sade and Beardsley.

Pornography is usually defined as that which is calculated to arouse sexual excitement. Since what arouses X repels Y, no two people are apt to respond in quite the same way to the same stimulus. One man's meat, as they say, is another man's poison, a fact now recognized by the American judiciary, which must rule with wearisome frequency on obscenity. With unexpected good sense, a judge recently observed that since the books currently before him all involved ladies in black leather with whips, they could not be said to corrupt the generality, since a taste for being beaten is hardly common and those who are aroused by such fantasies are already "corrupted" and therefore exempt from laws designed to protect the young and usual. By their nature, pornographies cannot be said to proselytize, since they are written for the already hooked. The worst that can be said of pornography is that it leads not to "antisocial" sexual acts but to the reading of more pornography. As for corruption, the only immediate victim is English prose. Mr. Girodias himself writes

like his worst authors ("Terry being at the time in acute financial
need . . .") while his moral judgments are most peculiar. With
reverence, he describes his hero Sir Roger Casement (a "superlative pederast," whatever that is) as "politically confused, emotionally unbalanced, maudlin when depressed and absurdly
naive when in his best form; but he was exceptionally generous,
he had extraordinary courage and a simple human wisdom
which sprang from his natural goodness." Here, Mr. Girodias
demonstrates a harmony with the age in which he lives. He may
or may not have described Sir Roger accurately, but he has
certainly drawn a flattering portrait of the Serious American
Novelist, 1966.

Of the forty selections Mr. Girodias has seen fit to collect, at
least half are meant to be literature in the most ambitious sense,
and to the extent that they succeed, they disappoint; Beckett's
Watt, Queneau's *Zazie,* Donleavy's *The Ginger Man* are incapable of summoning up so much as the ghost of a rose, to appropriate Sir Thomas Browne's handsome phrase. There is also a
good deal of Henry Miller, whose reputation as a pornographer
is largely undeserved. Though he writes a lot about sex, the only
object he seems ever to describe is his own phallus. As a result,
unless one lusts specifically for the flesh of Henry Miller, his
works cannot be regarded as truly edifying. Yet at Miller's best
he makes one irritably conscious of what it is like to be inside his
skin, no mean feat . . . the pornographic style, incidentally, is
contagious: the stately platitude, the arch paraphrase, the innocent line which starts suddenly to buck with unintended
double meanings.

Like the perfect host or madam, Mr. Girodias has tried to provide something for everyone. Naturally there is a good deal of
straightforward heterosexual goings-on. Mr. Girodias gives us
several examples, usually involving the seduction of an adolescent male by an older woman. For female masochists (and male
sadists) he gives us *Story of O.* For homosexual sadists (and
masochists) *The Gaudy Image.* For negrophiles (and phobes)
Pinktoes, whose eloquent author, Chester Himes, new to me, has
a sense of humor that sinks his work like a stone. For anal
eroticists who like science fiction there are passages from William

Burroughs' *Naked Lunch* and *The Soft Machine,* works that have appealed to Mary McCarthy. For devotees of camp, new to the scene, the thirty-three-year-old *The Young and Evil* by Charles Henri Ford and Parker Tyler is a pioneer work and reads surprisingly well today. Parenthetically, it is interesting to note the role that clothes play in most of these works, camp, kinky, and straight. Obviously, if there is to be something for everyone, the thoughtful entrepreneur must occasionally provide an old sock or pair of panties for the fetishist to get, as it were, his teeth into. But even writers not aiming at the fetishist audience make much of the ritual taking off and putting on of clothes, and it is significant that the bodies thus revealed are seldom described as meticulously as the clothes are.

Even Jean Genet, always lyric and vague when celebrating cock, becomes usually naturalistic and detailed when he describes clothes in an excerpt from *The Thieves' Journal.* Apparently when he was a boy in Spain a lover made him dress up as a girl. The experiment was a failure because "Taste is required . . . I was already refusing to have any. I forbade myself to. Of course I would have shown a great deal of it." Nevertheless, despite an inadequate clothes sense, he still tells us far more about the *travesti manqué* than he ever tells us about the body of Stilitano for whom he lusted.

In most pornography, physical descriptions tend to be sketchy. Hard-core pornographers seldom particularize. Inevitably, genitals are massive, but since we never get a good look at the bodies to which they are attached, the effect is so impersonal that one soon longs to read about those more modest yet entirely tangible archetypes, the girl and boy next door, two creatures far more apt to figure in the heated theater of the mind than the voluptuous grotesques of the pulp writer's imagination. Yet by abstracting character and by keeping his human creatures faceless and vague, the pornographer does force the reader to draw upon personal experience in order to fill in the details, thereby achieving one of the ends of all literary art, that of making the reader collaborator.

As usual, it is the Marquis de Sade (here represented by a section from *Justine*) who has the most to say about sex—or rather the use of others as objects for one's own pleasure, preferably at the expense of theirs. In true eighteenth-century fashion, he explains and explains and explains. There is no God, only Nature, which is heedless of the Good as well as of the Bad. Since Nature requires that the strong violate the weak and since it is demonstrably true that Nature made women weak and men strong, therefore . . . and so on. The Marquis's vision—of which so much has been made in this century—is nothing but a rather simple-minded Manicheism, presented with more passion than logic. Yet in his endless self-justification (un-Natural this: Nature never apologizes, never explains) Sade's tirades often strike the Marlovian note: "It is Nature that I wish to outrage. I should like to spoil her plans, to block her advance, to halt the course of the stars, to throw down the globes that float in space— to destroy everything that serves her, to protect everything that harms her, to cultivate everything that irritates her—in a word to insult all her works." But he stops considerably short of his mark. He not only refused to destroy one of her more diverting creations, himself, but he also opposed capital punishment. Even for a French *philosophe,* Sade is remarkably inconsistent, which is why one prefers his letters to his formal argument. Off duty he is more natural and less Natural. While in the Bastille he described himself as possessing an "extreme tendency in everything to lose control of myself, a disordered imagination in sexual matters such as has never been known in this world, an atheist to the point of fanaticism—in two words there I am, and so once again kill me or take me like that, because I shall never change." Latter-day diabolists have tried to make of his "disordered imagination in sexual matters" a religion and, as religions go, it is no more absurd than that of the crucified tripartite man-god. But though Nature is indeed nonhuman and we are without significance except to ourselves, to make of that same indifferent Nature an ally in behavior which is, simply, harmful to human society is to be singularly vicious.

Yet it is interesting to note that throughout all pornography, one theme recurs: the man or woman who manages to capture another human being for use as an unwilling sexual object. Obviously this is one of the commonest of masturbatory daydreams. Sade's originality was to try, deliberately, to make his fantasies real. But he was no Gilles de Rais. He lacked the organizational sense, and his actual adventures were probably closer to farce than to tragedy, more Charlie Chaplin trying to drown Martha Raye than Ilse Koch castrating her paramours at Buchenwald. Incidentally, it is typical of our period that the makers of the play *Marat/Sade* were much admired for having perversely reduced a splendid comic idea to mere tragedy.

Mr. Girodias's sampler should provide future sociologists with a fair idea of what sex was like at the dawn of the age of science. They will no doubt be as amused as most of us are depressed by the extent to which superstition has perverted human nature (not to mention thwarted Nature). Officially the tribal norm continues. The family is the central unit of society. Man's function is to impregnate woman in order to make children. Any sexual act that does not lead to the making of a child is untribal, which is to say antisocial. But though these assumptions are still held by the mass of human society in the West, the pornographers by what they write (as well as by what they omit to mention) show that in actual fact the old laws are not only broken (as always) but are being questioned in a new way.

Until this generation, even nonreligious enemies of irregular sexuality could sensibly argue that promiscuity was bad because it led to venereal disease and to the making of unwanted babies. In addition, sex was a dirty business since bodies stank and why should any truly fastidious person want to compound the filth of his own body's corruption with that of another? Now science has changed all that. Venereal disease has been contained. Babies need not be the result of the sexual act ("I feel so happy and safe now I take the pill"), while improved bathing facilities together with the American Mom's relentless circumcision of boys has made the average human body a temptingly hygienic contraption suitable for all sorts of experiment. To which the moralists can only respond: Rome born again! Sexual license and excessive bathing, as everyone knows, made the Romans effete and unable to stand up to the stalwart puritan savages from the German forests whose sacred mission was to destroy a world gone rotten. This simplistic view of history is a popular one, particularly among those who do not read history. Yet there is a basic point at issue and one that should be pondered.

Our tribal standards are an uneasy combination of Mosaic law and the warrior sense of caste that characterized those savage tribesmen who did indeed engulf the world of cities. The contempt for people in trade one still finds amongst the Wasp aristocracy, the sense of honor (furtive but gnawing), the pride in family, the loyalty to class, and (though covert) the admiration for the military virtues and physical strength are all inherited not from our civilized predecessors who lived in the great cities but from their conquerors, the wandering tribesmen, who planted no grain, built no cities, conducted no trade, yet preyed successfully upon those who did these contemptible, unmanly things. Today of course we are all as mixed in values as in blood, but the unstated assumption that it is better to be physically strong than wise, violent than gentle, continent than sensual, landowner or coupon clipper than shopkeeper, lingers on as a memorial to those marauding tribes who broke into history at the start of the Bronze Age and whose values are with us still, as the Gallup Poll attested recently, when it revealed that the President's war in Vietnam is most popular in the South, the most "tribal" part of the United States. Yet the city is the glory of our race, and today in the West, though we are all city dwellers, we still accept as the true virtue the code of our wild conquerors, even though our actual lives do not conform to their laws, nor should they, nor should we feel guilty because they don't.

In ten thousand years we have learned how to lengthen human lives but we have found no way to delay human puberty. As a result, between the economics of the city and the taboos of the tribe we have created a monstrous sexual ethic. To mention the most notorious paradox: It is not economically convenient for the adolescent to marry; it is not tribally correct for him to have sex outside of marriage. Solutions to this man-made problem range from insistence upon total chastity to a vague permissiveness which, worriedly, allows some sexuality if those involved are "sincere" and "mature" and "loving." Until this generation, tribal moralists could argue with perfect conviction that there was only one correct sexual equation: man plus woman equals baby. All else was vice. But now that half the world lives with famine—and all the world by the year 2000, if Pope Paul's as yet unborn guests are allowed to attend (in his unhappy phrase) the "banquet of life," the old equation has been changed to read: man plus woman equals baby equals famine. If the human race is to survive, population will have to be reduced drastically, if not by atomic war then by law, an unhappy prospect for civil liberties but better than starving. In any case, it is no longer possible to maintain that those sexual acts which do not create (or simulate the creation of) a child are unnatural; unless, to strike the eschatological note, it is indeed Nature's will that we perish through overpopulation, in which case reliable hands again clutch the keys of Peter.

Fortunately, the pornographers appear to be on the side of survival. They make nothing of virginity deflowered, an important theme for two thousand years; they make nothing of it for the simple reason we make little of it. Straightforward adultery no longer fascinates the pornographer; the scarlet letter has faded. Incest, mysteriously, seldom figures in current pornographies. This is odd. The tribal taboo remains as strong as ever, even though we now know that when members of the same family mate the result is seldom more cretinous or more sickly than its parents. The decline of incest as a marketable theme is probably due to today's inadequate middle-class housing. In large Victorian houses with many rooms and heavy doors, the occupants could be mysterious and exciting to one another in a way that those who live in rackety developments can never hope to be. Not even the lust of a Lord Byron could survive the fact of Levittown.

Homosexuality is now taken entirely for granted by pornographers because we take it for granted. Yet though there is considerable awareness nowadays of what people actually do, the ancient somewhat ambivalent hostility of the tribe persists; witness *Time* magazine's recent diagnosis of homosexuality as a "pernicious sickness" like influenza or opposing the war in Vietnam. Yet from the beginning, tribal attitudes have been confused on this subject. One the one hand, nothing must be allowed to deflect man the father from his procreative duty. On the other hand, man the warrior is more apt than not to perform homosexual acts. What was undesirable in peace was often a virtue in war, as the Spartans recognized, inventing the buddy system at the expense of the family unit. In general, it would seem that the more warlike the tribe, the more opportunistic the sexual response. "You know where you can find your sex," said that sly chieftain Frederick the Great to his officers, "—in the barracks." Of all the tribes, significantly, the Jews alone were consistently opposed not only to homosexuality but to any acknowledgment of the male as an erotic figure (cf. II *Maccabees* 4:7–15). But in the great world of pre-Christian cities, it never occurred to anyone that a homosexual act was less "natural" than a heterosexual one. It was simply a matter of taste. From Archilochus to Apuleius, this acceptance of the way people actually are is implicit in what the writers wrote. Suetonius records that of his twelve emperors, eleven went with equal ease from boys to girls and back again without Suetonius ever finding anything remarkable in their "polymorphous perverse" behavior. But all that, as Stanley Kauffmann would say, happened in a "different context."

Nevertheless, despite contexts, we are bisexual. Opportunity and habit incline us toward this or that sexual object. Since additional children are no longer needed, it is impossible to say that some acts are "right" and others "wrong." Certainly to maintain that a homosexual act in itself is antisocial or neurotic is dangerous nonsense, of the sort that the astonishing Dr. Edmund Bergler used to purvey when he claimed that he would "cure" homosexuals, as if this was somehow desirable, like changing Jewish noses or straightening Negro hair in order to make it possible for those who have been so altered to pass more easily through a world of white Christians with snub noses.

Happily, in a single generation, science has changed many old assumptions. Economics has changed others. A woman can now easily support herself, independent of a man. With the slamming of Nora's door, the family ceased to be the inevitable social unit. Also, the newly affluent middle class can now pursue other pleasures. In the film *The Collector,* a lower-class boy captures an educated girl and after alternately tormenting and boring her, he says balefully, "If more people had more time and money, there would be a lot more of this." This got an unintended laugh in the theater, but he is probably right. Sexual experiment is becoming more open. A placid Midwestern town was recently appalled to learn that its young married set was systematically swapping wives. In the cities, group sex is popular, particularly among the young. Yet despite the new freedoms that the pornographers reflect (sadly for them, since their craft must ultimately wither away), the world they show, though closer to human reality than that of the tribalists, reveals a new illness: the powerlessness that most people feel in an overpopulated and overorganized society. The sado-masochist books that dominate this year's pornography are not the result of a new enthusiasm for the *vice anglais* so much as a symptom of helplessness in a society where most of the male's aggressive-creative drive is thwarted. The will to prevail is a powerful one, and if it is not fulfilled in work or in battle, it may find an outlet in sex. The man who wants to act out fantasies of tying up or being tied up is imposing upon his sex life a power drive which became socially undesirable once he got onto that escalator at IBM which will take him by predictable stages to early retirement and the medically prolonged boredom of sunset years. Solution of this problem will not be easy, to say the least.

Meanwhile, effort must be made to bring what we think about sex and what we say about sex and what we do about sex into some kind of realistic relationship. Indirectly, the pornographers do this. They recognize that the only sexual norm is that there is none. Therefore, in a civilized society law should not function at all in the area of sex except to protect people from being "interfered with" against their will.

Unfortunately, even the most enlightened of the American state codes (Illinois) still assumes that since adultery is a tribal sin it must be regarded as a civil crime. It is not, and neither is prostitution, that most useful of human institutions. Traditionally, liberals have opposed prostitution on the ground that no one ought to be forced to sell his body because of poverty. Yet in our Affluency, prostitution continues to flourish for the simple reason that it is needed. If most men and women were forced to rely upon physical charm to attract lovers, their sexual lives would be not only meager but in a youth-worshiping country like America painfully brief. Recognizing this state of affairs, a Swedish psychologist recently proposed state brothels for women as well as for men, in recognition of the sad biological fact that the middle-aged woman is at her sexual peak at a time when she is no longer able to compete successfully with younger women. As for the prostitutes themselves, they practice an art as legitimate as any other, somewhere between that of masseur and psychiatrist. The best are natural healers and, contrary to tribal superstition, they often enjoy their work. It is to the credit of today's pornographer that intentionally or not, he is the one who tells us most about the extraordinary variety of human sexual response. In his way he shows us as we are, rather like those Fun House mirrors which, even as they distort and mock the human figure, never cease to reflect the real thing.

WILLIAM PHILLIPS

THE NEW IMMORALISTS

A specter is haunting modern literature, the specter of avant-garde homosexuality. Some people are thrilled, others frightened, by the morbid prospects. The leading figures of the new subversives are Jean Genet and William Burroughs, though there are many other lesser talents, less flamboyant talents, imitators, hangers-on, and plain phonies. One might think of them as the extreme Left of the advanced sexuality that has dominated fiction and the movies for some time now. But I think this is too superficial a view, almost a routine response of middle-class respectability disguised as sober criticism; and such lumping of sex, experiment, dissent, and new values promotes the appetite for sensationalism and makes it difficult to evaluate or to understand the new works.

Some day writers like Genet and Burroughs might be assimilated, but so far the reaction to both of them—particularly to Burroughs—has been uneasy, uncertain, and spotty. They have

139

been praised, dismissed, ignored, usually as a gesture or a public stand. Mary McCarthy, Robert Lowell, and Norman Mailer have hailed Burroughs as a major talent (I don't recall what they said about Genet); and there is Sartre's monumental tribute to Genet, *Saint Genet*. On the other hand, many critics have found Genet mediocre and distasteful, and Burroughs revolting, formless, and interesting mostly as pornography. Lionel Abel, who is not known for his conservative taste, said recently that Burroughs belongs to the "cult of utterness" which lies outside of literature. Even the word "sick," normally used only by the guardians of morality, has been applied to Genet and Burroughs by literary people. Rarely have judgments been so opposed, and for so long. What we have here is not difference of opinion, which usually varies only slightly and mainly in emphasis, but a difference of values. People are forced—not always consciously—to re-examine their values before being able to make up their minds about Burroughs or Genet, and sometimes there is a contradiction between how they feel and how they think they should feel. Hence sides are taken the way they are on political or ideological issues.

Genet is a much more complicated and more traditional writer than Burroughs, and, I think, a much more gifted one. But both of them have turned traditional values upside down. I do not mean that they have questioned only those conventions that make up the moral cant and the popular styles of our time. If this were all there was to their subversion, they surely would be part of the advanced establishment, especially now with the homage paid to the cult of novelty and rebellion. We all know about the attraction to "evil": the *Inferno* is more interesting than the *Paradiso*, and it is an old story that the Devil is usually more likable than God. The moral underground is a staple of the modern household, like civil rights or sexual freedom. Who dares question the thinking of the avant-garde—or what is by now its tradition? And by association with such extreme but accepted figures as Rimbaud or Baudelaire or Gide, Genet and Burroughs seem to be legitimate heirs to the tradition of dissent and experiment. But the resemblance is superficial. Baudelaire's concern with evil, for example, or Dostoevski's with crime, were attempts to assimilate the new psychology to traditional morality; while

Nietzsche, the great rebel of modern thought, seems tame today by comparison with Genet. Rimbaud talked of degrading the senses; Burroughs achieves it.

What distinguishes Genet and Burroughs is that they have broken almost completely with the past. Theirs is a distinct, self-contained world, one in which there are very few tensions or contradictions between the old and the new, scarcely any concessions to existing taste or sensibility in the choice of images or metaphors, very little guilt. There are few rests between the successions of shocks, few "normal" associations, of the kind we find even in someone like Kafka, in whom the irony and the ambiguity serve as links with the conventional world. It is hard to think of a single writer, however "advanced," who has not been full of dull and undistinguished passages, as though to remind us how habitual genius often is, and how ordinary is the experience of most art. Sometimes the commonplace has been programmatic, as in Pop art, which—like Dada earlier—has tried to make a style out of the connection between the bizarre and the blatant. With Genet and Burroughs, however, it is just the opposite: instead of relating to more traditional ideas, they force us to accept and to judge them on terms set by themselves.

Such submission through art to what is otherwise considered to be intolerable is, of course, in keeping with the guilt-ridden spirit of liberation that is riding high these days. To embrace what is assumed to be beyond the pale is taken as a sign of true sophistication. And this is not simply a change in sensibility; it amounts to a sensibility of chaos—for it means that every new work has an equal and irresistible claim on us, that it lies outside judgment. True enough, new works do not come into being simply to be judged. Still, we all know that in some way not easily defined we both judge and don't judge; we are open to new experiences for their own sake at the same time that we exercise some kind of selection by relating them to other things we think or have felt. Taste is actually a form of judgment.

Some of these questions are raised quite dramatically in a recent piece by Susan Sontag on "camp." Miss Sontag describes boldly and with much spirit a current mode, fairly general though mostly found among younger people, and largely homosexual in

origin, that puts style above meaning, taste above judgment, living above life. Her own attitude seems to be torn—since she is
reflecting as well as examining the new stance—between the
"moral seriousness" of high culture and the "aestheticism and
irony" of camp. And she is really not interested in reconciling
these two modern forces, nor does she see any advantage in
being consistent. Hers is obviously a radical and sophisticated
position and so advanced that one does not like to be excluded
from it. But those who have stronger roots in another style, one
that recognizes that morality has limits but is not ready to
abandon morality for any aesthetic stance, are even less prepared
to abandon themselves to pure play, or to pure experience, which
amounts to the same thing. One finds oneself *judging* as well as
experiencing the quality of the new work or the new idea. And it
is an axiom of criticism that in evaluating new art we cannot
avoid applying traditional standards, though these standards are
themselves altered by new works.

One of the difficulties in dealing with Genet is that there
are two Genets: the wild playwright and the almost documentary
novelist and memoirist. Ironically, it is the tamer, more prosaic
Genet I find not only less exciting but also less palatable. For
the autobiographical declaration, *The Thief's Journal,* like most
of the fiction, is little more than a saga of what Genet has done
and how he has felt. The "content" of these books is a recital of
the crime and perversity that make up Genet's being. Hence
one might expect some new form to accommodate the unusual
subject. But the journal and the novels are naturalistic, orderly,
conventional—the prose is traditional—in a way that suggests
some aesthetic perversity. What comes through is only one side
of Genet, his raw experience, in its most literal and routine
form, even though Genet the writer does emerge as part of the
person. His art consists of his having transformed his life into a
life-style. Hence the work has the compact facility of a self-
portrait. It is not truly an autobiography, nor a confession or a
justification of what he has done or felt; it reads more like a
condensed version of the murder, theft, sodomy, treason, disloyalty, sadomasochism, that make up his life, all presented as
though the world they come from might be different but not

abnormal. In this respect, Genet is really making the same assumptions most other writers do: that the scene of their work is one we are in or in which we can easily imagine ourselves, and can therefore take for granted.

Because *The Thief's Journal* is so consistent and so explicit, it can serve as Genet's moral and psychological dictionary. It defines his acts and his feelings and supplies the clues to his most perverse ideas; in this sense it traces his "moral" development. But more than that, the book reconstructs and gives shape to his life; it makes his life plausible by making it coherent, the way a work of art or a psychoanalysis makes an imaginary life real or endows a real life with imagination. The homosexual rites that fill Genet's novels are here, in all their clinical splendor, told with an innocent boyish exhibitionism. But they are also connected with Genet's absorption in crime and with other phases of his pathology, partly through the juxtaposition of incidents, partly by self-analysis, so that what emerges is essentially the evidence for Genet's ideal of himself. And not much more: for the autobiography is obsessively selective, and we learn very little about Genet's life beyond his passions and attachments and his compulsive interest in theft and murder. The reiteration of his petty criminal acts and his perverse feelings gives the impression that there are just a few themes, rotating around one another.

As Genet presents his life the core is in his homosexuality. I don't know whether this is the art or the truth of Genet, but it does explain many things. His total and abject submission to male ravishment clarifies his double attitude to authority: he likes to violate and to be violated, particularly by cops. His passion for killing or stealing is a passion for a pure act disconnected from "normal" acts and values, and mixed up with the betrayals, over wrought loyalties, and phallic associations that go with his homosexuality. "The only criterion for an act," says Genet, "is its elegance." Genet speaks with excitement of all forms of disloyalty, including treason, but always as though they were natural, innocent, and fulfilling, somehow necessary to his peculiar existence. The events of his life appear to have a pathological consistency as its abnormal components are fused, violently, as though they were mated. In the end, Genet's existence takes on a waif-like sexuality, complete, cut off, abandoned to its own deformed innocence.

Genet's criminal simplicity almost grows on one, so long as he remains an outcast who simply is everything that has happened to him. But the spell is broken when he appropriates a nobility and a moral purity that come from a civilization he has rejected. When, for example, Genet applies for sainthood—or it is bestowed on him by Sartre—it sounds inauthentic and literary. One hears echoes of the stale, romantic association of the depths with the heights, the marriage of heaven and hell. Whatever reservations one might have about most of Genet's work, it is not on the grounds of falseness. But when he says, "Saintliness means turning pain to good account . . . forcing the devil to be God . . . obtaining the recognition of evil . . ."—then he is only dressing up his life in the clichés of a sophisticated and fashionable approach to literature and religion: he becomes a moral transvestite. The one thing Genet is not is a saint, unless we assume that every talented and suffering criminal is *ex officio* a saint.

But even the pretense of sainthood does not make *The Thief's Journal* easier to assimilate. Nor does it rescue the book from the boredom of the homosexual catechism. What makes Genet's world at all palatable is the literary gift; it is through literature that the middle class flirts with the forbidden. And Genet's sensibility helps make his inferno seem almost respectable. For the clean, functional prose—the prose of journalism and exposition—is something we associate with the rigors and the responsibilities of middle-class society, with the idealizing of order and the therapeutic approach to disorder.

The other Genet, however, the Genet of *The Balcony* and *The Blacks*, is a different story. In the plays, which are marvelously suggestive and ambiguous because they do not pretend to be documentary, the metaphors that connect his life with other kinds of life are more mysterious and, therefore, ultimately, less disturbing. *The Balcony*, for example, has to do with perversity, but not literally or exclusively; and its meaning is enlarged because of the way the sexual idea the characters have of themselves runs in and out of their worldly idea of themselves. It might be said that Genet's novels are transformed into his plays, the way life is normally converted into art.

Our other underground man, William Burroughs, on the surface at least, is more experimental, less conventional, and wider in his fantasies than Genet even in the plays. Where Genet has a recognizable subject, Burroughs' subject is his fantasies. The new book, *Nova Express,* differs from *Naked Lunch* in that it is conceived in the mode of science fiction, but like his earlier work, it is essentially a biological nightmare. The cast, as usual, includes junkies, queers, criminals, wanderers of all sorts, but in *Nova Express* they are more explicitly insiders and outsiders, because Burroughs has created a fanciful opposition to "the police machine." Beyond this, it is almost impossible to explain what happens. (Because it cannot be paraphrased this would have made a good example of a prose text for the New Critics.) All one can say is that *Nova Express* is very much like the scenario of a battle, with the various bizarre characters jerking in and out of the set, flashing all kinds of lurid messages in junkie code, the whole scene blazing in images of death and destruction, merged with drugged states, hallucinations, queer dreams, images of feces, vomiting, etc. It is as though Burroughs had hit upon a way of seeing all of life in terms of a homosexual essence: the feeding, almost literally, of human flesh and organs on each other in an orgy of annihilation. The whole world is reduced to the fluidity of excrement as everything else: ideas, metaphors, objects, associations, memories, bodies, people, all melt into one another in a cosmic orgasm.

Burroughs' prose, too, though woollier than Genet's, is, like Genet's, always working—there are no wasted words, only wasted sentences—and as in the case of Genet, what he is writing about is blunted by making writing into a common denominator of experience.

A few years ago, when Burroughs was being dismissed because he was new and unrespectable, it might have been necessary to defend him against the philistines and the legions of decency. But now that unrespectability itself is becoming respectable, one can't go on talking about him as though he were a wild new talent, full of the promise and the faults of youth. It seems reasonable to expect Burroughs by now to have developed into something more than a permanent, however able, propagandist for his obsessions. His gifts as a writer of prose can carry him only so far—unless we are ready to reduce writing to its craft.

The ultimate test of a new work is its influence on other writers and its effect on our view of things. In the case of Genet's plays there is some indication that our imagination has been stirred and enlarged. But I do not think this is true of his novels. And I do not believe this happens at all with Burroughs. But there is also a more immediate and simpler test, boredom: and the truth is that Genet's fantasies in the form of confessions and Burroughs' confessions in the form of fantasies are bound to bore anyone outside that closed circle of experience. Boredom, after all, is a form of criticism. And the sophisticated reader's or professional critic's failure to be bored is a failure of personality —an overeagerness to become something other than what one is.

The trouble is that we are constantly changing. We can no longer be sure of what we think we are and what we believe. Scared by the speed with which the future seems to be coming at us, a new breed of literary vigilantes has sprung up to safeguard nonexistent values and warn against the dangers of the latest avant-garde. But, really, literature is dangerous only to those who, in the name of a morality they do not believe in, attack an art they do not like. Even if writers like Burroughs or Genet sometimes sound like spokesmen for what used to be considered immoral and abnormal, at most this can only be tiresome—almost as tiresome as pep talks about normal and healthy art. Extremes are bound to feed on each other. So we shouldn't be surprised to see an up-to-date version of the old gentility in reaction to a new avant-garde.

BENJAMIN DE MOTT

"BUT HE'S A HOMOSEXUAL . . ."

What is a homosexual artist? A devil and a liar, says the current noisy indictment—a desecrater, a self-server, a character nobody on earth should trust. Sly and sulky, he poisons hope and idealism with the mean flow of his resentment. Sick and exhibitionistic, he jams the media with neuroses, teaching that women are destroyers and heterosexual domestic life is hell. Worse by far, the man is power-mad. Skinnying his way onto established grant committees, prize panels, editorial boards, and other seats of authority, he spurns aspirants not of his clique, thereby creating a tyranny of taste that soon will have every center of imaginative expression—theater, opera, symphony hall, publishing house, museum, gallery—under its cheesy thrall. In sum: The homosexual artist is an enemy of the people, a threat to the quality of American life.

As every magazine reader knows, indictments like the foregoing have for some time been highly salable. For a representa-

147

tive sample, consider an article about Messrs. Albee, Warhol, et al.—the title was "Who's Afraid of Aunt Fanny?"—that appeared a while back in *Ramparts*. The initial stance of this piece was one of tolerant sophistication; the author, Gene Marine, gave assurances that he was no scandalmonger, no keyhole inquirer into celebrities' private lives, no naif eager to set up equations between, say, "longhaired hippies" and homosexuality:

> Let me put things straight [he wrote], for you and the libel lawyers. I don't absolutely know for certain the names of any famous homosexuals, though I probably make the same guesses you do, and if I did know any for certain, I wouldn't tell you. As far as I know, Edward Albee is a square family man, Andy Warhol is afflicted with satyriasis and California has no homosexuality south of the Santa Ynez river. I couldn't care less.

But having given these assurances, Marine went on to prove them spurious. Employing the tricks of an innuendo-cutie and a manner of sleazy downrightness, he developed an ever more expansive series of charges, and ended by dealing damnation round the entire American cultural landscape. Here are some steps in the progress:

> The point is that homosexual playwrights and homosexual directors and homosexual producers are having more and more to say about what can and can't be done in American theater.

> People who know more about it than I do . . . tell me that it's even worse in the world of art—by which I mean painting and sculpture. The galleries take what the decorators want them to take, and the decorators want them to take their gay friends.

> I'm getting damned tired of all the art being campy and all the plays being queer and all the clothes being West Fourth Street and the whole bit. Some I don't mind, but it's getting too close to all, and I have the feeling that there are healthier bases for a culture.

You can take almost any part of the world of culture, and there it is, in bold lavender. Dance and interior design, fashions (women's and men's), music—especially outside the relatively virile jazz and rock fields—and music promotion, novels and poetry, little theater and magazines.

The ploy in question is, predictably, more or less standard throughout the contemporary muckraking press. (*Fact* enlarged the area of presumed "domination" by printing a "study" of homosexuals in T.V.) And hints of the influence of this ploy—more about them in a minute—have been visible in journals of a quite different character: the Sunday drama section of *The New York Times*, highbrow periodicals like the *New York Review of Books* and the *Drama Review*.

That the subject of homosexual influence in the arts should engage attention at this moment isn't mysterious. American interest in matters cultural and aesthetic is on the rise. New levels of candor about sexual behavior seem to be achieved every other week. And, most important, the national reserves of credulity have not diminished much over the years. If this were not so, baiters of homosexual art probably would pull smaller audiences. For their charges are rooted in the belief that centralized control of the arts can be achieved by a nonpolitical, essentially nonideological nonorganization—and only the credulous can rest comfortably in such faith. Tyrannies of taste do occur, to be sure—they are inevitable whenever a professionally practiced art lacks multiple centers of power. (Serious music is the sector of the arts that most nearly meets the latter description at this moment. Outlets for the work of living American composers are extremely few, which means that homosexual cliquishness could—some informed people say it does—throttle free musical expression.) And homosexual centers of power do exist—a cluster of art galleries here, a group of experimental moviemakers there. (One famous Fifty-seventh Street gallery has even been, in fairly recent days, a center of homosexual poetry as well as of painting and sculpture.)

But countless other galleries flourish that are nothing of the sort, and a half-dozen low-budget cinematic experimenters con-

tinue to produce—and exhibit—films untouched by what is called
"homosexual fantasy." And in other sectors of the arts mixed
situations seem generally the rule. The financial backers of one
newly founded off-Broadway production firm are homosexuals;
those of several other newish producing firms are not. A few
trade publishing houses appear to be particularly well disposed
to homosexual writers; the majority have no clear policy save the
pursuit of profit. Given present complications and uncertainties
of taste and prejudice, and given the continued emergence from
time to time of new centers of activity (the American Place
Theatre is an example) the danger of total domination will
remain slight. Cliquishness cannot be abolished, and, as just
indicated, it can cause damage in fields of artistic endeavor
where opportunities for professional hearing are subject to auto-
cratic control. But, while complacency about these fields is inex-
cusable, they are less numerous than scourgers of "homosexual
tyranny"—and the more gullible of their readers—profess to
believe. And the heralded culture explosion should reduce their
number, not increase it, in the future.

But if the homosexual himself isn't a serious threat to cultural
vigor and variety, the same can't be said of those who harass
him in print. The point at issue here isn't, true enough, easy to
grasp. A piece writer who beats up "the fairies" for a few thousand words would seem, on the face of it, only another harmless
canny profiteer. It's plain, after all, that complaints about "homosexual art" will never mobilize hostility and frustration at the
destructive levels sustained in yesteryear by the Red-baiters.*
And conceivably "frank talk" in this area, no matter how woolly
and superstitious, can have beneficial effects. (The public needs
to be reminded some say, that reputations in the arts are made

* Two mythy items that figure in "thinking" about the coming
homosexualization of America are the concept of a nation asleep at
the switch, as it were, too absorbed in business to notice its sex is
changing, and the concept of a doomsday recognition scene, a moment
at which people discover to their horror that they have frittered
away their birthrate and are the last generation of their kind. Both
concepts figured, in slightly different form, in Senator McCarthy's
speeches on the Commie conspiracy a decade ago.

things, not miracles: edifices built by the continuous efforts not simply of a single artist, but of friends who sometimes praise a man's work when what they actually value is his personal charm. And the public needs the experience, others say, of talking about homosexuality—because such talk fosters the growth of tolerance: when homosexuality in one quarter of the community is freely and openly assessed, responses to homosexuality in the community at large should become less hysterical.) Why turn hypercritical toward characters who, whatever their own personal cynicism, may function as nourishers of American sophistication?

The answer is simple: At the center of most talk about "homosexual art" lies the assumption that books, pictures, poems created by homosexuals are private documents, narrow in range, incapable of speaking truly to anyone not himself a homosexual. The prime effect of this already widely disseminated idea has been to neutralize or denature several of the most provocative critical images of contemporary life to win mass audiences since World War II. And from this it follows that the self-appointed enemy of "homosexual art" isn't just a nuisance: he is a pernicious waster of an invaluable cultural resource.

As might be guessed, the ways of waste—the means by which commentators cheat the work of homosexuals and torture it out of strength—are nothing if not ingenious. Chief among them is a trick of medical inside-dopesterism that transforms texts clear enough on their surface into complex codes or allegories—productions whose deepest truths yield themselves only to psychoanalytic exegesis. Consider, for instance, the operations of clinical exegetes on Edward Albee's *Who's Afraid of Virginia Woolf?* In both the stage and film versions, the ending of this work seems a moment of poignance. Weary beyond fury, blasted (almost) into kindness, George and Martha have arrived at a nowhere world in which combat is pointless. The audience knows that cozy murmurs about reconciliation, forgiveness, happiness ahead would be puerile, but is nevertheless aware of a passage into an atmosphere of feeling less ridden by fantasy, more open, more yielding. Nobody has "won," but a loss has been suffered jointly: pity is in the room.

Enter the clinical exegete, and every "simplistic" reading of the play is laved in scorn. (Exegetes of this brand are printed in psychoanalytic journals as well as in magazines of art.) *Virginia Woolf*, wrote Dr. Donald M. Kaplan (a psychoanalyst) in the *Drama Review*, is in its essence a predictable homosexual claim that "genitality is . . . an unnecessary burden"; the closing scene is a moment of triumph, it signifies that a married man "can prevail through the tactics of pregenital perversity" and need not grow up to his role:

> The sexuality of the parental bedroom (Nick and Martha offstage) is no match for the multifarious derivatives of George's oral aggression, anality, voyeurism, masochism and procreative reluctance. In the end, Martha returns to George, as she so often has in the past. The enfant terrible again triumphs over the cocksmen of the outside world, and the nursery is preserved. . . .

Fitted into this pattern of homosexual aggression and glee, Albee's play is easily dismissed as a projection of dementia—a set of remarks about Rorschach cards, a collection of symptoms, nothing a "straight" could even begin to take straight.

Clinical exegesis isn't, of course, the harshest line of critique found in discussion of so-called homosexual art. Traditional American manliness makes itself heard in *Fact* and *Ramparts* ("I like women," Gene Marine said stoutly) and even in tonier periodicals—witness Philip Roth's attack on Albee's "pansy prose" that appeared in the *New York Review* following the opening of *Tiny Alice*. But the survival of tough-guyism is less interesting— and less regrettable—than the nearly universal acceptance of the central assumption just mentioned, namely, that art produced by homosexuals is irrelevant to life as lived by nonhomosexuals. A year or two ago the Sunday theater section of *The New York Times* printed a pair of articles by Stanley Kauffmann, then the newspaper's drama critic, on the "subject of the homosexual dramatist." A liberal, humane man, Kauffmann clearly had no terror of "perverts," no desire to suppress the work of the artists he was discussing. His articles, seen by many as another heroic breakthrough for frankness, dealt in passing with the matter of "homosexual style," and with the supposed tendency of the homosexual writer to treat theme and subject as immaterial and surface as all-important. They were partly conceived as defenses of the homosexual's right to freedom of expression, and they offered several telling observations about uses and abuses of that right.

Yet everywhere in his comments this critic signified his conviction that plays by homosexual dramatists should be regarded as codes to be deciphered, disguises to be seen through, private languages requiring continuous acts of translation by the audience:

> In society the homosexual's life must be discreetly concealed. If he is to write of his experience, he must invent a two-sex version of the one-sex experience that he really has.

Kauffmann blamed this situation upon society—not upon the homosexual writer. And he argued forcibly for an end to the repression and inhibition that harries these writers into deceit:

> If we object to the distortion that homosexual disguises entail, and if, as civilized people, we do not want to gag these artists, then there seems only one conclusion. The conditions that force the dissembling must change.

But, like the psychoanalyst quoted earlier, Kauffmann was committed to the notion that a homosexual's image of life is necessarily an expression of "homosexual truth"; the man has no choice to "transform [what he knows] to a life he does not know, to the detriment of his truth and ours."

Even those critics whose avowed purpose is to make a case for "homosexual art"—as it is—to rescue it from vulgar attack and place it in a dignified light—fall into modes of discourse that are reductive and evasive in discussing its meaning. Consider the approach adopted in Susan Sontag's "Notes on Camp." This critic announces herself to be "strongly drawn" to the kind of art she is setting out to describe; yet throughout her essay she speaks of that art always as a phenomenon of style alone; the worth of its statement, the nature of its view of life, even its cultural associations and origins are passed off as boring matters. ("One feels," says the critic, "if homosexuals hadn't more or less invented Camp, someone else would.") What counts about this art is its tonality, not the total experience offered and the meanings created through that experience:

> Camp and tragedy are antitheses. There is seriousness in Camp (seriousness in the degree of the artist's involvement), and, very often, pathos. The excruciating is also one of the tonalities of Camp; it is the quality of excruciation in much of Henry James . . . that is responsible for the large element of Camp in his writings. But there is never, never tragedy.

The obvious question is: Given the nature of the life represented in a so-called "Camp novel," is the quality of excruciation tendentious or appropriate? Can a man learn or confirm any truth of experience through a confrontation with Camp? When such questions aren't asked, much less answered, the implication is that this art may truly be empty of substance.

The point at stake bears restating. Dumb-ox or tough-guy or Philistine versions of works of art produced by homosexuals tend to be crudely dismissive—too crudely dismissive, often, for educated audiences to accept. But other dismissive lines have now become available. There is chic psychoanalytical chatter that evades the truth of a scene by seeing the scene as a symptom. There is a liberal critique that evades the truth of a scene by tolerantly viewing the scene, not as an image of life, but as a product of indirect censorship. And there is a brand of aesthetic criticism that evades the truth of a scene by focusing solely on matters of form. None of the approaches mentioned appears hostile to the so-called homosexual artist; each embodies different values and assumptions. But all are alike in espousing, or else in refusing to challenge, the dogma that the homosexual's representation of life can be only an expression of homosexual truth— "his truth" as opposed to "ours," as Kauffmann put it. And that dogma while comforting to the majority, is quite without foundation.

It is probable that most readers and theatergoers—save for the scandalmongers who shriek about homosexual tyranny—will accept the claim that the most intense accounts of domestic life and problems in recent years, as well as the few unembarrassedly passionate love poems, have been the work of writers who are not heterosexual. The problem of compulsive promiscuity, or Don Juanism—one that Jose Ortega y Gasset described as the most delicate and abstruse in contemporary human relations—has been examined with extraordinary force and directness by Tennessee Williams in several plays. And that intensity has time and time over proved to be an illumination of a kind. Some of the writers in question can be overpraised, to be sure. There is phony elegance and needless obfuscation in Albee's current manner, total dishevelment in the bulk of Ginsberg, too much self-indulgence in Williams, who seems bent on writing the same play four hundred times.

Yet a fair assessment of these writers, or of any of their relevant superiors—Genet and Auden for two—can hardly be wholly negative. With a few other poets and dramatists, they are the only compelling writers of the postwar period who seem to know anything beyond the level of cliché about human connectedness, whose minds break through the stereotypes of existential violence or Nietzschean extravagance into recognizable truths and intricacies of contemporary feeling. They are not purveyors of situation comedy of Bond banalities or *Playboy* virility or musical-marital bliss (*I Do! I Do!*) or mate-murders. A steady consciousness of a dark side of love that is neither homo- nor hetero-sexual but simply human pervades much of their work; they are in touch with facts of feeling that most men do not or cannot admit to thought. They know what Catullus knew about *odi et amo*—simultaneities of hatred and its opposite—and they know the special terms and strains of these simultaneities in modern experience, wherein prohibitions against self-indulgence have lost force. They know that love and suffering are near allied and that love ought not to be confused with the slumbrous affection or habitual exploitation that is the rule in numberless households. They know that the lover's demand for exclusive possession has vanity as one of its roots.

They have in mind, not as aphorisms but as potential behavior and gesture, knowledge of the kind compressed in Mme. de Staël's remark that love equals self-love *à deux,* or in Proust's claim that there are people for whom there is no such thing as reciprocated love, and that these people are by no means the most insensitive among us. They know that instability is a fact of love, as of human personality generally. And the tensions and furies arising from contradictory desires and impulses seem to them proper subjects for intelligence to probe.

As good an exhibit as any, perhaps, is Auden's much celebrated "Lullaby":

> Lay your sleeping head my love,
> Human on my faithless arm;
> Time and fevers burn away
> Individual beauty from
> Thoughtful children, and the grave
> Proves the child ephemeral:
> But in my arms till break of day
> Let the living creature lie,
> Mortal, guilty, but to me
> The entirely beautiful.
>
> Soul and body have no bounds:
> To lovers as they lie upon
> Her tolerant enchanted slope
> In their ordinary swoon,
> Grave the vision Venus sends
> Of supernatural sympathy,
> Universal love and hope;
> While an abstract insight wakes
> Among the glaciers and the rocks
> The hermit's sensual ecstasy.
>
> Certainty, fidelity
> On the stroke of midnight pass
> Like vibrations of a bell,
> And fashionable madmen raise
> Their pedantic boring cry:

Every farthing of the cost,
All the dreaded cards foretell,
Shall be paid, but from this night
Not a whisper, not a thought,
Not a kiss nor look be lost.

Beauty, midnight, vision dies.
Let the winds of dawn that blow
Softly round your dreaming head
Such a day of sweetness show
Eye and knocking heart may bless,
Find the mortal world enough;
Noons of dryness see you fed
By the involuntary powers,
Nights of insult let you pass
Watched by every human love.

Reductions of this poem to homily or "general truth" play into the hands of Auden's detractors—those given to abusing the poet for being overchic. But that risk can be run. Some of the distinction of the "Lullaby" lies in the steadiness of its refusal to exclude the narrative consciousness from the lyric consciousness; joy, love, enchantment are placed, in this poem as in life, in immediate, living, indismissible adjacency to their opposites. Another part of the poem's distinction lies in the capacity of the singer at once to inhabit the lullaby-trance of union, to experience it in its fullness and uniqueness, and to look on from outside, acknowledging, neither merely pityingly nor merely knowingly, the replicability (in an age of indulgence) of this "ordinary swoon." And everywhere in the poem there is an alertness to contrarieties and puzzles of response—the murderously brief and beautiful sense of moral being perfected in sensual delight.

Grave the vision Venus sends
Of supernatural sympathy,
Universal love and hope . . . .

In this small poem a densely instructive world of feeling is created, a world that is proof against the simplicities of desiccation (the typist in *The Waste Land*), as well as against those of romantic melancholy (Frederick Henry in *A Farewell to Arms*). And in Auden's *Collected Poems* there are a number of songs—see for instance the matchless lyric "Warm are the still and lucky miles"—worth equal praise.

Does the knowledge embodied in such poems qualify as unique? Is it in itself a guarantee of "profundity"? Of course not: most reflective men know what these poems know—namely that love is the only human entrance into an ideal world, and that life, a teaser and mocker, lets few men through to stay. Why then is such knowledge more vivid in homosexual art than elsewhere? Again quick answers are unsatisfactory. Heroicizing the "homosexual artist" is, certainly, as senseless as condescending to him as a case. It does need to be said, though, that the homosexual artist's aptitude for the presentation of certain human (not homosexual or heterosexual) complications of feeling can't be understood by people oblivious to the features of his situation that lend it a measure of dignity. "To be free is to have one's freedom perpetually on trial." It isn't necessary to endorse every line of existential scripture to see the application of this text from Sartre to the intelligent, responsive homosexual who has a gift for the formed re-creation of experience. The latter gift is, as everyone knows, distributed according to no visible plan; sexuality conceived as a pure and separable essence is not its determinant. But the homosexual who possesses it does have special occasion to exercise and refine it in fundamental, as well as in craft or professional, areas of life, owing to the peculiarities of his situation in the general culture. If I am a Citizen, Husband, Straight-Arrow, I easily can put myself on trial. I can speak for a troubling cause, enter upon a bout of promiscuity, teach in a turtleneck, grow my hair long in back. But I cannot escape the promise of ease, the possibility of subsiding into the accepted and the respectable; always an oasis of habitual, unexamined, unjudged life awaits me.

The intelligent homosexual, however, is in another situation. A tide of suspicion flows toward him, perpetually demanding that he justify his difference; relaxation into unthinking self-acceptance in the presence of other eyes is prohibited. If he is rich and shrewd, he may manage to create for himself the illusion of a life unexposed to antipathetic scrutiny—but sustaining that illusion is hard work. If he isn't rich and shrewd, his immediate confrontations with hostility—the interruptions of his taken-for-granted daily existence—will be numberless. And these interruptions will induce in him a heightened awareness of the feelings and assumptions of others—an immediate living consciousness of the fragility of the shields that hide human cruelty from general view.

To say this isn't for a moment to suggest that lives can, by any system of categorization, be precisely compared in terms of their remoteness from challenge: we measure with inklings and intuitions here, and confidence isn't in the equation. Neither is it to suggest that the intelligent and sensitive homosexual is the only man who is ever thrust into tasking encounters with himself and others. It is to say that these encounters are probably more difficult for the homosexual to avoid than for other men. And the encounters do have "excruciating" value to anyone whose art depends upon his ability to experience dailiness rather than simply pass through it, to inhabit moment-to-moment reality, to be aware of present time and know it not as something between yesterday and tomorrow but as the edge of his life. Admittedly a man of strong mind can close himself off from the coarseness that teases the homosexual in his round of errands in any town or suburb other than a gay colony—schoolchildren mincing behind his back as their elders have more or less instructed them to do, overheartiness or dropped eyes among tradesmen, slyness and lubricity in the cleaning woman. And the danger of sentimentalizing experience of this kind, assigning more value and meaning to embarrassment than it possesses, is real. Everyone knows about homosexual arrogance; everyone knows that aristocratic poses fend off "nights of insult"; everyone knows that flights of defensive scorn or resentment—the familiar gestures of mediocrity—are common in homosexual conversation.

But self-deception and mediocrity are, after all, everywhere the rule—and the writers and artists spoken of publicly as homosexuals, and thus looked down upon, are by and large not mediocrities. They are men who have been provoked into dwelling on the relative emptiness and unthinkingness of most men's commitments to the terms of their own lives. They are people whom we put on endless tiral, because our manner declares that no condition of moral being except our own can be approved, because our explicit claim is that love can only be a permanent attachment, and because we dare not detach ourselves from our "institutions" even though we know they derive in great part from superstition. They are people forced to face up to the arbitrariness of cultural patterns—arbitrariness that we insist on regarding as altogether unarbitrary, a logical bidding of nature, a sane, wholly explicable pattern, like the movement of the earth. The fury that lifts James Baldwin's prose to eloquence, when that writer has before him the cruelty of cultural arbitrariness, stems not alone from Baldwin's experience as a Negro. And the racking power of those moments in Genet, when this writer has the same spectacle in sight, arises not only from a career as a thief. The usefulness of the instruction offered through this eloquence and power doesn't vary in accordance with the condition of the reader's sexuality. We need not be "perverts" to see into the life of that moment when Genet's Divine enters the cafe, smiles round the room in "her" crazy aloneness, tests the blade of hate:

> She smiled all around, and each one answered only by turning away, but that was a way of answering. The whole cafe thought that the smile of (for the colonel: the invert; for the shopkeepers: the fairy; for the banker and the waiters: the fag; for the gigolos: "that one"; etc.) was despicable. Divine did not press the point. From a tiny black satin purse she took a few coins which she laid noiselessly on the marble table. The cafe disappeared, and Divine was metamorphosed into one of those monsters that are painted on walls— chimeras or griffins—for a customer, in spite of himself, murmured a magic word as he thought of her:
> "Homoseckshual."
>
> [*Our Lady of the Flowers*]

The making of a monster—a demon fabricated by simple habitual acts of learned disgust—is the theme momentarily in view here.

And the reader who regards his imperviousness to it as a badge
of moral distinction is at best a pious fool.

The case I am urging is, needless to say, open to a hundred
misunderstandings. Someone says: You pretend that you aren't
claiming that the homosexual is more sensitive to certain aspects
of human relations than the heterosexual. But haven't you just
been saying that homosexuals have insights that are denied to
heterosexuals? Answer: Not quite. The notion of denial over-
simplifies the issue, leaves out important parts of the full context. The difference between what the homosexual sees and what
the heterosexual sees can't be explained in narrow physiological
terms. Neither kind of sexuality can be separated from the culture and regarded as a physical or neurological thing-in-itself
determining degrees of insight. Homosexuality, like heterosexuality, is a situation, a complex set of relations between self
and society: the nature of these relations determines to some
extent the special quality of the perceptions that each perceptive
man can have. The relations vary with time and place; surely
there are few significant likenesses between the situations of
homosexuals in the arts in New York City now and the situations
of their counterparts in, say, Paris in 1815 or London in 1600.
There isn't, in short, any abstract entity properly called "homosexual insight" or "heterosexual insight"; there are only differences in the kinds of life situations in which intelligence tests
itself. And these are the differences that shape the artist's
vision.

Again, another query: You seem almost to imply that someone
reading a poem or play dealing directly with homosexual experience could nevertheless achieve—through his encounter with this
work of art—deeper understanding of aspects of strictly heterosexual relationships. Do you really mean this? Answer: Yes. Look
for a minute at the poem by Tennessee Williams called "Life
Story."

After you've been to bed together for the first time,
without the advantage or disadvantage of any prior acquaint-
        ance,
the other party very often says to you,
Tell me about yourself, I want to know all about you,

what's your story? And you think maybe they really and
 truly do
sincerely want to know your life story, and so you light up
a cigarette and begin to tell it to them, the two of you
lying together in completely relaxed positions
like a pair of rag dolls a bored child dropped on a bed.
You tell them your story, or as much of your story
as time or a fair degree of prudence allows, and they say,
 Oh, oh, oh, oh, oh,
each time a little more faintly, until the oh
is just an audible breath, and then of course
there's some interruption. Slow room service comes up
with a bowl of melting ice cubes, or one of you rises to pee
and gaze at himself with mild astonishment in the bathroom mirror.
And then, the first thing you know, before you've had time
to pick up where you left off with your enthralling life
 story,
they're telling you their life story, exactly as they'd intended
 to all along.
and you're saying, Oh, oh, oh, oh, oh,
each time a little more faintly, the vowel at last becoming
no more than an audible sign,
as the elevator, halfway down the corridor and a turn to the
 left,
draws one last, long, deep breath of exhaustion
and stops breathing forever. Then?
Well, one of you falls asleep
and the other one does likewise with a lighted cigarette in
 his mouth
and that's how people burn to death in hotel rooms.

Not a masterwork to be sure, much too easily and sardonically
knowing a poem, too pleased by its own blackishness, and perhaps too needlessly "daring" in its sequence of third-person
masculine pronouns. But "Life Story" is a sharp perception of
relations between promiscuity and the self-regard and self-
absorption of an age gone mad for Identity—and the sense of

this relatedness is as much an illumination for the straight world as for the queer.

And one more hostile question: You ask for pity, understanding, admiration for homosexual artists—thus suggesting that these are badly mistreated people of this day. Are they? Aren't they in reality all the cry just now? If we put them under pressure, they, for their part, do find excellent means of freeing themselves. And, finally: Suppose it is granted that the best "homosexual art" is indeed art—art without modifier; are we obliged to be decent to the worst? When we go off for a night at the theater and encounter something amounting simply to a play in drag, must we smother resentment?

The answer is that of course homosexual artists, like other ones, can be inferior, and that of course these artists have invented ways of easing the pressure we put them under. They do on occasion compose fantasies. They do on occasion express their resentment. They do on occasion revenge themselves through sexual disguises in plays and poems. They mock our solemnities with Happenings and joke pictures and weirdo flicks. They parody the ceaseless commercial agitation of "straight" sexual appetites. They create an art heavily dependent (see Genet) on magic and metamorphosis, an art usually thin in political content, relatively unconcerned with what are called "public issues." And they can give themselves over to glee at the thought that whatever we think of them, few among us match them in brio or brilliance.

But these satisfactions can scarcely outweigh all torments—and, in any event, the fact that an achievement has earned a reward usually is not thought of as ground for discounting the achievement. And there are achievements here—this is the point of moment. A portrait of a man exacerbated by a woman need not be only a thrust at a generalized Enemy; in at least one American play such a portrait faced a mass audience with truths about the new world of sexual equality and universal self-absorption quite inexpressible either in Ibsen or Bernard Shaw. An image of egos dependent upon a fantasy child can be more than a faggish leer: in one American play such an image showed mean uses of the family and, in addition, the vapidities of the doctrine that procreation in itself equals fulfillment. And, by the same token, artists with extensive experience of respectable marriage and child rearing may write with seeming authority about subjects the homosexual can "never know," and yet be worthless—because they are blind to the truth that the acceptable life, the embrace of heterosexuality, can become a cliché, an automatized rather than freely created value.

The canard that negation is not necessarily stupidity and affirmation not necessarily illumination does, in fine, need summoning once more—in discussion of "homosexual art." Nobody is obliged to accept Nietzsche's claim that "every good thing, even a good book which is against life, is a powerful stimulant to life." But the sort of mind that seeks to place all hostility to established institutions as proof of disease does dirt on the revolution of candor that we claim to prize. Failure to hear out the homosexual artist with a seriousness matching his own, over-eagerness to dismiss him as ignorant or perverse, assurance that we know what we are—this behavior at a time when Don Juans by the thousand jam the week-night motels and divorce rates soar and children everywhere are flogged into meaningless ambition —this is worse than senseless. It is a mockery not only of art and of the suffering that art rises out of and seeks to comprehend: it is a mockery of our famous, preening new liberation as well.

STANTON HOFFMAN

THE CITIES OF NIGHT: JOHN RECHY'S
CITY OF NIGHT AND THE AMERICAN
LITERATURE OF HOMOSEXUALITY

I

The recent American literature of homosexuality, allowing for
certain personal themes and eccentricities, can be characterized
by reference to two poles: the image of the "gay world"; and
the image of the personal homosexual relationship. The connection between these two images is essential to this fiction. The
"gay world"—that part of homosexual life which is a world in
itself, which is an organized society with its own language and
manners, and the part of homosexuality which most conforms
to and provides the stereotypes of homosexual life, the "queen,"
the "queer bar," "the world of swish"—begins as a threat to individual homosexuals in love or trying to love, but is transformed
into a metaphor which in turn transforms a theme of homosexual love into a theme of the impossibility of love in America.
The "gay world" comes to represent something like the "under-
world" of which James Baldwin speaks in "The Male Prison,"

where the homosexual "never meets either men or women, where it is impossible to have either a lover or a friend, where the possibility of genuine human involvement has altogether ceased."

In three important novels of the American literature of homo- sexuality—Gore Vidal's *The City and the Pillar,* Baldwin's *Giovanni's Room,* and John Rechy's *City of Night*—there is a changing relationship between these two poles, with the "gay world" as an emerging metaphor. The culmination of this emer- gence occurs, I think, in Rechy's novel, where the "gay world" and all its parts overwhelm not only the possibility of any rela- tionship implying human involvement, but also the existence of the particular characters who would form this relationship if they could, and especially the existence of what is meant to be the center of focus in that novel, the narrator as character, and where it functions as a metaphor for a destructive and despair- ridden American reality. The America of these novels is the possibility of a vast hell always defining a smaller and intense personal hell.

That the "gay world" is seen literally as the threat to the individual homosexual trying to love and to define himself is understandable. The "gay world" not only is the only place where the individual homosexual is made to feel he can exist, but also is the result of his guilt over his choice of a way of life, the result of his acceptance of the stereotypes of a culture and an obsessive consciousness of effeminacy and masculinity. That the "gay world" has been chosen to represent American reality, and that it in relationship to the individual, homosexual and non- homosexual alike, is perhaps also understandable. For the "gay world" is a complete society seen to mirror in its forms and institutions—such as the "queer bar," its excessive effeminacy and its concern for the categories "feminine" and "masculine," its casual attitude towards relationships, its interest in celebrity, its concern for form as separate from content, its superficiality and interest in trivia, its materialism, its obsession with youth, and its indifference to either a politically motivated or socially responsible life—the forms and institutions of the larger Ameri- can society, although in sometimes exaggerated or parodic terms. The feeling is that this world can explain both how hard it is to love in America and how necessary it is to love in America. In this last respect, the function of the "gay world" in these novels is in part rhetorical, serving to establish the necessity of love (not to love is to achieve this terrible world), and in part sociological, serving to establish causes for the failure of love.

The human beings who emerge, then, from these novels are beings who exist in a lonely, love-mad culture, and who seek to define themselves in the destructive context of that culture. This contest manifests itself in their consciousness through a sense of lost innocence, a fear of experience, of love and the dangers of love, and through a sense and fear of emasculation. Their behavior is presented in terms of unbreakable patterns. And as characters they are ultimately unable to love, thus reflecting the culture which surrounds them and creates and destroys them. That on a literal level, although they sometimes resist the "gay world," they are in some way or another attracted to elements of this same world, such as a "gay" party, or a bar, or a succession of bars, signifies their relationship to this culture. A hesitating approach in Vidal's novel becomes a real fascination in *Giovanni's Room*, and a total entry and submergence in *City of Night*.

II

The City and the Pillar, Giovanni's Room, and *City of Night* represent, I think, stages in the discovery and development of the possibilities of using a part of homosexual life as a metaphor for an American reality. What seems in Vidal's novel indirectly handled and tentatively related to the action of that novel is more fully developed in Baldwin and more closely and significantly made a part of the action, more clearly made a part of the literal level of *Giovanni's Room*. In *City of Night* the metaphor seems corrupt and out of control.

In *The City and the Pillar* a homosexual at a "gay" party clearly defines the role of the "gay world" in that novel. "I think," he says, "the American man, normal or not has been utterly castrated by the women he has been made, by his mother, to worship. The homosexual is, generally, the man who has

revolted completely from the rule of the women; yet women
have defeated him since he is a castrate and can never love a
woman as an equal; I think homosexuality in America is less the
result of Teutonic primitiveness than it is the result of negation:
not so much a healthy love for other men than a hatred of
women, a repugnance, a revolt against their authority. That, I
think, is the American homosexual." The homosexual is then at
least implicitly the figure for the heterosexual, or for both the
homosexual and the heterosexual; and the "gay world"—seen as
a place of excessive effeminacy—is the figure for an America
where men are emasculated, and robbed of the possibility of
"healthy love." Characters such as Jim Willard, or his two lovers,
Sullivan and Shaw, see their homosexuality as separate from
this world, as if to say it were a matter of love and not a matter
of categories. But also they are not able to love, because they in
their own pasts were emasculated and robbed of their manhood.
The importance of the "gay world" in their consciousness serves
to amplify their excessive concern with the categories they wish
to avoid in protesting their separation from that same world.
And that they are sometimes literally attracted to a homosexual
bar where easy pick-ups may be made, or are attracted to a party
such as the one which figures prominently at the novel's end,
suggests more strongly the emasculation their desire to establish
their masculinity already implied. This pattern can be best seen
in the history of Shaw the actor. Still dominated by his mother
and the myth of his mother, he progresses through one relationship after another, approaching and finally entering the "gay"
bar, approaching one-night and anonymous pick-ups in the context of this bar.

But for the most part in *The City and the Pillar* the metaphorical potential of the "gay world" is somewhat undiscovered,
and too much contained in statements, and not apparent enough
as important in the novel's plot. For what emerges especially
from the presentation of the characters of Jim Willard and
Sullivan and their inability to love and the destruction of their
love is not so much a fact of emasculation as a fact of their living
their lives in terms of rigid and apparently inescapable patterns
(their repeating of experiences). This might certainly relate to

emasculation, but also to what in the case of Jim Willard is central in his being, and thus central in the novel, a desire to recapture a single experience in his adolescence. This obsession with a single moment and a fall from grace (Sullivan also relives a single moment in adolescence, a betrayal) is certainly part of the American reality Vidal wishes to portray. But this part of this American reality is not contained in the "gay world," which is made to represent another part of that same reality. Thus one comes to feel what I have already implied is only the partial discovery of the metaphorical potential of the literal "gay world."

James Baldwin in his *Giovanni's Room* is able to discover this potential, and to develop it quite fully, making the manifestation of the "gay world" in his novel more important to the plot of the novel, and to the lives of his characters. In fact the novel seems to move between Guillaume's bar, a homosexual bar in Paris, and Giovanni's room, a place of love. Furthermore, Baldwin is able to make this bar important in terms of his two concerns in this novel—to write about the nature of love and to write about the nature of love in America. That the relationship between these two concerns is not always certain or definite is perhaps no matter. What is important is that Guillaume's bar serves to explain the reasons for the failure of love and to make terrifying the effect of its failure. David, the novel's hero, is unable to love. And yet he must love.

For Giovanni it often seems that the sources of David's betrayal and rejection seem to lie in David's being "Monsieur l'Americain," and Giovanni often ridicules what seem to him to be particular American obsessions, like "finding oneself." David appears to accept the clichés of American experience and his reasons for rejecting the first experience of love he ever had—an experience with a boy named Joey during his adolescence—are tersely stated in the phrase, "But Joey is a boy." David also has a preoccupation with proving his manhood, and a preoccupation with a myth of the fall from innocence. He fears experience and more precisely the dangers of love—the confused and intense space of Giovanni's room.

David spends much time in Guillaume's bar which implies his relationship to that bar. And that bar is the opposition to the room in which David lives with Giovanni. This bar is Baldwin's image of the "gay world," a world further seen in two characters, Guillaume, the owner of the bar, and Jacques (an American) who is very much a part of this bar. These men, pursuers of boys are repulsive, callous, sad, cruel, old. And their repulsiveness, callousness, sadness, cruelty, and middle age are the components of this bar and the world it represents.

David fears homosexuality, which, we really see, is his fear of the dangers of love, or selfhood and experience; and he is attracted to a homosexual bar, which identifies him with those things characteristic of that bar, and which identifies those things characteristic of that bar with him. His attraction to that bar and his entry into that bar is the context for his rejection of Giovanni and his room. The world of Guillaume and Jacques is implicit in him. Implicit in David the American is the "gay world," which is the metaphor for him, and for that which defines him, his being American, and thus the metaphor for America, as well as the metaphor for the end of love. His heterosexuality—an American obsession—in being a question of proving something to himself, and as he uses a pathetic girl named Sue to prove this thing, implies the "gay world"; and his heterosexuality is closer to that world than Giovanni's room could ever be. It is interesting in this respect that Hella, David's mistress, is made somewhat ridiculous by Baldwin, and is disliked by the French women of the village where they go, David to escape Giovanni, and to betray him.

Thus Giovanni's room and the possibility of love between David and Giovanni stands surrounded by and threatened by, at times overwhelmed by, the "gay world," by Guillaume and his boys, by America, David's guilt, his American identity, his clichés of experience, his fear of love, and his attraction, literally and metaphorically, to that bar. That love's failure should lie in love's nature may be felt by Baldwin, but he qualifies this by presenting the nature of an American who betrays his lover for reasons part of a definite cultural reality. As the room in which David and Giovanni live is the metaphorical equivalent to love, so the bar to which David (and ultimately Giovanni) goes is the metaphorical equivalent to the failure of love. And as the failure of love is felt to reside in that which is American in David, so the metaphor for the failure of love is a metaphor for an American failure of love, for that which defines an American reality. For Giovanni, David is too often and too much "Monsieur l'Americain."

A part of Guillaume's bar was male prostitution. In John Rechy's *City of Night* the world of the male hustler seems the extension of the "gay world," and is used essentially in the same way—metaphorically—as the latter is used in the earlier novels. And this hustler's world is almost the totality of the novel, for the novel's hero's relationship to this world is not one of attraction, but is one of complete entrance and submergence, so that he is always seen from within this world.

The presence then of the "I," the narrator, of this novel is rather implicit than explicit, and seems throughout to be overwhelmed by a large body of material which can only be held together in two respects—by the metaphorical implications of that material, and by the presentation on the literal level of plot of a fairly precise relationship between the individual homosexual and the hustler's world which he encounters. The particulars of the hustler's world, with its many parts, repetitions and variations, are intended to be related to an image of America in the novel which reveals that the hustler's world and the larger American context are analogous to each other, and that the male prostitute's world—really an extension of the "gay world"—is the metaphor for that larger context. The theme of Rechy's "I," in the guise of autobiography, beginning the novel with a remembrance of childhood, and ending the novel with a dialectic on love and a personal Ash Wednesday, is rarely felt in the body of this work, and then is brought in almost perfunctorily, as for instance in the novel's Los Angeles section. But it seems to be Rechy's intention to make each of the geographical sections of the novel mark a stage in the development of the "I." That is, all the experiences and incidents related (along with all the biographies of the novel's many characters) are organized, I suspect, into stages or aspects of a single awareness of a personal hell and a single theme of the failure of love in the "I," part of a theme of the failure of love in America. As the personal consciousness and the American reality are then meant to meet, the hustling and the "gay world" become important, for that will be the actual place the hero enters and the metaphorical place which explains his entry.

That Rechy means his reader to make an identification between the hustler's world and the American reality, to see the one as representing the other, is perhaps clear from the relatively brief Chicago section of his novel. His image of Chicago is not a hustler's Chicago—rather it is a city seen in terms of various images of poverty, drunkenness, and loneliness. Rather than a Chicago seen in terms of bars and parks where quick pick-ups can be made, it is a place seen in terms of tenements, people staring out of windows, of old derelicts, of burlesque theatres, and talent night in run-down taverns. Most important to this section is a five-dollar talent night in a derelict bar, where wrecks of people live out various final fantasies—and all this is placed in the context of a searchlight atop the Tribune Tower. "And crazily excited I wonder if that spotlight swirling nightly is not trying somehow to embrace it all—to embrace that fusion of savage contradictions within this legend called America." And like Chicago, Rechy's Pershing Square (in his Los Angeles section) is also a "Hybrid of all the tarnished fugitives of America." For his Pershing Square is inhabited by pensioners, revivalists, their listeners, as well as by hustlers, "queens," "scores," and cops. It is a place where all the lonely come, and a place which is meant to bring together all kinds of incongruities into an image of despair.

And that Rechy means to see his male prostitute's world as mirroring in its specifics the specifics of the larger context of America is perhaps clear from an awareness that in the elaborateness and fullness of the presentation of the hustler's world there is some kind of vague scheme operating. For instance, the Los Angeles section has numerous parts and sub-sections—the stories of Miss Destiny, Chuck, Skipper, Lance, and Dean, and the married man the hero meets on the beach at Santa Monica. What one gets are the components of an American reality (and in this they become the components of the "I"). In Miss Destiny there is the despair of doing what one cannot help doing and the madness of the masculinity-femininity obsession; in Chuck there is the desire to "play it cool," to get simply through life, and the dream of innocence one once had, in this case, a dream of horses; in Lance and Dean there is the obsession with youth, narcissism, and the use of love to gain objects; and in the man on the beach there is repression and fear. The other major sections of the novel attempt to do the same thing. San Francisco extends the image of the "gay" hustling world to include boot fetishists, cultists, masochists, and sadists. It ends with a cry, which seems central to the entire presentation of the "gay world," America, and the novel's hero. " 'Oh, yes—but you know why I'm unhappy?' he repeated, 'Because—' he said, enunciating slowly, 'because—I wanna—wanna—lover. Yes! A Lover!' "

III

The failure of *City of Night* seems to me to lie in the unconvincing manner in which Rechy attempts to use a metaphor and to create a metaphorical level in his novel. Here there is the paradoxical situation of a failure to make the metaphor work coupled with an overconsciousness that it should be there working. Thus in *City of Night* there exists a confused and inadequate literal level and an overabundance of reminders (other metaphors—such as the city of night, and the Inferno; the excesses of a style where buildings rise in supplication, where buildings are "knife-pointed," and parks are "lonesome") that the novel is to have a metaphorical level. In this last respect, the novel's Chicago section seems especially crude.

The novel's literal level involves the encounter of the individual male prostitute and the world of male prostitution, meant to represent the encounter between the individual and the American reality in terms of the possibility of or destruction of love. That for the most part the novel's hero seems present implicitly— almost as if the self were obliterated in its encounter—might seem to represent the relationship between the individual and the reality which surrounds him and envelopes him. But in three places, Rechy makes his hero exist explicitly. And what Rechy does in these three places only confuses the relationship between the individual homosexual and the hustling world and seems to contradict what sections like the novel's Chicago appear to assert. The relationship is never clear.

City of Night begins with a chapter of childhood remembrance. But one soon discovers there is no real character created here, despite the emphasis on an "I" which rarely appears elsewhere in the novel. This chapter is a chapter created around five or six incidents and images which will occasionally appear in various forms elsewhere, and which are too patently symbolic, and yet as symbols too fragile for the weight of the experiences and incidents of the novel. The past of "I" seems too heavily manipulated, too artificial. Incidents such as the young boy's sitting on his father's lap, receiving money and affection, are inadequate in two respects. They force upon us the various identifications we are to make; and they obscure the literal relationship of the "I" to the hustling world.

But throughout the novel one does not know what this "I" really is. In the Jeremy section (in bed with a youngish man who has picked him up, and with a Mardi Gras outside which brings together the homosexual world and the "straight" world, and thus works something like Pershing Square and the novel's Chicago section, Rechy's hero engages in a dialectic on love), Rechy's hero discovers that his desire to be loved and his refusal to give love in return is really a form of love. This, in part, is meant to explain his existence in the literal hustler's world. But this has little relationship to what is presented elsewhere of the encounter of the individual and the American reality—or what is presented elsewhere of Rechy's hero. It, in fact, is gratuitous, and does not seem at all meaningful. And in the very last section of his novel, at the end of Mardi Gras, on Ash Wednesday, and in New Orleans (where a church broods over the city), after an orgy of anonymous sex, and where Rechy's "I" encounters more and more voices which reveal the "ice age of the heart"; a resolution for the "I" is imposed upon the novel, as if the conclusion to a carefully created development of character, Rechy's hero undergoes a personal anguish, penitence, and desire for redemption. We are given then an image of the "I" hardly in keeping with any other image we have been given of the "I." The "I" is removed from the context of the other elements of the novel, and the novel's literal level is further confused.

This divorcing of elements can be seen in the way in which Rechy presents his hustler's world, despite the hint of a vague scheme controlling the materials of this world. The manner in which this world is presented seems to overwhelm its own metaphorical function, and thus to be separate from such parts of the novel as the Chicago section, the description of the Mardi Gras in the New Orleans section, and the description of Pershing Square, as well as being separate from the chapters which attempt to create a character out of the novel's narrator. For the multitude of details, the immensity of details concerning the hustler's world and the "gay world" are ultimately a part of a journalistic impulse, their justification no longer lying in an attempt to create a metaphor for an American reality and to present and cope with that reality, seeing it in terms of specific characteristics, describing and judging it. The real relationship between the "I" and the hustler's world is that of a tour guide to his homosexual travelogue.

What exists on this novel's literal level has little to do with what should exist on its literal level, if the terms of that literal level are to represent the terms of the novel's real theme—the individual confronting an American reality, and the individual unable to love in this reality. Yet, in sections like the Chicago section, and in a prose reminiscent of "America has a thousand lights," Rechy urges upon us his real theme and his literal level as metaphor. *City of Night* is filled with a style which, Henry Heifitz has noted in his review in a recent issue of *Studies on the Left*, "drools," and in which Rechy "sprays images everywhere." And it is filled with obvious devices to remind us that a world of hustlers and "scores" is like a world of pensioners in a park, or ruined people in a run down bar, or married people at a Mardi Gras. In James Baldwin's *Giovanni's Room* the realization that a "gay" bar and the "gay world" are to represent the America from which David comes and the America that is within him is subtly suggested. In Vidal it is in one place stated. And in Rechy's novel, it is stated again and again.

IV

The manner of viewing the "gay" and hustler's world which exists in these novels, I have been discussing and which I think characterizes and defines an American literature of homosexuality is not, however, the only possibility. In Jean Genet's fiction, for instance, the "gay world," where men are named in the feminine, is presented paradoxically as the most masculine of worlds, freed from an effeminacy-masculinity obsession, not seen as a threat to love, but as its source, because it is recognized as an underground, where one lives with danger, and death, and it is akin to the world of the thief, or the prostitute, or the murderer, or the police. (In a similar sense, the French director Jean Luc Godard chose for his film *My Life to Live* the image of prostitution as the source of the growth of love.)

The limitations of this American fiction of homosexuality, beyond the limitations of the specific books, result in part from this defining characteristic. A part of homosexuality is opposed to another part of homosexuality. That part is ultimately to be converted into a metaphor for the malaise of a society. It is also a metaphor which translates homosexuality and homosexual love into a too restricted social phenomenon. This concern with the problem of an American reality is to return, as far as homosexuality is concerned, to a kind of conventionality implicit in a type of justification inherent in this subject as an American concern. By this I mean homosexuality is never homosexuality, and it is always something else. It is love, America, the failure of love, loneliness—always part of a case for something.

To view these novels a bit perversely is to see a vengeance operating. For an earlier mode of the fiction of homosexuality in America saw a different threat for the homosexual and was plotted around the conventional conflict between the sensitive homosexual or homosexual relationship and the "straight," or normal, world, which was incapable of understanding that individual, that relationship, or the fact of homosexuality. The heroes of such books as Fritz Peters' *Finistere* or Gerald Tesch's *Never the Same Again* were the victims of this world. But what has happened is that a cliché which saw the homosexual only in terms of the "gay world," and as "fairy," has been turned against the users of that cliché. It has been separated in a sense from the homosexual and made the metaphor for and one with the "straight" world. Thus, the American novelist of the literature of homosexuality, no doubt sincerely involved with facing an American reality and a failure or absence of love in our culture, restricts his material and himself in his desire to be polemical with reference to society as well as with reference to homosexuality. This polemical quality leaves one with a strange sense of paradox, that while in this American literature we really do have a literature of homosexuality, we at the same time do not really have a literature of homosexuality. The latter might be a literature concerned with all kinds of experiences which are part of the homosexual's life, and also, and possibly more important, the interior life of homosexuality, and of the homosexual. It would not be a literature limited to presenting a case against its culture or limited to attempting to make statements about love and its possibilities in a cultural context. And even in the existence of the "gay world" it could find a larger world than it suspects, with variations and a multiplicity of forms, of subtle shadings and distinctions.

Finally, with all this is the most serious limitation of all—a confining of homosexuality in a too restricted and somewhat monotonous range of experience. The possibilities for variation and for the perception of a larger variety of experience, explicit in such different non-American novels as Yukio Mishima's *Confessions of a Mask*, Eric Jourdan's *Les Amitiés Particulières* (especially in its portrayal of Father de Trennes), or even Martyn Goff's *The Youngest Director*, are ignored. For instance, Mishima's novel depicts the internal life of its homosexual hero as a life which is a progression through a number of images, a life filled with slight distortions. In fact, the life depicted in this novel never manifests itself in external sexuality, but rather in a delicate yet erotic fascination with such things as a painting of the martyrdom of Saint Sebastian. These latter novels, besides having definite senses of cultural contexts, are in any case able to be novels which seem to me primarily imaginative rather than polemical. They are novels which portray homosexuality as a world of some vastness and imagination, seeing possibilities the American literature avoids.

Perhaps we are left then with the conclusion that the only real American literature of homosexuality exists in the underground of fantasy and pornography, where novels like those of Jay Little or K. B. Raul couple large sex organs with young and beautiful boys to create young and beautiful boys with large sexual organs.

GEORGE PLIMPTON

PHILIP ROTH'S EXACT INTENT

Of a number of questions addressed earlier this month to Philip Roth, his concern was to answer specifically those that dealt with the literary issues raised by the publication of *Portnoy's Complaint*—namely the extreme use of language and the graphic recounting of Portnoy's thought processes. He does so without the petulance one might expect of an established author going over the familiar ground of obscenity and sexual explicitness; quite to the contrary: he wishes to make it very clear to his audience exactly his intent—regarding both the form and execution of his book.

Would you say something about the genesis of "Portnoy's Complaint"? How long has the idea of the book been in mind?

Some of the ideas that went into the book have been in my mind ever since I began writing. I mean ideas about style and

179

narration, about form and procedure. The book, for instance, proceeds by means of what I began to think of while writing as "blocks of consciousness," chunks of material of varying sizes piled atop one another, held together by association rather than chronology. I attempted something like this in *Letting Go*, and have wanted to try coming at a narrative in this way again—or breaking a narrative down in this way—ever since. Then there's the matter of style; specifically I suppose I mean here language and tone. Ever since *Goodbye, Columbus*, I think I've been attracted by a prose that had the turns and vibrations and intonations, the spontaneity and ease, of spoken language, at the same time that it was solidly grounded on the page, weighted with the irony, precision and ambiguity, the patience and thoughtfulness that we associate with a more traditional literary rhetoric. I'm not the only one who wants to be able to write like this, obviously, nor is it a particularly "new" aspiration on the planet: but that's the kind of literary idea, or ideal, I found myself pursuing in this book.

I was thinking more in terms of the character and his predicament when I asked how long you had in mind "the idea of the book."

I know you were. That's partly why I answered as I did.

But surely you don't intend us to believe that this volatile novel of sexual confession, among other things, had its conception in purely literary motives?

No, I don't. But the conception is really nothing, you know, beside the delivery. My point is that until my "ideas," about sex, about guilt, about childhood, about Jewish men and Gentile women, were absorbed by an over-all fictional strategy and goal, they were not ideas unlike anybody else's. Everybody has "ideas" for novels; the subway is jammed with people hanging from the straps, their heads full of "ideas" for novels they cannot begin to write. I am often one of them.

Given the book's openness, however, about intimate sexual matters, as well as its frank use of obscenity, do you think you would have embarked upon such a book in a climate unlike today's? Or is the book appropriate to these times?

As long ago as 1958, in *The Paris Review*, I published a story called "Epstein" that some people found very disgusting in its intimate sexual revelations; and my conversation, I have been told, has never been as refined as it should be. I think that many people in the arts have been living in "a climate like today's" for some time now; the mass media have just caught up, that's all, and with them, the general public. Obscenity as a usable and valuable vocabulary, and sexuality as a subject, have been available to us since Joyce, and I don't think there's a serious American writer in his thirties who has felt restricted by the times particularly, or suddenly now feels liberated because these have been advertised as "the swinging sixties." In my writing lifetime, the use of obscenity has by and large been governed by one's literary taste and tact and not by the mores of the audience.

What about the audience? Don't you write for an audience? Don't you write to be read?

To write to be read and to write for "an audience" are two different matters. If you mean by "an audience," a particular readership which we can describe in terms of its education, or politics, or religion, or even by its literary tone, the answer is no. When I'm at work I don't really have any group of people in mind whom I want to communicate with; rather, what I want is for the work to communicate itself as fully as it possibly can, in accordance with its own intentions. Precisely so that it can be read, but on its own terms. When one has an audience in mind, it is not any special interest group whose beliefs and demands one either accedes to or challenges, but a kind of ideal reader whose sensibilities have been totally given over to the writer, in exchange for his seriousness.

Let me give an example of what I mean, which will also get us back to the issue of obscenity. My new book, *Portnoy's Complaint*, is full of dirty words and dirty scenes; my last book, *When She Was Good*, had none. Why is that? Because I've suddenly become "a swinger"? Because I'm no longer "uptight"? But then I was apparently "swinging" all the way back in 1957, with "Epstein." And what about all those dirty words in *Letting Go?* No, no. The reason there is no obscenity, or blatant sexuality either, in *When She Was Good* is because it would have been beside the point, gratuitous, ridiculous—above all, destructive of what I was up to. *When She Was Good* takes place among very conventional Westerners; their uprightness and conventionality shaped not only their own language, but my own. In order to create a certain moral susceptibility in the reader (and in myself) to these plain people, I tried in my prose to come up with a slightly heightened version of their own bare language, for instance to employ their clichés and banalities in the narration itself. Not to satirize them, you see, but to communicate as fully as I could their way of seeing and judging; it occurs to me that I was trying to create a certain respect for them in their ordinariness. As for obscenity, I was careful, even when I had Roy Bassart, the young ex-G.I. in the novel, reflecting—had him safely walled-up in his own head—to show that the furthest he could go in violating a taboo was to think "f. this and f. that." Roy's inability to utter more than the initial of that famous four-letter word, even to himself, was the very point I was making.

Chekhov makes a nice distinction, in discussing the purposes of his art, between "the solution of the problem and a correct presentation of the problem"—and adds, "only the latter is obligatory for the artist." I would say that using "f. this and f. that" instead of The Word Itself, was an attempt on my part, small to be sure, to make "a correct presentation of the problem." To be serious with the reader.

Are you suggesting then, that in "Portnoy's Complaint"
"a correct presentation of the problem" requires a frank
revelation of intimate sexual matters, as well as an extensive

use of obscenity? That this is a way of being "serious," as you put it, with the reader?

Yes, I am. Obscenity is not only a kind of language that is used in *Portnoy's Complaint*, it is very nearly the issue itself. The book isn't full of dirty words because "that's the way people talk"; that's one of the lesser reasons for using obscenity in fiction. Very few people actually do talk the way Portnoy "talks" in this book—this is a man speaking out of an overwhelming obsession: he is obscene because he wants to be saved. An odd, maybe even mad, way to go about getting saved; but, nonetheless, the investigation of this passion, and the combat it precipitates with his Conscience, is what's at the center of the book. Portnoy's pains arise out of his refusal to be bound any longer by taboos which, rightly or wrongly, he experiences as diminishing and unmanning. The joke on Portnoy is that for him the breaking of the taboo turns out to be as unmanning in the end as the honoring of it. Some joke.

So—I wasn't just after a simple verisimilitude here, as far as language is concerned; my hope was to raise obscenity to the level of a subject. You may remember that at the conclusion of the novel, the Israeli girl (whose body Portnoy has been wrestling her for on the floor of his Haifa hotel room) says to him, and with loathing, "Tell me, please, why must you use that word all the time?" I gave her this question to ask—and to ask at the end of the novel—altogether deliberately: Why he must is what the book is all about.

Do you think there will be Jews who will be offended by the book?

I think there will even be Gentiles who will be offended by this book.

I was thinking of the charges that were made against you by certain rabbis after the appearance of "Goodbye, Columbus." They said you were "anti-Semitic" and "self-hating," did they not?

In an essay I published in *Commentary*, in December, 1963, called "Writing About Jews," I replied to those charges, and at length. Some critics also said that my work furnished "fuel" for anti-Semitism. I'm sure all these charges will be made again— though the fact is (and I think there's even a clue or two to this in my fiction) that I myself have always been far more pleased by my good fortune in being born a Jew than any of my critics may begin to imagine. It's a complicated, interesting, morally demanding and very singular experience, and I like that. There is no question but that it has enriched my life, but when I say "enriched" I don't know that I mean the same things that my rabbinical critics may mean when they use that word. What I do mean is that I find myself in the historic predicament of being Jewish, with all its implications. Who could ask for more? But as for those charges you mention—yes, they will doubtless be made again. Because of the U.N. condemnation of Israeli "aggression," and anti-Semitic rage flaring up in the black community, many American Jews must surely be feeling more alienated right now than they have in a long time; consequently, I don't think it's a moment when I should expect a book as unrestrained as this one to be indulged or even tolerated, especially in those quarters where I was not exactly hailed as the messiah to begin with. I'm afraid that the temptation to quote single lines out of the entire fictional context will just about be overwhelming on upcoming Saturday mornings. After all, the rabbis have got their indignation to stoke, just as I do. And there are sentences in that book, alas, upon which a man could construct a pretty indignant sermon.

I have heard some people suggest that your book was influenced by the nightclub act of Lenny Bruce. Would you consider Bruce, or other stand-up comics such as Shelly Berman or Mort Sahl, or even "The Second City" comics, an influence upon the comic methods you employ in "Portnoy's Complaint"?

Not really. I would say I was somewhat more strongly influenced in this book by a sit-down comic named Franz Kafka and a very funny bit he does called "The Metamorphosis." Interestingly, the only time Lenny Bruce and I ever met and talked was in his lawyer's office, where it occurred to me that he was just about ripe for the role of Joseph K. He looked gaunt and driven, still determined but also on the wane, and he wasn't particularly interested in being funny—all he could talk about or think about was his "case." I never saw Bruce work, by the way, though I've heard tapes and records, and since his death I've watched a movie of one of his performances and read a collection of his routines. I recognize and admire in him what I used to admire in The Second City Company at its best, that joining of precise social observation with extravagant and dream-like fantasy. It seemed to me also that Bruce was a beautiful mimic of all kinds of American speech, but then I'm a sucker even for somebody like Jules Feiffer, who does a fairly good Walter Brennan.

What about the influence of Kafka that you mention?

Well, of course, I don't mean I modeled my book after any work of his, or aspired to write a Kafka-like novel. At the time I was beginning to play around with the ideas for what turned out to be *Portnoy's Complaint,* I was teaching a good deal of Kafka in a course I gave once a week at the University of Pennsylvania; when I look back now upon the reading I assigned that year I realize that the course might have been called "Studies in Guilt and Persecution"—"Metamorphosis," *The Castle,* "In the Penal Colony," *Crime and Punishment, Notes from Underground,* "Death in Venice," *Anna Karenina.* . . . My own previous two novels, *Letting Go* and *When She Was Good,* were about as gloomy as the gloomiest of these blockbusters, and fascinated, obviously, as I still was by these dark books, I was actually at that time looking for a way to get in touch with another side of my talent. Particularly after three arduous years spent on *When She Was Good,* with its unfiery prose, its puritanical, haunted heroine, its unrelenting concern with banality, I was aching to write something extravagant and funny. It had been a long time between laughs. My students probably thought I was being deliberately blasphemous or simply entertaining

them when I began to describe the movie that could be made of
The Castle, with Groucho Marx as K. and Chico and Harpo as
the two "assistants." But I meant it. I thought of writing a story
about Kafka writing a story. I had read somewhere that he used
to giggle to himself while he worked. Of course! It was all so
funny, this morbid preoccupation with punishment and guilt.
Hideous, but funny. Hadn't I recently sat smirking through a
performance of *Othello?* And not just because it was badly done
either, but because something in that bad performance revealed
how dumb Othello is. Isn't there something ludicrous about
Anna Karenina throwing herself under that train? For what?
What after all had she done? I asked my students; I asked myself.
I thought about Groucho walking into the village over which
the Castle looms, announcing he was the land surveyor; of course
no one would believe him. Of course they would drive him up the
wall. They had to—because of that cigar! Now—the road from
these random and even silly ideas to *Portnoy's Complaint* was
more winding and eventful than I can begin to describe here;
there is certainly a personal element in the book, but not until I
had got hold of guilt, you see, as a comic idea, did I begin to feel
myself lifting free and clear of my last book and my old concerns.

This answers a little more fully, doesn't it, the question you
raised to begin with, about "the genesis," "the idea," for the book?

It does.

Fine then. That gives us a beginning, a middle and an end.
That would please Aristotle.

Would your book?

I don't know. Was he Jewish?

ROBERT BOYERS

ATTITUDES TOWARD SEX
IN AMERICAN "HIGH CULTURE"

Thirty-five years ago, in his remarkable novel *Towards a Better Life*, Kenneth Burke admonished us to remember "that as the corrective of wrong thinking is right thinking, the corrective of all thinking is the body." Set as it is in the context of an elegant and extremely high-toned fiction, Burke's sentence could not have meant for his original readers what it says for us. More perhaps than he knew, Burke anticipated an inclination which has become almost a formalized convention of the serious literature at present being written and discussed in this country. The body has become for our writers that oracle wherein lie value and truth, and balm for the pains of consciousness. Our literature is created under the same star which has guided the fantasies of pornographers since the origins of that frequently black, yet somehow sacred profession. If our more serious writers are more than pious pornographers, there is at the same time no doubt that they represent experience largely "as seen through the eye of a penis."

Steven Marcus' sniggering, even condescending, indictment of pornography on this ground, as on others (in his book *The Other Victorians*), serves as well to describe manifestations rampant in contemporary high culture, though it is possible that we disagree on what is "high" and on what is "culture."

So that there shall be no mistaking what we are observing here, it may be necessary to mention that for our purposes the word "culture" is to be taken in its narrowest sense, signifying the collected presence and impact of all works of the creative imagination in every medium, as well as that body of criticism and philosophy which seeks perpetually to alter or encourage or simply to explain the work with which it deals. It is not easy to locate what we mean by "high" culture, and any definition will inevitably seem exclusivist to those more or less serious practitioners of an art, or their defenders, who cannot comfortably be placed within the magic circle, as it were. Acquiescently to extend the circumference of such a circle is no answer, however, for this would constitute an evasion of standards, and a sacrifice of that taste which it is the duty of every critic vainly to parade before his readers, as the badge both of his conviction and his fallibility. The serious literature to which I shall refer, then, will indicate my impressions of what is significant in contemporary culture. So that our focus will not be overly dispersed, we shall concentrate primarily on a few recent books of fiction which readily illustrate particular attitudes toward sex that I should like to explore.

To return, then, to the body—we having successfully, one would hope, mastered that inclination to be content with mere sex in the head which a no less renowned sexual reactionary than D. H. Lawrence could propose as a viable possibility for mature men and women—to that body which beckons to us, no longer sinful, nor even dirty, nor yet beautiful, but brimming nonetheless with promise, the promise of deliverance from all that is inauthentic or smugly innocent. What courses through our literature is this promise, rarely if ever kept, yet never wholly abandoned, as if all other frontiers had been reached, all other modes of knowing explored and nothing left to do but plug on in search of that ultimate body which we plunder in our dreams, or that apocalyptic orgasm in which all barriers are magically removed, all connections passionately restored.

It is curious that a countertendency may be discerned in the literature of our high culture, though a tendency which similarly exalts the importance of the body. Among the writers of this second group, there is a conviction of the body as a limitation, a limitation which must be pursued. Here involvement with the body represents not a path to vitality nor a means to making contact with what is most real and complex in oneself. Instead, the body is seen as a mode of escape from painful realities, a mode of forgetfulness, in a sense a mode of a blessed nonbeing. In both tendencies, the body is cultivated as a means of redirecting energy and attention—in the one case, away from what is lying, hypocritical, convenient, inauthentic; in the other case, away from what may, in fact, be too utterly authentic, too much a pattern of experience in which one has been rendered the passive spectator of one's own inglorious dissolution.

I

Probably the most talented, serious, and proclaimed champion of apocalyptic sexuality in this country is Norman Mailer, whose recent works of fiction have been received with howls of dismay and disbelief. *An American Dream* is a pop-art caricature of ideas which Mailer has held for some time, but which somehow never seemed quite so banal and ludicrous as they now largely appear. This is not at all to suggest what so many critics have insisted upon: that the novel is simply bad. Mailer can do more with a line of English prose than any man currently writing fiction. His imagination is teeming with invention, and his metaphors have the reach of genius. But Mailer's great gifts cannot conceal the fact that Mailer is a rather corny romantic who has been posing for years as a kind of big bad boy, possessed by visions of brutality and voracious sexuality. Elizabeth Hardwick has observed, "no heat arises from [the novel's] many brutal couplings." Through everything, one sees Mailer himself, sweating to make us feel something he himself cannot feel. His characters have no real lives of their own to which we can

respond. They are plastic creatures, whom Mailer consistently
fails to motivate adequately. Mailer is pathetically anxious for
us to believe in his vision, and his earnest entreaties are frequently embarrassing.

Mailer's protagonist Stephen Richards Rojack is a war-hero, a
former congressman, a one-time friend of Jack Kennedy, and an
intellectual who compares the pain of a shrapnel wound to the
"delicious pain clean as a mistress' sharp teeth going 'Yummy'
in your rump." Clearly, an extraordinary character! In every way,
he appears to be a libertarian type, but in the first pages of the
novel he gives himself away. His wife Deborah has committed
five confessed adulteries during the eight years of their marriage,
and Rojack recognizes each of these adulteries, with its subsequent revelation, as "an accent, a transition, a concrete step in
the descent of our marriage." Rojack values fidelity as an index
of love, in the most conventional way possible. For all his brutal
frankness, Rojack is as puritanical as one might expect him to be,
given his swagger and his panting insecurities. He speaks of the
sexuality implicit in the act of murder, with its thrill of violent
release, and Rojack indeed does murder his wife. But there is
nothing erotic in the actual murder. The woman's neck is broken
and her corpse thrown out of a window, without any voluptuous
emotions attendant upon the scene. In fact, the whole thing is
not even titillating in the way one expects of a good horror story.
Rojack is practically unconscious throughout the proceedings,
moving from step to step almost in a trance. Nowhere is there a
trace of passion or conviction.

Inevitably, he rushes to climb into bed with the German maid,
whom he surprises, "all five fingers fingering like a team of mag-
gots at her open heat. She was off in that bower of the libido
where she was queen." They make violent love, Mailer permitting
us to imagine for ourselves just how Rojack managed to pry those
fingers from that "open heat." Rojack's bout with Ruta may best
be described as a hysterico-comic exercise in advanced gymnastics. Back and forth Rojack springs from orifice to orifice, fore and
aft, "a raid on the Devil and a trip back to the Lord." Ultimately,
full of guilt, Rojack drops his load at the door of the Devil.

It is appropriate that a book espousing apocalyptic sexuality should employ a reasonably flexible religious terminology. What is important for Rojack is making the correct connections during and as a result of his sexual transports. He views the sexual act as a kind of test in which he is gravely judged, not for his virility or endurance, but for his courage and profundity. Rojack's very soul is somehow at stake even in the most casual encounters. He worries over his commitment to life, and sees in each sexual lapse or crudity an acquiescence in that death-wish which laps at our very heels.

Rojack wants to be a Faustian type, but he is too much a victim of conventions that he thinks he has passed beyond. He wants to fly in the face of a civilization for which he would like to have righteous contempt. In identifying his stubborn reluctance to abandon anal intercourse with an attraction to the Devil, Rojack is passing a severe judgment on himself. For him, there is something sinful in following his own instinct or whim, for such indulgence denies man's fundamental responsibility to subject himself to a will more general and embracing than his own. In denying Ruta her orgasm, when she had every right to expect that Rojack would "think of her," he calls down a judgment upon his head. Rojack's happiness, or his right to experiment with human life, whether on a purely physical or emotional level, cannot be positive values in themselves, but must subserve the more basic requirement of preserving respect for the feelings and even for the gratification of others. In the light of Rojack's bowing before such an ethic, it is rather appalling to think how little he suffers over the murder of his wife. One can only conclude that, for Rojack, the taking of a life is a minor matter compared with the integrity of one's performance between the sheets.

There is something faintly touching and not a little bit absurd in attributing to poor coitus a burden of such momentous gravity. Indeed, Mailer's characters display the sort of elaborate, one might almost say literary, awareness of themselves and the symbolic significance of their every genital thrust which renders the possibility of their experiencing true passion or release highly unlikely. At its most intense, Mailer's characters seem to feel sexual activity has the capacity of conferring on both participants an awareness of grace, of that still point in the midst of flux in which the sorrows of the world wash by, are lamented, but cannot really disturb the fundamental equilibrium so tenuously achieved. In *An American Dream,* predictably, Rojack falls in love with a girl named Cherry, no less. Naturally, the full magnitude and depth of their feeling for one another is understood during intercourse. Rojack and Cherry barely know each other as people, but there is something bittersweet in Cherry's juices which tells Rojack he has found the thing he has needed. Cherry is for Rojack a symbol of the eternal victim, a perpetual child in a world that plunders and corrupts and uses those who cling to their innocence. When Cherry spreads her mournful legs, it is consolation she seeks, not an electric charge. For Rojack and Cherry, sex is an activity which ideally takes one out of the body, and enables a communion with the diverse and determinedly unresponsive elements in the universe.

A reader must ask himself whether such projections can be valid. What the question really comes down to, of course, is whether Mailer has been able to make them appear, if not reasonable, then at least conceivable for us. It is difficult to consider Mailer's vision of human sexuality other than as symptomatic of a kind of pathological attempt to impose will on an experience which ought to be less a matter of will than of untrammeled emotion. Undoubtedly, there is something unpleasantly expedient, if not crude, in attempting to draw a distinction between aspects of human behavior which never function wholly independently of one another, and yet I think it is a distinction which must be drawn if we are to see what Mailer and other writers have done.

Rojack experiences a sexual gratification in which his partner is appreciated to the degree that she fits conveniently into a symbolic pattern which confers peculiar value wholly apart from any actual human qualities the partner may have. We are here in the presence of a phenomenon which is more than familiar, which may, in fact, be a predominating characteristic of Western sexuality. Moreover, it involves a mechanism which is intrinsic to an understanding of the Western love ethic that exalts marriage and fidelity as keys to fulfillment. In his deservedly classic work *Love in the Western World,* Denis de Rougemont argues that marital fidelity is based upon a construct which has no particular merit of its own that should recommend it to lovers, aside from the fact that it is a construct which they have decided upon and determined to respect. In de Rougemont's own words:

> I propose to speak only of a troth that is observed by virtue of the absurd—that is to say, simply because it has been pledged—and by virtue of being an absolute which will uphold husband and wife as persons. Fidelity . . . contradicts the general belief in the revelatory value of both spontaneity and manifold experiences. . . . It denies that its own goal is happiness. It offensively asserts first, that its aim is obedience to a truth that is believed in, and secondly, that it is the expression of a wish to be constructive.

In de Rougemont's view, then, the love ethic by which most men in the Western world measured themselves, and according to which they have structured their lives, has not been supportive of untrammeled emotion, but has worked as a counterforce to passion. Marital fidelity is profoundly unnatural for any normal human being. Its capacity to gratify lies precisely in the opportunity it affords the individual of transcending the demands of his own ego, the demand, for example, to be happy on the most instinctual level. In marriage, there is a pride in renouncing that one would desire if permitted to do so, and a commitment to an alternative object which is viewed as more important—the willed making of a relationship, despite contingency, despite desires which would thwart one's project. The marital partners are permitted to grow only through obedience to the particular laws and requirements of the relationship that binds them, in a subjection to which they actively consent.

Rojack's view of human sexuality is closely related to and, one would suppose, derivative from this Western love ethic. To the degree that sexual pleasure is purely or even largely physical, he considers it base and dehumanizing. He can have little affection for Deborah because "making love she left you with no uncertain memory of having passed through a carnal transaction with a caged animal." Rojack rejects carnal transactions in which he is unable to attach symbolic, even transcendent importance to his partner, and to their shared roles as part of some vast, if arbitrary, scheme. In his earliest sexual encounter with Cherry, Rojack is again disappointed: "We paid our devotions in some church no larger than ourselves." It is the prison of the self from which Rojack wishes to escape. He is embarrassed by the insistent demands, frequently perverse or sadistic, of his ego. For Rojack, sex is a means of replenishing the universe, of infusing the universe with the vitality of original creation. In its most authentic form, sex, like love itself, transcends particular personalities, just as there is a devaluation of particular sexual organs. All that matters is the vow to believe in the value of something which is, at its root, arbitrary and absurd. Rojack makes what one might properly term an extreme statement of this view, after discovering the authenticity of his love for Cherry: "Love was love, one could find it with anyone, one could find it anywhere. It was just that you could never keep it. Not unless you were ready to die for it, dear friend."

The nature of Mailer's apocalyptism has never been clearer. For Mailer, it is not sex itself which opens the gates to Paradise, nor is it the monumental orgasm which shatters forever one's allegiance to the shoddy and banal and mundane. He sees nothing liberating per se in the sexual act. In fact, there is almost nothing in Mailer's view of sex that one would expect of a sexual apocalyptist. For Mailer, authentic sexuality is a task, a difficult commitment, for it imposes a terrible burden upon both participants. It is the burden of perpetually mythologizing the nature of an experience which could so easily represent nothing more than sheer forgetfulness and release. The apocalyptic element in Mailer's vision has to do with the liberating potential of any act of the creative imagination, the imagination which perceives the ostensibly crucial obstacles to harmony among men and things as basically superficial and capable of being transcended. As an activity which enlists the total energies and attention of participants, sex has the capacity to tap man's deepest resources of feeling and thought, which, as an artist of considerable distinction, Mailer identifies with the imagination. Far from being an end in itself, sex is merely a kind of catalyst which releases a unique degree of zeal and energy that, in their turn, may alter man's pattern of existence. Moreover, not all or even most sexual activity can make such rewards available. Only sex in which the burden of consciousness is unrelentingly pursued, and in which the full weight of the beloved as an object of, in many ways, impenetrable density is accepted for himself, can promise the fulfillment which Mailer admires. As in de Rougemont's notions of marriage, what is important for Mailer is not happiness, nor the immediate gratification of instincts. Sex, like marriage, is a means to realizing qualities of the human personality which are resolutely unnatural, though qualities which the processes of civilization, and the refinements of culture, have conditioned responsible men to value.

II

How utterly sophisticated all of this is, despite so much that is ludicrous and crude in Mailer's novel, when one compares it to the fiction of several other talented people who work from a related orientation. Jeremy Larner is a younger writer, whose first novel *Drive, He Said* contains passages of singular virtuosity and extraordinary humor. It fails, however, to give one a clear sense of what Larner really feels on various subjects, not least among these the question of human sexuality. The alternation of heavy-handed satire and an almost hysterical sincerity is handled rather sloppily, so that one cannot quite be certain as to what Larner wishes us to take seriously, and what satirically. Parts of the novel even strike one as patent adolescent wish-fulfillment, as mature, beautiful women permit themselves to be regularly ravished by young students who really have little to recommend them but their ardent desires and, one assumes, healthy erections.

There is considerable attention devoted in this novel to the possibilities of apocalyptic orgasm. The actor Tony Valentine, for example, is known as an orgasm man, who has "fuzzy intimations of how the orgasm might be just one feature of a hitherto unthought of psychic politics that could swing our desperate world into a new wild millennium of pleasure." Unfortunately,

Valentine is a preposterous figure, whose intimations are deservedly bestowed with the epithet "fuzzy." Even more unfortunate though is that Larner never really tries to come to grips with Valentine's ideas, to which he is inexorably attracted, despite the satirical detachment he manages to affect. Larner's protagonist Hector Bloom takes his sexual transports very seriously indeed, and his friend Gabriel Reuben is driven insane by his inability to combine sexual passion with what he considers true feeling, something apparently distinct from passion in his view. Both Hector and Gabriel view sex in terms of instant revelation, though neither of them is clear on what it is they expect to have revealed. Proper orgasm is supposed to effect all kinds of remarkable transformations not only on a personal level, but in the social and political spheres as well, with attendant metaphysical vibrations. But it is all so much a matter of rhetorical indulgence that one is unable to discuss the ideas in Larner's novel seriously.

In a way, this should not be surprising, either with regard to *Drive, He Said* in particular, or to American writing in general. We have a great tradition of writers who have been consistently unable to deal seriously with sex, particularly with mature sexual relations between fully developed male and female characters. Leslie Fiedler contributed the demonstration of this thesis in *Love and Death in the American Novel*, a book of criticism which perhaps says as much about the American psyche as any book of recent years. Even in the fiction of the 1960's, there is little or no evidence that Fiedler's thesis could not be easily extended. And it is not that we simply lack serious writers. Saul Bellow is a novelist of undeniable genius, but, as V. S. Pritchett has pointed out, his women characters fail to impress as real people. We cannot approach them as we are able to approach Bellow's male protagonists. There is in Bellow's entire fictional output no convincing illumination of the nature of normal sexual relations in American society. In *Herzog*, Bellow makes a valiant effort, but his sexual encounters are bathed in a kind of pathos, or a kind of dreary if occasionally quaint sentimentality which renders them almost ineffably idyllic. On the other hand, the female character who has most to do with the direction taken by the novel's protagonist is in the tradition of the all-American bitch-goddess, a figure whom we need never consider too closely, for we know she is a mere creature of those dire fantasies which we maintain to justify our inexplicable terrors.

To be sure, then, the rhetorical extravagance we have come to associate with most treatments of sex by American writers is understandable as an evasion of fundamental issues which they are still unable or unwilling to treat. It is almost impossible to conceive of an American novelist treating sex with the sort of spare, relentlessly analytic style of certain French masters who can philosophize about sex without wallowing in sentimentality or yielding to grandiloquence. The one American writer of distinction who, in her criticism at least, has managed to discuss erotics as a fundamental element in the consideration of any art form is Susan Sontag. Perhaps Miss Sontag's distinction in this area is partially attributable to her profound absorption in European, and especially French, literature. In a recent article entitled "On Pornography," Miss Sontag dealt at length with several pornographic novels, including one entitled *Story of O* by a pseudonymous author who is conveniently called Pauline Reage. This French novel has had a wide distribution in this country, and has evoked rather sober discussion in the more prestigious intellectual and literary publications—perhaps a sign of a new receptivity to the notion of pornography as potentially serious literature.

There is no need at this point to go into *Story of O,* nor into its predecessors in the distinguished tradition of European pornography in any great detail; but it might prove instructive to suggest possible affinities with works of American fiction which have been popularly characterized as lewd, if not deliberately pornographic. According to Miss Sontag, what one may justifiably respond to and appreciate in a work like *Story of O* is the integrity with which the author consistently pursues a largely diabolical vision. There is no inclination on the part of the author to justify his vision, or the fantasies of characters, as in some way representative of a widely held position. The author is not primarily interested in impressing us with the universal implications of his work, but is more concerned with impressing upon us the passion and singularity of his absorption in a vision which may be uniquely his. Nor is the author worried lest we should think him deranged. What is important is "the originality, thoroughness, authenticity and power of that 'deranged consciousness' itself, as it is incarnated in a work."

What the more creative and original writers in the European tradition have understood and accepted is that sex is not a normal activity. Miss Sontag, as we have learned to expect of her, makes the statement in the most extreme and yet most cogent way: "Even on the level of simple physical sensation and mood, making love surely resembles having an epileptic fit at least as much, if not more, than it does eating a meal or conversing with someone." In American literature, even when sex is described in patently brutal or perverse terms, one is almost always conscious of an attempt to mediate the extremity of the vision, to assure us that only very rare (if not actually deranged) people are capable of a sexual response of inordinate violence. Even Mailer's Rojack, whom one would not ordinarily expect to make explicit confessions of inhibition, is driven to cry out in the extremity of physical and emotional passion, when his involvement with Cherry has become consuming: "Let me love her some way not altogether deranged and doomed. . . . Let me love her and be sensible as well." Unlike the author of a work like *Story of O*, Mailer is not possessed by a vision, but is instead the extremely self-conscious writer balancing several visions of possibility at once. Whatever Mailer says about the demoniacal energies inherent in sexual activity, his own understanding of these energies is mainly literary, and consequently limited in conviction.

III

There is no lack of conviction in Ken Kesey's *One Flew over the Cuckoo's Nest*, but neither is there an attempt to deal with human sexuality as a complex phenomenon. Kesey's novel is wholly successful as an indictment of modern society, and as an exploration into the kind of subtly repressive mechanisms we help to build into the fabric of our daily lives. Kesey's solution to our common problem is the opening of floodgates, the releasing of energies which have too long lain unused or forgotten. Chief among these are the twin resources of laughter and uninhibited sexuality, the linkage between which Kesey manages to clarify in the course of his novel.

The novel is set in a mental institution which is, in many respects, a microcosm of the society-at-large. It is to Kesey's credit that he never strains to maintain the parallel at any cost— it is a suggested parallel at most, and, where it suits his novelistic purposes, Kesey lets it go completely. His protagonist is one Patrick Randall McMurphy, pronounced psychopathic by virtue of being "overzealous in [his] sexual relations." His purpose in the institution, as in life apparently, is both to have a hell of a good time, and to defy "ball cutters," defined by McMurphy himself as "people who try to make you weak so they can get you to toe the line, to follow their rules, to live like they want you to." McMurphy is a truly monumental character—a gambler, a braggart, a fantastic lover, and a gadfly who insults and goads those who resist his charismatic injunctions. While he is something of a sensualist who dwells regularly on the ecstasies of sexual transport, and even goes so far as to bring his whores into the hospital to restore the vitality of his moribund fellow-psychopaths, McMurphy feels himself and his comrades the victims of women, not their lords and masters as his rhetoric would have it. His techniques of resistance and defiance are mostly pathetic, as they can achieve what are at best pyrrhic victories. One is never tempted to question the validity, the nobility, or even the necessity of McMurphy's defiance, but no mature reader will be convinced that his techniques can realistically accomplish what Kesey claims for them at the novel's end—the reclamation of numerous human beings who had grown passive and torpid before McMurphy's arrival.

At one point, McMurphy characterizes the inmates of the hospital as "victims of a matriarchy." In Kesey's view, modern society is a reflection of womanish values—archetypically responsible, cautious, repressive, deceitful, and solemn. One must look to the spirit of the whore if one would know what is best in women, and what can best bring out what is vital in men. There is no doubt that Kesey labors under a most reactionary myth, involving the mystique of male sexuality, which sees men as intrinsically better than women in terms of the dynamism and strength they can impart to the universe. Unable rationally to account for the disparity between such a projection and the puny reality of our male lives, Kesey waxes fatalistic, though never submissive, and sees "ball cutters" everywhere. It is a kind of paranoid, conspiratorial view of things, not without its measure of accuracy, but it somehow evades the crucial issues which Kesey and others have raised.

At the heart of Kesey's notion of what is possible for modern liberated man is a phenomenon which one may call porno-politics. It is a phenomenon which resides primarily in the imagi-nation of a few thousand people, most of them young and bright, and which is occasionally manifested in the hysterical behavior of certain radical partisans of unpopular causes, a behavior which, by the way, many would call resolutely antipolitical, for all its pretensions to the contrary. Advocates of porno-politics are usually utopian socialists who lack the vision and patience to realize their goals politically: that is, they are youthful dream-ers who are frustrated by the customary routines through which men achieve power or influence in order to alter the political relations which obtain in their society. Frequently, the retreat into varieties of porno-politics results from people relying too heavily on the flexibility of a given political system, and on the sheer magnetism of their own sincerity, which they and their asso-ciates had always considered irresistible. When the erstwhile utopian realizes how restrictive and closed the political structure of his society is, despite its aggressive disclaimers, and when he is made aware of the basic indifference to his ideals and to his attrac-tiveness among the masses of people, he is suffused by a kind of anger and dread. As the society affords him virtually no outlet for these feelings, which rarely become specific enough to fix legitimate targets anyway, the befuddled utopian permits his vision of the possible to undergo a remarkable transformation. Unable to affect masses of men or to move political and social institutions, he transfers the burden of realizing a perfectly har-monious society to sex.

In Kesey's novel, we have what seemingly amounts to a *re-ductio ad absurdum* of familiar Freudian propositions. It is repressed sexuality which ostensibly lies behind every psychosis, and which is responsible for the acquiescence of all men in the confining conventions of Western society. It is in the spirit of random and thoroughly abandoned sexuality that Kesey's Mc-Murphy would remake men, and subsequently the world. What is a little frightening in a novel like this, though, is that such a projection does not at all operate on a metaphorical level. Sex is not here a mere metaphor for passion, nor for any positive engagement with one's fellow human beings. There is a literalism in Kesey's suggestions of sexual apocalypse, with its unavoidable ramifications into a political and social context, which cannot be lightly taken. Other talented people are caught up in such projections, and are delivering gospels of sexual salvation with a hysterical dogmatism that is, for many of us, laughable and pathetic. This is so particularly for those who have observed the failure of libertarian sexual experimentation and random coupling to affect substantially the pettiness and self-absorption even of those who are most easily committed to libertarian modes and who have no need perpetually to justify such commitments ideologically. How futile it is for intelligent people seriously to expect their sexual programs and practices to have a liberating effect on masses of men, when what these people want is to be left alone to enjoy what they have. What porno-politics essentially amounts to is a form of entertainment for a middle-class audience, which alternatively writhes and applauds before the late-night news, and welcomes the opportunity to indulge and express postures it considers intrinsic to its worth as modern men: tolerance and righteous indignation.

Kesey's brilliance is evidenced by his ability to be seduced by porno-political utopianism, and yet not to yield to it entirely. What saves him are his sense of the ridiculous and his understanding of men as fundamentally dishonest and irresolute. Kesey wants to believe that the source of all terror and passivity is somehow sexual, that the liberation of sexual energies in the form of primal fantasies will enable men to conceive of themselves as more passionate and autonomous individuals. But his intelligence forces him, as it were, against his will, to tell a truth which is more complex and disheartening. He recounts a group therapy session which had taken place in the institution some years before McMurphy's arrival. Unlike the usual dispirited proceedings, this particular session stood out for the violent release of confessions that it evoked from the habitually desultory and tightlipped inmates. Once the momentum is established, the inmates begin shouting confessions: "I lied about trying. I did take my sister!" / "So did I! So did I!" / "And me!" "And me!"

At first, all of this seems satisfying, at least from a conventionally clinical point of view: repressed memories are rising to the surface, where they can be handled therapeutically. But, almost immediately, we are shown that not only did such events never occur in the lives of these men; they do not even represent their fantasy lives. Such "confessions" have nothing at all to do with the wish-fulfillment that is a strong component of compulsive fantasies. What the inmates have done is simply to exploit certain readily available clichés issuing from standard interpretations of modern man as the perennial victim of sexual repression. The inmates are victims of something much more embracing and diversified than simple sexual guilt or repression, though the sexual element may be particularly significant in the case of two or three inmates among many. What is sickening is their desire to please the therapists by revealing what they are supposed to, rather than what is really inside them. Finally, they are shamed by the resounding announcement of hopeless old Pete: "I'm tired," he shouts—a confession so simple and true that it puts an abrupt end to the rampant dishonesty of the others. Kesey loves McMurphy, and identifies with his aspirations—he wants men to be free, to laugh the authorities down, to refuse to be manipulated. He wants, moreover, to go along with McMurphy's sexual orientation, and to be as optimistic as McMurphy about the effects of sexual liberation on the reigning political and social atmosphere. But McMurphy is not a mask for Kesey, nor is any single character in the novel. In fact, as much as Kesey admires McMurphy's stratagems for outwitting the matriarch par excellence who goes under the title Big Nurse, we are never quite certain whether to laugh at McMurphy as well as with him. Big Nurse, as the personification of "the system" at its most callow, repressive, yet ostensibly enlightened, represents a tendency toward antiseptic desexualization which is abhorrent. We want McMurphy to bewilder her, to kill her with his charming nonchalance and boyish exuberance, and to parade his own aggressive sexuality before her. We want her to be teased and tempted so that she will be provoked to try to castrate McMurphy, if not actually, then symbolically, as she has successfully whipped the other inmates. We want to see McMurphy put to the test of the vitality and resilience he proudly proclaims, as if he could redeem us from any misgivings we might have about our own potency.

And yet, throughout this novel, we know that nothing McMurphy does, or encourages his comrades to do, will make any substantive difference to the system that we all despise. McMurphy, through an ideological predisposition, which in his case is more instinctive than learned, attributes to sex what even he knows it cannot accomplish. His is a heroic endeavor in every way, but McMurphy is at bottom a little lost boy who gets into the big muddy way up over his head. The picture of him, in bed with his whore at last, almost at the end of the novel, is utterly revealing: ". . . more like two tired little kids than a grown man and a grown woman in bed together to make love." McMurphy can behave as brashly as he likes, and speak with utter abandon of sex, but for him it has still an element of mystery, of vows exchanged, even if only for a brief duration. His libertarian apocalypticism is sincere, but in McMurphy's own character we can see that a libertarian sexual orientation ultimately has little to do with making men free as political and social beings. McMurphy needs no sexual swagger to be free, though, in his case, it is a believable accoutrement of his personality. What is indispensable in McMurphy's character is his propensity to laugh, in his lucid moments to see himself as something of a spectacle, not wholly detached nor different from the other inmates who have failed to retain their resilience. When he loses his laugh, he grows desperate, and places upon sex that burden of hope for transcendence which the reality of sexual experience must frustrate. When, at the very conclusion of the book, McMurphy rips open Big Nurse's hospital uniform, revealing, for all to see, her prodigious breasts, we see where McMurphy's porno-political vision has led him. Unable to affect a world that victimizes him, a civilization which, in the words of the British psychoanalyst R. D. Laing ". . . represses not only 'the instincts,' not only sexuality, but any form of transcendence," McMurphy is driven to rape the reality incarnated in Big Nurse. In his fear and frustration, he does not see what, of all things, should be most obvious to him: that he cannot make another human being aware of his humanity by destroying or suppressing those elements of his own humanity that have made McMurphy a beautiful person. By his action, he demonstrates the original futility of his project, the necessary brutalization of his sexual ethic, and the dehumanization implicit in the act of invoking an Eros which is imperfectly understood and crudely employed.

IV

Among writers who treat sex as a means of relief from painful reality, though not as a means of transforming that reality, several contrasting approaches are discernible. These approaches are largely a function of the individual writer's temperament, rather than a reflection of any ideological point of view. All of these writers are concerned with that crisis of identity which Western writers have been engaging for forty years or more; all of them are cynical of the solemnity with which educated people customarily bow before conventions of thought and concern that they ought to have outgrown; and all of them view sexuality as a necessary evasion of issues which civilization has unfortunately encouraged us to confront.

John Barth is one of the most cynical, serious, and accomplished writers of this inclination. While his recent, extremely ambitious fiction has been given a great deal of attention, his earlier work is equally interesting, and especially rewarding for our present purposes. In particular, his 1958 novel *End of the Road* is a superb exploration of attitudes that we cannot overlook. Barth's protagonist is Jacob Horner, who fears he has no identity as a man, that he is, in fact, nothing more substantial than his moods, which are many and various. He adopts postures or roles, and holds on to them as long as they satisfy his requirements in given situations. A quack doctor who helps him in time of need strengthens his predilections toward what is an extreme relativism. All that is important for both the doctor and Horner is that man retain his ability to make choices, to act. There is only one wrong choice—the choice which leads to immobilization, an unresolved tension.

Such an orientation, of course, will lead a man to value noninvolvement, unless his character becomes so strong over an extended period of time that he learns to identify himself with a particular course of action which implicates every aspect of his being. Where Horner is concerned, the doctor advises against both marriage and love affairs, which are too complicated and might involve a man in painful tensions. Masturbation is recommended as a wise choice.

In the course of the novel, Horner pursues and goes to bed with two women, with whom we become familiar. In his sexual relations, the true ugliness of Horner's inclinations and aversions becomes gruesomely manifest. He is an inverterate son of a bitch, though he says some brilliantly witty things, and does manage even to suffer a bit. In his relations with poor Peg, who, in early middle-age, is desperate for a man, Horner's behavior is disgusting. He has always been uncomfortable with "women who took their sexual transports too seriously." Moreover, he sincerely exalts sexual relations in which he is not thought of as a human being, so that it does not become incumbent upon him to consider his partner as human.

Barth is not Jacob Horner, but Barth's attitudes toward sex and toward human involvement in general emerge rather clearly in *End of the Road.* These attitudes emerge in the form of a tension established between Horner and his opposite number, a fellow named Joe Morgan. Joe takes himself very seriously. He is a brilliant young professor, hard at work on a book. His relations with his wife Rennie are terribly self-conscious and absorbing. They are, in a sense, each other's project, and their pride in what they accomplish in their relationship spills out into their communications with others, and, in fact, dominates their secondary relationships.

At first, Horner can do no more than sneer at Morgan, but his

aversion quickly turns to admiration, then to jealousy, and finally
into a compelling desire to expose Morgan's integrity and discipline as essentially dishonest. Convinced that no one can be
genuinely decent, or devoted to another human being as he is
devoted to the gratification of his own needs, Horner has an
affair with Joe's guilt-ridden wife, and grows curious as to how
the inordinately generous and open-minded Joe Morgan will
respond to the revelation of his cuckoldry. But before they have
a chance to apprise him, Joe is caught literally with his pants
down, or at least with his zipper opened. What Barth gives us
is an unforgettable tableau which can stand as an image, complete unto itself, of what Barth thinks of high-mindedness, total
commitments, and pretensions of having transcended the demands of the diabolical self. Joe Morgan is observed by wife
and friend executing military commands, mugging ridiculous
faces at himself in the mirror, then, finally, simultaneously picking his nose while masturbating. It is one of the funniest scenes
in all of literature, heightened as it is by Barth's sheer stylistic
virtuosity, but it is not at all poignant. We are not shattered by
this revelation of Joe, for we knew all along somehow that Horner, and even Barth, would have it this way. Morgan was too
good to be true, too much an obstacle in the ready flow of cynicism that pours like syrup over Barth's fictions, and sticks to
everything it touches.

Barth's attitude toward sex, then, as one might suppose, is
very much bound up with his total view of things. A line of
Horner's says it rather succinctly: "Maybe the guy who fools
himself least is the one who admits that we're all just kidding."
One requires a great deal of irony and a great deal of courage to
feel this way about oneself, as about men in general, it seems to
me. But perhaps when one grows sick enough of man's pervasive
hypocrisy, and tired enough of one's own inability to commit
one's self to anything beyond one's own pleasures, perhaps then
the defensive irony and detachment come easily, and the cynicism grows into a mask not readily removed. What we are left
with is the image of man as masturbator, mechanically satisfying
his needs, unwilling to romanticize those needs in terms of suggesting that they might be more profound or consuming than, in

fact, they are. And Barth, to be sure, sees nothing demonic or even obscene in the various expressions of sexuality. Nothing in his universe is sacred or taboo: it is a landscape with which we have suddenly become all too familiar.

V

In the hands of lesser writers than Barth, such materials and attitudes are worked on more casually, and more superficially. Barth's fiction has an energy and a relentless logic which is truly remarkable, given the bizarre creations that are the very texture of his work. In a writer like James Purdy, one cannot but feel that we are dealing with a man who has attitudes at second hand, and who writes novels with the express purpose of having a platform from which he can crudely denounce the popular deities. The attitudes are not all that different from Barth's, but their expression is puerile and lax by comparison with Barth's presentation. *Cabot Wright Begins,* to select but one example, is a novel about a rapist, and incidentally about everything in the modern world—everything, that is, that Purdy can think of, which are usually the most apparent things. I mention him at all only because his reputation is very high among some responsible critics, and because he has managed to treat the problems of human sexuality with some maturity, if not with precision.

The crux of Purdy's "message" is that, for all the abandoned talk of sex, for all that liberalism has accomplished, "there isn't a stiff pecker or a warm box in the house." Of course, Purdy may be right, but I doubt it—I doubt even the sense of his character's assertion. What is more important, though, is that it really does not matter very much, for, in Purdy's view, sex is an experience which suggests an extreme impoverishment of other faculties that might instill vigor into the personality. Characters in Purdy frequently resort to sex almost as a last resort, and the novel challenges the very notion of sex as closely related to passion. Cabot Wright is a prodigious rapist not because he is in thrall to his passion, but because he has tried everything else and has been bored to distraction. Finally, of course, the sex fails adequately to satisfy, and Purdy can attribute to it nothing more than minimal significance, which is perhaps as much as it deserves. As one of Purdy's main characters engages in a casual homosexual affair, he is politely set straight by his partner: "A little pressure here, a little pressure there lifts the weight of the world from the heart, but no need to celebrate it by way of explanation." It is difficult to argue with so temperate a statement.

It is not at all surprising that the point of view with which we have here been dealing tends to consider both masturbation and homosexuality as not in any way deviant, nor especially different in the satisfaction they can afford, from "normal" heterosexuality. Some of our better writers, of course, retain a more traditionalist position, though this, too, has its complexities. In a recent story entitled "Whacking Off," Philip Roth recounts an adolescence and a young adulthood tainted by the spectral presence of masturbation and the fear of exposure. For Roth's character, who speaks in the first person, "My wang was all I really had that I could call my own!" Beset by a world which has destroyed his confidence in his ability to make choices for himself, which has instilled in him a fear of life itself, he escapes into the privacy and sanctity of his room to work variations on his monomaniacal obsession. What is unfortunate in the story is Roth's need to explain the bleak and cowardly world view with which he has been impressed as a peculiarly Jewish phenomenon. How frayed and worn the "Jewish mother" gambit has become, with its images of the perennial nag, neurotically concerned to prevent diseases and see to it that the members of her family eat appropriately. One wonders whether Jewish writers like Roth do not believe that Irish mothers frequently express such concerns, and that Irish sons sometimes resort to masturbation as a means of evading a depressing environment.

In that case, what is important for us is that Roth's character implicitly harbors a view of "normal" sexuality as potentially satisfying to the degree that it represents adjustment to the world, engagement with its realities, and the ability to overcome a heritage of petty fears. Masturbation he views as a necessary mode of disengagement in which the masturbator ceases to recognize the unreality of the fantasy that grips him. Roth's character is compelled to reside in the realm of the imagination, but he is fundamentally dissatisfied because he cannot stave off the encroaching reality that surrounds him. The dream of omnipotence is shattered by his social instincts, which advise him to join the world and to consider his evasion immoral and cowardly.

VI

It is perhaps difficult to conceive that there is anything new left to say on the subject of sex. To be sure, our avant-garde writers, including artists as well as social scientists, have more or less exhausted considerations of the possible varieties of sexual experience. What is remarkable, though, is the degree to which emphases have been shifted and primary allegiances re-examined. This is largely the work of a few influential neo-Freudians, including Herbert Marcuse and Norman O. Brown, though it would be misleading to suggest that such men work from a common orientation or proceed in similar directions. What Brown is especially responsible for is a criticism of sexuality as essentially a matter of genital organization. In *Life Against Death* and the more recent *Love's Body*, Brown has articulated an elaborate, if largely fragmented and incoherent, theory of the body as the proper medium for mystical experience, and has tried to move beyond our notions of the genital orgasm either as central or indispensable to human sexuality. To reach his conclusions, Brown has exploited and extended familiar Freudian concepts, particularly Freud's observations of polymorphous perversity identified in the behavior of infants.

Brown has been widely read and discussed in recent years, and his work has been praised in all quarters of our high culture. Even where Brown's proposals have been questioned or vilified, he has been taken seriously, and ideas which we associate with him and with other influential people have become part of our circulating intellectual currency. This influence is reflected in the way that many of these ideas arise in the creative work of some of our best young writers, who cannot ignore their fascination even though they may be repelled or dubious. One example is the novel *Beautiful Losers* by a Canadian writer named

Leonard Cohen. The book has been so popular in the literary community as well as among generally literate readers in the United States, and it is so pervaded by a tone which is undeniably American, that we need not apologize for treating it as a product of American culture. Cohen speaks as one of us, alternately bemused, bewildered, and appalled by the dimensions of experience which our writers and artists have tempted us to explore.

Cohen's is not a balanced vision. The tone of *Beautiful Losers* is shrill and hysterical, reflecting Cohen's conviction that we have become inured to so much that we have almost lost the capacity to feel the numbness that creeps over us. Cohen's pessimism is so embracing as to leave almost no loophole for the soul. He is driven, as it were, to extreme positions, but these do not seem tenable once they are considered in real terms, rather than as abstractions. Cohen's characters exalt playfulness, but they are determinedly unplayful. They are attracted to Brown's theories of the adult body as fundamentally erotogenic, but in describing their participation in various erotic rites, Cohen lapses into a parody of Brown that ultimately suggests Cohen's scepticism. Cohen presents a series of hysterical passages in which characters make love by stuffing their index fingers in one another's ears, to the amazement and dismay of a conventionally jealous husband: "You did it to each other? With your bare fingers? You touched ears and fingers?" / "You begin to learn." / "Shut up. What did her ears feel like?" / "Tight." / "Tight!" / And so on. Notions of orgasm are to be expanded to include a wide range of sensation: "All flesh can come! Don't you see what we have lost? Why have we abdicated so much pleasure to that which lives in our underwear? Orgasms in the shoulder! Knees going off like fire crackers!"

In fact, the range of human sensation may be extended by a conscious and habitual application of such principles to one's experience, but what this cannot do is counteract other tendencies in experience which tend to desexualize human beings and to detach them from the roots of human behavior. The industrialization of Cohen's native Canada involves a destruction of the primitive cultures that Cohen associates with the American

Indians. "They are pouring roads over the trails," his character cries, and later, "I've poisoned the air, I've lost my erection." For Cohen, one cannot separate existence into discrete categories of things which do not interact. What Cohen wants, but knows he cannot have, is a reassertion of the possibilities of love among men, but he feels that such possibilities must remain remote so long as we commit ourselves to them only tangentially. What Cohen ideally envisions is a humanity prostrate before all varieties of experience, yet still somehow able to discriminate, to make choices based on a perception of what is most authentic.

Sexuality will involve a thrust toward an impossible, because complete, engagement with the love object, which may be a real person or an imaginary projection of various ideal qualities. What matters for Cohen is the individual's willingness to accept immolation as a necessary concomitant of genuine engagement. All distinctions between subject and object must cease to be operative, as one becomes what he envisions through the act of willing and naming the terms of his immolation. Sexual activity is an enabling agent in this process, for as it gratifies, it also makes one receptive to the possibility of harmony among things. For Cohen, however, one does not achieve this purely on an imaginative level, through a passive receptivity potentiated by the release of sexual energies. Unlike Mailer's, Cohen's is an activist ethic, in which sexuality must ideally bring one back to the world, and back to the body, but a body which is loved to the degree that it incorporates qualities of all bodies, and is a pathway to the love of all men. Cohen's activist ethic has a communal basis, and sexual activity, as part of this ethic, must implicate masses of men in a process which renews them as individuals and unites them as a collectivity.

In *Beautiful Losers*, Cohen's protagonist is thrown against a girl in the midst of a swarming political rally. Without a word passing between them, they grope for and find each other's sexual organs, as the frenzy of the crowd begins to mount. As Cohen puts it, "We began our rhythmical movements which corresponded to the very breathing of the mob, which was our family and the incubator of our desire." For Cohen, sex is gratifying insofar as it directly involves men in the task of rebuilding their society. It is a beautiful thought, and if it ignores what we have come to take for granted in human behavior, perhaps it is time that we began to envision possibility in the image of our desire.

In any case, what our best writers and artists have demonstrated is that the engagement of the creative imagination with the materials of sexual experience can be a fruitful process, both for art and for our appreciation of the range of human resources. Though it has been impossible here to do more than suggest certain broad tendencies, it is clear at least that, for our most gifted people, human sexuality cannot be considered apart from other essential elements of the human personality. Where the vision of sexual encounter has been reducible to the grating of organs, at least we have been made aware of our impoverishment as men. We can say with gratitude that we have not been taken lightly.

THE FUTURE

Autumn is also seedtime. . . . A period which can reasonably be seen as decadence in relation to what is ending can be seen quite differently in relation to what is beginning.
Eric Bentley. "The Naked American."

The ideas of one generation become the instincts of the next.
D. H. Lawrence. "Making Love to Music."

Out of chaos comes a dancing star.
Friedrich Nietzsche.

STROTHER PURDY

ON THE PSYCHOLOGY
OF EROTIC LITERATURE

There are few mental states without representation in imaginative literature, and few works of imaginative literature that do not in some way embody their author's sexual psychology: Dodgson's Alice as well as Pope's Eloïsa; Nabokov's Lolita as well as Virgil's Dido; Homer's Achilles as well as Valmiki's Rama. But the study of sexual psychology, not to mention sexual physiology, has been and still is being handicapped by artificial limitations—most simply described as "the question whether such things ought to be studied at all." Most of us, of course, carry on a lifetime study, directed toward the satisfaction of our instincts, our curiosity, and our need to adjust our image of ourselves to what we can learn about our fellows. The artificial limitations tend to keep us from comparing results of our studies with others. Books give information without asking for any in return, and imaginative books are the easiest, because the most interesting, to read; the result is that erotic fiction, often of a proscribed nature, is a main source of sexual data of all kinds.

At the same time the writers of erotic literature may be no more advanced in sexual knowledge than many of their readers, for they face the same limitations. Like the novelist looking in a door at some French Protestants eating their dinner, and deciding she had grasped the essence of French Protestant life, they depend on imagination as well as experience. Because there has been almost no scientific study of sex, and wide literary censorship, until recently; because there still is social resistance to pooling of experiential data, tradition has been strong in erotic literature, generally outweighing individual talent. The writer of an erotic novel has fewer sources of trustworthy information against which to compare his own experience, so unless he has great, or psychopathic, confidence in that experience he is more apt than a writer in another genre to follow the safe and easy path of originating little and borrowing a lot from what has been done before.

Another result of the situation is that there has been very little qualitative or scholarly criticism of erotic literature. Social taboo has kept it down, of course—how many learned journals would, or even will, print such studies?—but so has the already mentioned dearth of specialist background studies. We have enough of that critical information now, little enough, but so much more than we had a few years ago that we might get started on the outlines of critical theory in this area.

The easiest critical task is that of exposing errors, and they abound in erotic literature—from misapprehension of the nature of the female orgasm and the role of drugs, to mistaking the effects of masturbation, continence, incest, fellatio, or multiple orgasm. I should like to comment on just one, the phallic fallacy, or the idea of "the bigger the better" as applied to the male sex organ. This is a physiological fallacy, but not so simple psychologically. There it is more a locus of related phantasies, and in literary terms we might speak of "phallic phantasies." How deeply they are ingrained in human culture I need hardly mention: folklore abounds with such marvels as that Dillinger's penis was 22 inches long and is now kept in the Smithsonian (shades of Jonathan Wild!). The man with the large penis is almost everywhere and at every time considered more of a man

by other men, and considers himself superior. This latter feeling
is an effect of the former, for a man would hardly have any
reason to admire the size of his penis if it were not for signs of
admiration he picked up from other men—or from women, or
from books. More about those sources in a moment.

Yet the average man has little chance to do comparative
studies; as a heterosexual he may go throughout life without
seeing any penis in an erect state but his own. And once he
accepts the basic premise about size equalling merit he is caught
up in a circle of anxiety ("Do I match up?") that seals his lips
in the presence of other men. Stag films provide a neat illustration: when men watch them together they rarely remark on the
size of the penises shown on the screen, which generally look
much larger than they are, for each man fears he will expose
himself as insufficiently equipped if he were to do so. On the
other hand, when such films are viewed by married couples, some
husband will probably profess astonishment at the size of the
man in the film, for he doesn't want his wife to think him sub-
normal. Once he speaks, the other men will relievedly join in his
exclamations, for they have, again, been silently wondering. But
let me turn to a literary example, from the Arabic classic, *The
Perfumed Garden of Sheik Nefzawi:*

> It is also said that the poet Farazdak met one day a woman
> on whom he cast a glance burning with love, and who for
> that reason thus addressed him: "What makes you look at
> me in this fashion? Had I a thousand vulvas, there would
> be nothing to hope for you!" "And why?" said the poet.
> "Because your appearance is not prepossessing," she said,
> "and what you keep hidden will be no better." He replied,
> "If you would put me to proof, you would find that my
> interior qualities are of a nature to make you forget my outer
> appearance." He then uncovered himself, and let her see a
> member the size of the arm of a young girl. At that sight
> she felt herself burning hot with amorous desire. . . . Then
> she uncovered herself. . . .

and so forth; they fall into each other's arms.

This little story is utterly charming, timeless (it is exactly

parallel to the Mickey Rooney–Ava Gardner joke), and almost
utterly fallacious, showing the telltale signs of a masturbatory
daydream (male) rather than of reality. "What a joy to have a
penis the size of a young girl's arm," muses the author. "All
women would be instantly available to me—no delays, no arduous
courtship, but instantly." The ultimate male wish. This is the
justification of the dream of size: the larger the member, the
more pleasure it gives the woman. If it is of unutterable size it
gives unutterable pleasure; it will conquer any woman at any
time—a virtuous matron in the middle of the street at high noon,
for instance. This is the support from women I mentioned earlier,
and it is quite without physiological basis. And almost entirely
without psychological verity, for women simply don't think that
way, unless they have been affected by male thinking to an
abnormal degree. There is no need for them to think that way,
penis size, within normal limits, having very little to do with
pleasure in sexual intercourse.

Why did Nefzawi write a story that his experience, or enquiry,
could tell him had no basis in the actual relations of men and
women? Partly because of the daydream element I mentioned,
partly because he is as much the victim of the phallic fallacy as
men 1000 years before him and men 1000 years after, and partly
because he is working within a literary tradition. His is not the
only such Arabic work, and he makes reference to the earlier
Sanskrit treatises on his subject. Without suggesting that he knew
specifically the *Kamasutra,* the oldest and most renowned of
them, we may take its approach as typical—and as influential.
The *Kamasutra* states that women may be classified by the depth
of their vaginas, and men by the length of their phalluses: an
"Elephant" woman has the largest vagina, a "Rabbit" man has
the smallest phallus; if they have sexual intercourse the pleasure
will be slight. "Hence a man with a small penis fails to endear
himself to a woman." The opposite is not stated, that the largest
man will give the smallest woman the greatest pleasure, but it is
noted that the small- and medium-sized women are given more
pleasure by the man of the size above theirs than by the man of
their own size. The pattern is thus set; there is no other erotic
manual to deny it until Masters and Johnson's *Human Sexual*

Response, although experience denied it all along. Nefzawi used his book to strengthen a concept already established in books.

Another example: the *Jou-p'u-t'uan* of Li Yü, a Chinese work published in 1634 and outstanding for its humor, imagination, and, in general, for its sexual psychology. There are not many other erotic novel–erotic manual combinations in world literature—*Lady Chatterly's Lover, The Perfumed Garden,* the *Sermonis Aloisiae Sigaea,* Aretino's *Raggionamenti* all in some way combine narrative with instruction, but the *Jou-p'u-t'uan* easily surpasses them. Except in the matter of phallic phantasy, where it seems just as bound to perpetuating hoary error.

I say "seems" because the way the story starts could be used as a parable to illustrate the truth: the hero, the Before Midnight Scholar, marries and gives himself and his bride the highest kind of nuptial pleasure, once he has thawed her prudish reserve by getting her to scan some erotic books (a humorous frame reference here). But he is sadly taken with the Don Juan obsession: to find and enjoy the most beautiful women in the world. So he abandons his wife and sets out, only to meet with a devastating setback when he joins forces with a robber. The robber promises his assistance in fraudulent entry to the bedchambers of even the most closely guarded castle, but he insists first on an inspection of the Before Midnight Scholar's penis, "just to set my mind at rest. I shall be able to take your part with a clearer conscience once I've seen for myself that everything is satisfactory." Unwillingly, but with a certain self-esteem, our hero draws out his weapon. The robber roars with laughter:

> "Your equipment is not even a third as large as that of the average man. And with that you planned to invade strange houses and seduce other people's wives. Ha ha! Does it seem likely that a woman whose gate is as wide as a shoe and who is dissatisfied with her husband's last would attempt to fill out the gap with your pitiful stylus . . . ?"

The Before Midnight Scholar is crushed, forgets all the pleasure he has given and received with the penis Nature gave him, and retires into seclusion. The story might be a satire on the phallic fallacy: when the approval of other men, here a man he respects, is withdrawn, our hero feels, and thus becomes, a failure. Even more satirical appears the utterly grotesque remedy he finds: he engages a surgeon to graft the erect penis of a large dog onto his own, and returns to society with a member that excites universal awe. But the satire in the book lies elsewhere; in the adventures that follow, our hero receives ample proof that the monster penis gains him entry where his original equipment would have merited him only scorn and rejection. He learns his lesson at the end, but it is the lesson of Don Juan, that obsessive philandering brings damnation, death and horror, rather than that for a man to aspire to a huge penis, or despair over a small one, is absurd.

Let's return to the matter of support from women. I hazarded the generalization that such support does not come from women, because they have no physiological basis from which to arrive at it. Ideas without factual support are often dearly cherished, racial supremacy and masturbation-as-pathogenic being examples. Women are clearly swayed by male concepts, especially in male-dominant societies, but couldn't we expect to find the women in erotic novels approximating women in life in this respect—that is, the great majority of them unconcerned with this peculiarly male phantasy? The examples I have cited so far, the lady in *The Perfumed Garden* and the women of the *Jou-p'u-t'uan*, are very much concerned; and they are more the rule than the exception. It might be said that in the majority of works where women are presented commenting on penises they adhere to the rule of "the bigger, the better." That is, in works of normal heterosexuality; in de Sade, by contrast, the monstrous phalluses are viewed by owners and by victims as means of inflicting pain. *The Autobiography of a Flea* is a modern case in point: the heroine, who has had her first sexual experience merely hours before, receives a glimpse of the enormous member of her father confessor and murmurs, "Holy Mother, this is already Heaven!"

The same is true in books that purport to be written by women or show a variety of sexual events entirely through a woman's eyes. Fanny Hill, Josefine Mutzenbacher, the narrator of *Le Foutromanie*, all, in one way or another, express admiration for size, if not scorn for lack of it. These books, and all others like them I have seen, were written by men. It is not true that women take no interest in erotic literature, and it must be true that women have written erotic books of frankness equivalent to those I have mentioned, but it is difficult to find such a book of which feminine authorship is quite certain. I might add that *The Story of O,* though not the kind of book I mean, is currently the subject of a masculine-feminine authorship debate; if it were indeed written by a woman, that woman thinks exactly like a sado-masochistic male!

So we are back where we started: what is not in male experience is in male projection. And we are forced to a partial realization of why so much erotic literature is bad: although it deals with the basis of life, censorship and guilt force it out of the normal course of life and literature, and it makes a virtue out of its handicap, strengthening rather than seeking to control and diminish its departure from verisimilitude. Social impulse and view outside oneself are abandoned in it; its most characteristic effect becomes solitary, narcissistic, and masturbatory—primarily male. A solitary reader in rapt admiration of his erect penis.

What we call great literature lacks almost all erotic physicality; let me cite two short examples:

> She was so beautiful, with her gown half torn off, and stirred to such a pitch of passion, that Fabrizio could not refrain from following an almost unconscious impulse. No resistance was offered him.

> That for which Vronsky had been almost a whole year the one absorbing desire of his life, replacing all his old desires; that which for Anna had been an impossible, terrible, and even for that reason more entrancing dream of bliss, that desire had been fulfilled. He stood before her, pale, his lower jaw quivering, and besought her to be calm, not knowing how or why.

There are few novelists in any literature that can equal Stendhal's mastery of human psychology; there are no novelists that equal Tolstoy. Except in the description of the making of love, for Tolstoy does not describe that. Nor does Stendhal, nor does Proust, nor does Homer, nor does Virgil, nor does Valmiki—the physiology of love is not their province. We might presume that they would naturally have taken it to be had they not been prevented from doing so; it is idle, but fascinating, to speculate what Tolstoy could have done with the passion and descriptive power he put into the physical presence of Vronsky's mare, and the race that proved fatal to her, had he felt able to direct it upon the central figure of *Anna Karenina*. Of course, Tolstoy's omission saves him from demonstrating an ignorance that the circumstances of his domestic life indicate he might well have had. And it saves *Anna Karenina* from presenting such psychological and physiological nonsense as that I have quoted from Nefzawi and Li Yü. We can thus say, "*Anna Karenina* presents no misinformation about physical relations between men and women," but that isn't much to say; it's too close to saying, "*Anna Karenina* presents no information about the physical relations between men and women." It is rather poignant that our greatest Western novels about the love of men and women tell us nothing about how that love is made, particularly when we consider the extent to which we derive knowledge of life from the novels we read. Is there no mid-point between *Anna Karenina*, where a horse must do the work, and the *Jou-p'u-t'uan*, where a dog penis occupies center stage? Both novels point the moral of irresponsible sexuality, specifically adultery, with consummate skill, but one offers the sexuality itself in disguised, indirect terms, and the other in a directness flawed with grotesque errors of observation.

A modern candidate for such mid-way, ideal status is the work of D. H. Lawrence, who with *Lady Chatterley's Lover* pushed the psychological novel a great distance closer to sexual awareness, with an awareness in turn that this is what the novel *should* do. In it Lawrence states "the novel, properly handled, can reveal the most secret places of life: for it is in the *passional* secret places of life, above all, that the tide of sensitive awareness needs to ebb and flow, cleansing and freshening." And that, sadly, is the great weakness of *Lady Chatterley's Lover;* its nature of erotic novel is undermined by its status as program for the erotic novel, which for Lawrence must be a diatribe against modern civilization and a glorification of phallic power blasting to atoms the dangerous absurdity of female will. As beautiful as the lovemaking scenes are, they bear an underlying strain of misogyny; Connie must be taught by them to switch off the "cold and derisive" qualities of "her queer female mind." It is no wonder that Simone de Beauvoir dismisses Lawrence as the victim of "phallic pride," his male phantasy may spare us Li Yü's marriage of man and beast, but its inclusion of the feathered serpent and the woman who rode away cause its glorification of sex to verge dangerously on its degradation into sadism.

But Lawrence's work has another kind of value: it gives a key to the sexual psychology that dominates erotic literature to the extent of distorting physiology. The *Kamasutra, The Perfumed Garden,* the *Jou-p'u-t'uan, The Autobiography of a Flea* are essentially as mute as a Japanese pillow-book illustration: they present the giant phallus, but give no clue as to why, and perhaps even whether, they think it exists. When *Lady Chatterley's Lover* reveals the male organ, although normal sized, as the weapon with which the destruction of the female will is to be carried out, we are able to see what is both obvious and occult: the penis psychologically corresponds to the muscle of the male arm as an agent of domination; the larger it is the more effective it is in visually demonstrating the difference between the sexes, in spiking the *vagina dentata,* and in subduing the threatening female.

On this basis we might better see the real nature of two masterpieces of erotic literature, perhaps the two greatest erotic works. The first is the 16th-century Chinese *Chin P'ing Mei,* or the tale of Hsi Men and his six wives, which sets realistic and delightful descriptions of lovemaking inside a wide view of society and human motivation—not as wide a view as Tolstoy's, though, for the hero is as luxuriantly idle as the *Kamasutra's* ideal gentleman, and the action centers around him. Nevertheless, Cordier's *Bibliotheca Sinica* considered that the translation of the novel "would render superfluous any other book upon the manners of the Chinese"; in its own terms the work is very nearly perfect.

But not in ours, alas, for the women in it are simply concubines, sexual instruments of male pleasure, so that for all its preeminence the book is as limited in its presentation of women as the *Decameron* or the *Cent Nouvelle Nouvelles.* Thanks to unquestioned male dominance the male sexuality is true and the phallus size normal; the female sexuality is free from male projection, but hardly exists.

The second erotic masterpiece is James Joyce's *Ulysses,* a book that has gone from condemnation as a dirty book to such institutional prestige that most contemporary discussion of it stresses its characterization, its social comment, its use of music, its linguistic form—almost anything but its sexuality. That sexuality has not been sufficiently explored, especially within the tradition of erotic literature, for *Ulysses* is not an epic parody as it is commonly seen, setting up a comic contrast between the heroism of old and the drab city life of our century, but a sexual epic, achieving its comic force by translating traditional heroism into entirely sexual terms—a series of infidelities, a comic masturbation, the heroine in bed throughout, a masochistic orgy in which the hero changes his sex, and so forth. The book's message is not "How degraded and stale is modern life!" but "How inescapably sexual is life!" The female point of view is almost as strong in it as the male; with Molly Bloom Joyce made as great an effort as a male writer ever has to faithfully represent female sexuality. This element makes it superior to the *Chin P'ing Mei* in the matter of inclusiveness, in passages like this from Molly Bloom's long soliloquy:

> yes because he must have come three or four times with that tremendous big red brute of a thing he has I thought the vein or whatever the dickens they call it was going to burst though his nose is not so big . . . like iron or some kind of a thick crowbar standing all the time he must have eaten oysters I think a few dozen . . . no I never in all my life felt anyone had one the size of that to make you feel full up he must have eaten a whole sheep after whats the idea making us like that with a big hole in the middle of us like a stallion driving it up into you because thats all they want out

of you with that determined vicious look in his eye I had to
half shut my eyes still he hasnt such a tremendous amount of
spunk in him when I made him pull it out and do it on me
considering how big it is so much the better in case any of it
wasnt washed out properly the last time I let him finish in
me nice invention they made for women for him to get all
the pleasure. . . .

Joyce's effort has received a great deal of praise—C. G. Jung
wrote him that he rivalled the devil's grandmother to write with
such knowledge of the thoughts of women—on the other hand,
his wife, who never read his work, once said of him, "He knows
nothing at all about women." He knew a lot, I think, but certain
things about the passage I quoted leave me unsatisfied. First, it
contains the most complete description in the book of lovemaking, and that forces us to conclude that the book, for all its dangerous reputation, is stingy where the least pretentious erotic
novel is generous. Secondly, the way in which Molly thinks of
her lover, Hugh Boylan, is in terms of his penis, and—can it be
true?—what interests her most about that penis is its size. I am
strongly tempted to conclude that Joyce's artistic creation of a
woman's mind is based more on his reading of erotic books and
his knowledge of male jokes and stories than on a careful interro-
gation of women themselves. That *Ulysses* nevertheless is an
erotic masterpiece is a tribute to Joyce's power of suggestive
description, and another indication of the lack of competition.

In conclusion, that we have a male-dominated erotica is perhaps a surprise to no one, but that we have an erotica with powerful means of perpetuating psychological and physiological mis-
conception is perhaps not so well known. That John Fowles
could write *The Magus* (1965) is an indication that the higher
level of sexual knowledge currently prevailing may enable the
creation of a superior erotic literature; it is perhaps time as well
that we have a superior criticism of erotic literature.

KATE MILLETT

SEXUAL POLITICS:
MILLER, MAILER, AND GENET

I

I would ask her to prepare the bath for me. She would pretend to demur but she would do it just the same. One day,
while I was seated in the tub soaping myself, I noticed that
she had forgotten the towels."Ida," I called, "bring me some
towels!" She walked into the bathroom and handed me them.
She had on a silk bathrobe and a pair of silk hose. As she
stooped over the tub to put the towels on the rack her bathrobe slid open. I slid to my knees and buried my head in her
muff. It happened so quickly that she didn't have time to
rebel or even to pretend to rebel. In a moment I had her
in the tub, stockings and all. I slipped the bathrobe off and
threw it on the floor. I left the stockings on—it made her
more lascivious looking, more the Cranach type. I lay back
and pulled her on top of me. She was just like a bitch in heat,
biting me all over, panting, gasping, wriggling like a worm

on the hook. As we were drying ourselves she bent over and
began nibbling at my prick. I sat on the edge of the tub and
she kneeled at my feet gobbling it. After a while I made her
stand up, bend over; then I let her have it from the rear.
She had a small juicy cunt, which fitted me like a glove. I
bit the nape of her neck, the lobes of her ears, the sensitive
spot on her shoulder, and as I pulled away I left the mark of
my teeth on her beautiful white ass. Not a word spoken.

This colorful, descriptive prose is taken from Henry Miller's
celebrated *Sexus,* first published in Paris in the forties but out-
lawed from the sanitary shores of his native America until the
recent Grove edition. Miller, alias Val, is recounting his seduction of Ida Verlaine, the wife of his friend Bill Woodruff. As an
account of sexual passage, the excerpt has much in it of note
beyond that merely biological activity which the narrator would
call "fucking." Indeed, it is just this other content which gives
the representation of the incident its value and character.

First, one must consider the circumstances and the context of
the scene. Val has just met Bill Woodruff outside a burlesque
theater where Ida Verlaine is performing. In the rambling fashion
of Miller's narrative, this meeting calls up the memory of the
hero's sexual bouts with Ida ten years before, whereupon follow
eleven pages of vivid reenactment. First, there is Ida herself:

She was just exactly the way her name sounded—pretty,
vain, theatrical, faithless, spoiled, pampered, petted. Beautiful as a Dresden doll, only she had raven tresses and a
Javenese slant to her soul. If she had a soul at all! Lived
entirely in the body, in her senses, her desires—and she
directed the show, the body show, with her tyrannical little
will which poor Woodruff translated as some monumental
force of character. . . . Ida swallowed everything like a py-
thoness. She was heartless and insatiable.

Woodruff himself is given out as a uxorious fool: "The more
he did for her the less she cared for him. She was a monster
from head to toe." The narrator claims to be utterly immune to

Ida's power but is nonetheless subject to coldly speculative curiosity:

> I just didn't give a fuck for her, as a person, though I often wondered what she might be like as a piece of fuck, so to speak. I wondered about it in a detached way, but somehow it got across to her, got under her skin.

As a friend of the family, Val is entitled to spend the night at the Woodruff house, followed by breakfast in bed while husband Bill goes off to work. Val's initial tactic of extracting service from Ida is important to the events which follow:

> She hated the thought of waiting on me in bed. She didn't do it for her husband and she couldn't see why she should do it for me. To take breakfast in bed was something I never did except at Woodruff's place. I did it expressly to annoy and humiliate her.

In accord with one of the myths at the very heart of a Miller novel, the protagonist, who is always some version of the author himself, is sexually irresistible and potent to an almost mystic degree. It is therefore no very great surprise to the reader that Ida falls into his hands. To return to the picking, then, and the passage quoted at length above. The whole scene reads very much like a series of stratagems, aggressive on the part of the hero and acquiescent on the part of what custom forces us to designate as the heroine of the episode. His first maneuver, for example, is to coerce further service in the form of a demand for towels, which reduces Ida to the appropriate roles of a hostess and a domestic. That Ida has dressed herself in a collapsible bathrobe and silk stockings is not only accommodating, but almost romance-like. The female reader may realize that one rarely wears stockings without the assistance of a girdle or garter belt, but classic masculine fantasy dictates that nudity's most appropriate exception is some gauze-like material, be it hosiery or underwear.

Val makes the first move: "I slid to my knees and buried my

head in her muff." The locution "muff" is significant because it
is a clue to the reader that the putative humility of the action
and the stance of petition it implies are not to be taken at face
value. "Muff" carries the tone, implicit in the whole passage, of
one male relating an exploit to another male in the masculine
vocabulary and with its point of view. What is considerably more
revealing of the actual character of the action is the comment
which follows: "It happened so quickly she didn't have time to
rebel or even to pretend to rebel." Since the entire scene is a
description not so much of sexual intercourse, but rather of
intercourse in the service of power, "rebel" is a highly charged
word. Val had already informed the reader that "she wanted to
bring me under her spell, make me walk the tight-rope, as she
had done with Woodruff and her other suitors." The issue, of
course, is which of the two is to walk a tight-rope, who shall be
master?

Having immediately placed Ida under his domination, Val acts
fast to forestall insubordination. This prompts the next remarkable event—Val brings her into his element, as it were, and places
her in the distinctly ridiculous position of being in a bathtub
with her clothes on. Again the language indicates the underlying
issue of power: "I had her in the bathtub." The reader is also
advised that credit should be given to the narrator for his speed
and agility; Ida is swooshed into the tub in a trice. Having
assumed all initiative, Val then proceeds to divest his prey of her
redundant bathrobe and throw it on the floor.

The display of stockings and nudity is brought forward for
aesthetic delectation; it contributes to make Ida "more lascivious
looking, more the Cranach type." The frail perfection of a Cranach
nude had been mentioned earlier as Ida's comparable body type.
Juxtaposing the innocence and rarity of this image with the traditional "girlie" figure in silk stockings is an eminent bit of
strategy. The word "lascivious" implies a deliberate sensuality and
is dependent upon a relish for the prurient, and particularly for
the degrading, in sexual activity, which, in its turn, relies on the
distinctly puritanical conviction that sexuality is indeed dirty
and faintly ridiculous. Webster defines "lascivious" as "wanton;
lewd; lustful" or a "tendency to produce lewd emotions." The
Cranach in question is most like to be the delicate and rather

morbid Eve of the Genesis Panel, now depreciated to a calendar girl.

Val proceeds—his manner coolly self-assured and redolent of comfort: "I lay back and pulled her on top of me." What follows is purely subjective description. Ceasing to admire himself, the hero is now lost in wonder at his effects. For the fireworks which ensue are Ida's, though produced by a Pavlovian mechanism. Like the famous programmed dog, in fact "just like a bitch in heat," Ida responds to the protagonist's skilled manipulation: ". . . biting me all over, panting, gasping, wriggling like a worm on the hook." No evidence is ever offered to the reader of any such animal-like failure of self-restraint in the response of our hero. It is he who is the hook, and she who is the worm: the implication is clearly one of steely self-composure contrasted to lower-life servility and larval vulnerability. Ida has—in the double, but related, meaning of the phrase—been had.

In the conventional order of this genre of sexual narrative, one position of intercourse must rapidly be followed by another less orthodox and therefore of greater interest. Miller obliges the reader with a quick instance of dorsal intercourse, preceded by a fitting interlude of fellatio. But more pertinent to the larger issues under investigation is the information that Ida is now so "hooked" that it is she who makes the first move: ". . . she bent over and began nibbling at my prick." The hero's "prick," now very centerstage, is still a hook and Ida metamorphosed into a very gullible fish. (Perhaps all of this aquatic imagery was inspired by the bathtub.)

Furthermore, positions are significantly reversed: "I sat on the edge of the tub and she kneeled at my feet gobbling it." The power nexus is clearly outlined. It remains only for the hero to assert his victory by the arrogance of his final gesture: "After a while I made her stand up, bend over; then I let her have it from the rear."

What the reader is vicariously experiencing at this juncture is a nearly supernatural sense of power—should the reader be a male. For the passage is not only a vivacious and imaginative use of circumstance, detail, and context to evoke the excitations of sexual intercourse, it is also a male assertion of dominance over a weak, compliant, and rather unintelligent female. It is a case of sexual politics at the fundamental level of copulation. Several satisfactions for hero and reader alike undoubtedly accrue upon this triumph of the male ego, the most tangible one being communicated in the following: "She had a small juicy cunt which fitted me like a glove."

The hero then caters to the reader's appetite in telling how he fed upon his object, biting ". . . the nape of her neck, the lobes of her ears, the sensitive spot on her shoulder, and as I pulled away I left the mark of my teeth on her beautiful white ass." The last bite is almost a mark of patent to denote possession and use, but further still, to indicate attitude. Val had previously informed us that Bill Woodruff was so absurd and doting a groveler that he had demeaned himself to kiss this part of his wife's anatomy. Our hero adjusts the relation of the sexes by what he believes is a more correct gesture.

Without question the most telling statement in the narrative is its last sentence: "Not a word spoken." Like the folk hero who never condescended to take off his hat, Val has accomplished the entire campaign, including its coup de grace, without stooping to one word of human communication.

The recollection of the affair continues for several more pages of diversified stimulation by which the hero now moves to consolidate his position of power through a series of physical and emotional gestures of contempt. In answer to her question ". . . you don't really like me, do you?" he replies with studied insolence, "'I like this,' said I giving her a stiff jab." His penis is now an instrument of chastisement, whereas Ida's genitalia are but the means of her humiliation: "I like your cunt, Ida . . . it's the best thing about you."

All further representations conspire to convince the reader of Val's superior intelligence and control, while demonstrating the female's moronic complaisance and helpless carnality; each moment exalts him further and degrades her lower: a dazzling instance of the sexual double standard:

> "You never wear any undies do you? You're a slut, do you know it?"
> I pulled her dress up and made her sit that way while I finished my coffee.

"Play with it a bit while I finish this."

"You're filthy," she said, but she did as I told her.

"Take your two fingers and open it up. I like the color of it."

. . . With this I reached for a candle on the dresser at my side and I handed it to her.

"Let's see if you can get it in all the way. . . ."

"You can make me do anything, you dirty devil."

"You like it, don't you?"

Val's imperious aptitude sets the tone for the dramatic events which follow, and the writing soars off into that species of fantasy which Steven Marcus calls "pornotopic," a shower of orgasms:

> I laid her on a small table and when she was on the verge of exploding I picked her up and walked around the room with her; then I took it out and made her walk on her hands holding her by the thighs, letting it slip out now and then to excite her still more.

In both the foregoing selections the most operative verbal phrases are: "I laid her on a small table" (itself a pun), "made her walk on her hands," "She did as I told her," and "I pulled her dress up and made her sit that way." Ida is putty, even less substantial than common clay, and like a bullied child is continually taking orders for activity which in the hero's view degrades her while it aggrandizes him.

Meanwhile, the hero's potency is so superb and overwhelming that he is lost in admiration: "It went on like this until I had such an erection that even after I shot a wad into her it stayed up like a hammer. That excited her terribly." And emerging from his efforts covered with so much credit and satisfaction, he takes account of his assets: "My cock looked like a bruised rubber hose; it hung between my legs, extended an inch or two beyond its normal length and swollen beyond recognition."

Ida, who has never demanded much of his attention, nor of ours, is quickly forgotten as the hero goes off to feast in his inimitable adolescent fashion: "I went to the drug store and swallowed a couple of malted milks." His final pronouncement on his adventure also redounds to his credit: "A royal bit of fuck-ing, thought I to myself, wondering how I'd act when I met Woodruff again." Royal indeed.

During the course of the episode, Val obliges the reader with intelligence of the Woodruffs' marital incompatibility, a misal-liance of a curiously physical character. Mr. Woodruff possesses a genital organ of extraordinary proportions, "a veritable horse cock." "I remember the first time I saw it—I could scarcely be-lieve my eyes" whereas Mrs. Woodruff's dimensions have already been referred to under the rubric "small juicy cunt." But lest this irreconcilable misfortune in any way excuse her in seeking out other satisfaction, it is repeatedly underlined, throughout the section of the novel where she figures, that she is an uppity woman. Therefore the hero's exemplary behavior in reducing her to the status of a mere female. Moreover, we are given to under-stand that she is an insatiable nymphomaniac—thus his wit and prosperity in discovering and exploiting her.

The figure of Ida Verlaine appears to have haunted Miller's imagination. It is not enough that his hero should discover her "whorish" nature and bring her to paroxysms of sensual capitula-tion while congratulating himself on cuckolding her adulating husband. In an earlier work, *Black Spring*, she appears as a woman discovered at prostitution and properly chastised. Here Miller's didactic nature obtrudes itself and one is made to per-ceive the validity of his claim that his is a deeply moral imag-ination.

Bill Woodruff's brilliant reaction when the news is passed along to him by another buddy is narrated at length and with obvious relish. The narrator, again a version of Miller, regards the anecdote as "cute":

> This night, however, he waited up for her and when she came sailing in, chipper, perky, a little lit up and cold as usual he pulled her up short with a "where were you to-night?" She tried pulling her usual yarn, of course. "Cut that," he said. "I want you to get your things off and tumble into bed." That made her sore. She mentioned in her round-about way that she didn't want any of that business. "You

don't feel in the mood for it, I suppose," says he, and then he adds: "that's fine because now I'm going to warm you up a bit." With that he up and ties her to the bedstead, gags her, and then goes for the razor strop. On the way to the bathroom, he grabs a bottle of mustard from the kitchen. He comes back with the razor strop and he belts the piss out of her. And after that he rubs the mustard into the raw welts. "That ought to keep you warm for to-night," he says. And so saying he makes her bend over and spread her legs apart. "Now," he says, "I'm going to pay you as usual," and taking a bill out of his pocket he crumbles it and then shoves it up her quim.

Miller concludes the saga of Ida and Bill with a last joke at the cuckold's expense, for Bill is still a cuckold, and a maxim for the reader, in capital letters, is put forward as "the purpose of all this"—merely, "To prove what has not yet been demonstrated, namely that

THE GREAT ARTIST IS HE WHO CONQUERS THE ROMANTIC IN HIMSELF."

Miller's educational intentions in the passage are abundantly clear. Females who are frigid, e.g. not sexually compliant, should be beaten. Females who break the laws of marital fidelity should also be beaten, for the barter system of marriage (sex in return for security) must not be violated by outside commerce. Rather more informative that this sober doctrine of the cave is the insight it provides into Miller's sexual/literary motives and their undeniably sadistic overtones. They are closer to the vicarious politic of the cock-pit than of the boudoir, but the latter often casts considerable light on the former.

II

"I have nothing in me," she said. "Do we go ahead?"
"Who knows," I said, "keep quiet."
And I could feel her beginning to come. The doubt in me

had tipped her off, the adjuration to be quiet had thrown the bolt. She was a minute away, but she was on her way, and just as if one of her wily fingers had thrown some switch in me, I was gone like a bat and shaking hands with the Devil once more. Rare greed shone in her eyes, pleasure in her mouth, she was happy. I was ready to chase, I was gorged to throw the first spill, high on a choice, like some cat caught on two wires I was leaping back and forth, in separate runs for separate strokes, bringing spoils and secrets up to the Lord from the red mills, bearing messages of defeat back from that sad womb, and then I chose—ah, but there was time to change—I chose her cunt. It was no graveyard now, no warehouse, no, more like a chapel now, a modest decent place, but its walls were snug, its odor was green, there was a sweetness in the chapel, a muted reverential sweetness in those walls of stone. "That is what prison will be like for you," said a last effort of my inner tongue. "Stay here!" came a command from inside of me; except that I could feel the Devil's meal beneath, its fires were lifting through the floor, and I waited for the warmth to reach inside, to come up from the cellar below, to bring booze and heat up and licking tongues, I was up above a choice which would take me on one wind or another, and I had to give myself, I could not hold back, there was an explosion, furious, treacherous and hot as the gates of an icy slalom with the speed at my heels overtaking my nose. I had one of those splittings of a second where the senses fly out and there in that instant the itch reached into me and drew me out and I jammed up her ass and came as if I'd been flung across the room. She let out a cry of rage.

The foregoing is a description of heterosexual sodomy from Norman Mailer's *An American Dream*. The practice is not only one of the book's primary attractions, it is so central to the action that one might even say the plot depended on it. Mailer's hero, Stephen Rojack, has just finished murdering his wife and is now relieving his feelings by buggering his maid.

Mailer transparently identifies with his hero, who has little motive for the killing beyond the fact that he is unable to "master" his mate by any means short of murder. The desire for such mastery is perfectly understandable to Mailer and even engages his sympathy. So does Rojack's surprisingly old-fashioned stance of the outraged husband. Mrs. Rojack, to whom Mr. Rojack's many affairs are perfectly well known, has found the temerity to advise him that since separation she too has indulged herself. Moreover, and here is where one must depend on the forceful role of sodomy in the book, she admits that she has been enjoying this very activity with her new lovers. Now sodomy is a speciality in which our hero takes personal pride. Though he boasts to her face that his mistresses far excel her in this activity, the notion that his wife is committing adultery is evidently too severe a trial on his patience. It is the final blow to his vanity, his sense of property, and, most material of all, his fancied masculine birthright of superordination, and he promptly retaliates by strangling the upstart. As Mrs. Rojack is one of those Celtic sporting women, it is not easy work and Rojack is exhausted when he finishes—and all the more triumphant: "I was weary with a most honorable fatigue, and my flesh seemed new. I had not felt so nice since I was twelve. It seemed inconceivable at this instant that anything in life could fail to please."

Now to get back to the maid. Rojack had entered her room to find her busily masturbating, surely a fortuitous circumstance. The rest is easy. He calmly removes her hand from her genitals and replaces it with his bare foot "drawing up on the instant out of her a wet spicy wisdom of all the arts and crafts of getting along in the world." The comment is indicative of the heavy heuristic value which the hero is to obtain from his sexual exploits. For an instant Rojack toys with the idea of simply murdering the maid—"I was ready to kill her easy as not, there was an agreeable balance in the thought that I was ready to kill anyone at this moment"—but he decides instead to take her on. Three pages of sexual activity then follow before a word is spoken; and, as the hero boasts, "it must have been five minutes before I chose to give her a kiss, but I took her mouth at last." In doing so, he undertakes to absorb her soul, which is that of a German proletarian. It appears that Mr. Rojack's employee smells, and

it is chiefly through her odor that Rojack, a Harvard man, a
college professor, a United States congressman, a television personality, and the very recent widower of a rich woman, stumbles
upon the understanding outlined in the next statement.

> But then, as abruptly as an arrest, a thin high constipated
> smell (a smell which spoke of rocks and grease and the
> sewer-damp of wet stones in poor European alleys) came
> needling its way out of her. She was hungry, and it could
> have spoiled my pleasure except that there was something
> intoxicating in the sheer narrow pitch of the smell, so strong,
> so stubborn, so private, it was a smell which could be mel-
> lowed only by the gift of furs and gems.

Though her patron, Rojack is almost too repelled to continue:
"it could have spoiled my pleasure." Then he decides that even
this unworthy creature can serve him in some way: "I had a
desire to skip the sea and mine the earth, a pure prong of desire
to bugger, there was canny hard-packed evil in that butt, that
I knew."

It is at this point that the first word is spoken; the servant
resists the will of her master. But Ruta's "verboten" makes little
impression on Rojack. He has convinced himself that her essence
lies in her rectum and that it is a quality which might be convenient to him. As a newly arrived homicide, he is in immediate
need of a bit of that canny lower-class self-preservation Ruta is
presumed to contain. For if nothing else, she has the invaluable
"knowledge of a city rat." Furthermore, Rojack regards himself
in the light of a moralist in search of wisdom and Ruta's anus
can teach him about evil.

How evil resides in her bowels or why Ruta has a greater share
of it than her master may appear difficult to explain, but many
uncanny things are possible with our author. In most of Mailer's
fiction sexuality has such a mystical and metaphysical import
that genitals acquire personalities. Ruta's "box," as Rojack refers
to it, has very little to offer; nothing resides therein but "cold
gasses from the womb and a storehouse of disappointments." In
An American Dream female sexuality is depersonalized to the

point of being a matter of class or a matter of nature. Ruta be-
haves like a guttersnipe, Deborah, the former Mrs. Rojack, like
a cruel duchess. Cherry, the mistress Rojack later wins, has the
virtues of nature, unavailable to poor Ruta, and excelling those
of the privileged female who is now too dangerously insubor-
dinate to stay alive. As the hero and a male, Rojack, of course,
transcends any such typology.

Finding where Ruta's true serviceability lies, the hero disdains
her vagina to continue rooting in her nether orifice. (Her name
appears to be a cruel English pun on this: in German, "Rute,"
pronounced nearly the same as Ruta, refers both to the switch
or birch of chastisement as well as to the penis, and perhaps more
than mere linguistic coincidence is involved.) As her resistance
renders her difficult to penetrate, Rojack hits upon the device of
pulling her hair, noting with fastidious justification that, anyway
it is dyed red: "I could feel the pain in her scalp strain like a
crowbar the length of her body and push up the trap, and I was
in, that quarter-inch more was gained, the rest was easy." As
further justification for his inquiry into her he resorts again to
the odor of her presumably vicious, but now fascinating, character:

> What a subtle smell came from her then, something back of
> the ambition, the narrow stubbornness, the monomaniacal
> determination to get along in the world, no, that was re-
> placed by something tender as the flesh but not as clean,
> something sneaky, full of fear.

Just as homicide produced an honorable fatigue in him, Rojack
now hits on the glittering idea that in forcibly buggering his
servant he is actually performing an act of patriotism because
Ruta is a "Nazi." The reader may have some difficulty in accepting this; twenty-three years old and therefore a child during the
war, Ruta is hardly a fit subject for Rojack's instant justice. But
the hero continues to take an uncommon satisfaction in his racial
revenge: "There was a high private pleasure in plugging a Nazi,
there was something clean despite all—I felt as if I were gliding
in the clear air about Luther's jakes." And through this shift,

Rojack, a wizard at manipulative ethics, arrives at a position of moral leverage for any further exploits.

Sodomy has a number of possible meanings in Rojack's mind: homosexuality (he confesses to Cherry that he has some doubts about his heterosexual vocation); a forbidden species of sexuality at which he is an expert and over which he holds copyright; or anal rape, which is his way of expressing contemptuous mastery. It is the acting out of this last attitude which is reserved for Ruta.

Throughout the rest of the passage, Rojack entertains the reader with his contrasting impressions of Ruta's rectum, "a bank of pleasures," and her vagina, "a deserted warehouse, that empty tomb." But this virtuosity is accomplished with certain misgivings. As one might expect, these have nothing to do with her pleasure, which is never the issue, but with Rojack's peculiar notion of sexual honor. After all, he muses, her womb might contain "one poor flower growing in a gallery." Because he has deprived her of the opportunity to bear his seed, a substance Rojack regards with reverential awe, he feels obliged to regard himself as a "great thief." Later he will indulge in a number of "might have beens" about the ill fortune of "that empty womb," that "graveyard which gambled a flower and lost." The fact that his precious semen has been discharged in her rectum and not in her cervix is a source of bemusement, not uncomfortably experienced as guilt. Ruta has missed the radiant opportunity to be impregnated by a high power and he can only pity her: "I had thought then of what had been left in her. It was perishing in the kitchens of the Devil." And then he wonders: "Was its curse on me? . . . Was that the cloud of oppression which had come to me in the dark? That the seed was expiring in the wrong field? Perhaps it is this monomania about his own sexual discharge that has made Rojack a specialist in existential dread."

As for Ruta, she responds magically, just as the relevant masculine fantasy dictates. Indeed, her gratitude at being sodomized is positively astonishing: "I do not know why you have trouble with your wife. You are absolutely a genius, Mr. Rojack." Accordingly, the final stages in which this man has his will with his maid take place under the most compliant conditions. Ruta now responds quite as masculine egotism would prescribe: ". . . she was becoming mine as no woman ever had, she wanted to be part of my will." It would seem that she could want nothing better for herself, and at once her "feminine," or again "true woman," instincts emerge and she acquires what her master relays to be ". . . the taste of power in her eyes and mouth, that woman's look that the world is theirs." This delusion of success is, of course, most advantageous to her lord's purposes.

Sexual congress in a Mailer novel is always a matter of strenuous endeavor, rather like mountain climbing—a straining ever upward after achievement. In this, as in so many ways, Mailer is authentically American. Rojack is presently doing very well at his cliff-face, but Ruta begins to waver. She turns with guilty admission of possible failure, "a little look of woe was on her face, a puckered fearful little nine-year-old afraid of her punishment, wishing to be good." In his vast composure, Rojack orders her to "keep quiet." Not only is he more conscious than she of the state of her orgasm, he enjoys a complacent sadistic awareness of what "punishment" might ensue, if she isn't "good."

What follows is the passage I have quoted at the outset, almost exclusively a description of Rojack's activity—and properly so—as the coitus is simply his accomplishment as enacted upon Ruta, and therefore its value is precisely its value to him. Very much a solo flight, it is by no means inappropriate that the imagery employed is aeronautic, "I was gone like a bat," etc. It is also a summary of Rojack's major interests: sport—"I was ready to chase," "leaping back and forth in separate runs for separate strokes," "an icy slalom with the speed at my heels"; alcohol— "to bring booze and heat up and licking tongues"; and religion.

By now it is hardly surprising that his orgasm should take on cosmic and metaphysical implications: "a choice which would take me on one wind or another," "one of those splittings of a second where the senses fly out" and give rise to visions of a "huge city in some desert, was it a place on the moon?" What is more noteworthy are the elaborate configurations in the act of the Lord and the Devil. The Devil is manifestly an anal force. The Lord smiles upon Rojack's high mission to fertilize the humble and bring the "spoils and secrets" of his semen to the "sad womb" of this lowly woman through the favor of his visitation.

Indeed, Ruta's "cunt," as Rojack calls it, has prospered through association with him and has grown more worthy: "It was no graveyard now, no warehouse, no more like a chapel now." But despite the purloined phrases from William Blake it is still no great shakes, simply ". . . a modest, decent place, but its walls were snug," and appropriately, it is aware of its exalted, if only sporadic, honor in housing Rojack himself, who deigns to find in it "a muted reverential sweetness." But having defined the organ in question in terms of several types of public buildings, Rojack finally comes to detect in it a prison with "walls of stone."

The result of this discovery is that, at the last moment, he escapes back to the free-wheeling Devil of sodomy. The chief function of this pasage is to provide a way for Rojack to commit his crime a second time in symbolic circumstances. Given the often emphasized choice between the Devil (sodomy) and the Lord (procreation), or death and life, Rojack once again opts for death. Just as he refuses what we are asked to believe is a portentous existential opportunity to sweeten Ruta's womb with his magical semen (infallible in its power to bring about conception), so too does Rojack refuse the choice of acknowledging his crime, accepting responsibility for it and going to prison. Ruta's vagina has constituted his foretaste of prison. "That is what prison will be like for you; said a last effort on my inner tongue. 'Stay here!' came a command from inside of me." But the Devil has more exotic and dynamic attractions. Rojack claims that he is compelled to his decision and he explains it in terms of a generosity which pertains only to himself: "I had to give myself, I could not hold back." Ruta and prison must do without the hallowed presence of the hero so that Rojack may have his ultimate satisfaction: "I jammed up her ass and came as if I'd been flung across the room. She let out a cry of rage." It seems that Mailer is both a romantic manichean and a romantic diabolist.

After receiving his servant's congratulations on his dazzling performance, Rojack proceeds calmly to the next floor and throws his wife's body out of the window. He has elected to remain with the Devil and stay alive. Ruta has been a vessel of considerable utility. Through her, or rather through her "ass," the hero has made his major decision: to pass the murder off as an accident. And as Ruta was compliant to an outlandish degree, so is the rest of the world. All obstacles melt before Rojack who hereafter is a miracle of tough dispatch. Once almost a "loser," he is rejuvenated and remade through the act of murder: he wins a fight with a black gangster who cowers before him, a fortune at the tables at Las Vegas, and the love of a nightclub singer who wants him to make her a lady (the last detail a fatuity which is better passed over in silence). Even the police look on Rojack with eyes blinded by admiring camaraderie, and he is permitted to escape to Yucatan. In fact, Mailer's *An American Dream* is an exercise in how to kill your wife and be happy ever after. The reader is given to understand that by murdering one woman and buggering another, Rojack became a "man."

The humanist convictions which underlie *Crime and Punishment* (the original and still the greatest study in what it is like to commit murder) may all go by the board. Both Dostoyevsky and Dreiser, in *An American Tragedy,* gradually created in their murderers an acceptance of responsibility for the violation of life which their actions had constituted, and both transcend their crimes through atonement. Rojack has some singularity in being one of the first literary characters to get away with murder; he is surely the first hero as homicide to rejoice in his crime and never really lose his creator's support. In *Native Son* Richard Wright understood Bigger Thomas's crime while never condoning it and made of it a prototypical fable of the logic of rage in a racist society. Mailer also appears to find in Rojack a symbolic figure whose crime is diagnostic of conditions in American society. But the condition appears to be simply a hostility between the sexes so bitter that it has reached the proportions of a war waged in terms of murder and sodomy. And Mailer is to be on the winning side, to which end he has created in Rojack the last warrior for a curious cause, none other than male supremacy. Rojack is a far cry from Wright's underdog from a Chicago slum acting only through desperation in a novel that is both a plea for racial justice and a threatening vision of what may come to pass should the hope of it fail. Rojack belongs to the oldest ruling class in the world, and like one of Faulkner's ancient retainers of a lost cause, he is making his stand on the preservation of a social hierarchy that sees itself as threatened with extinction. His Jewish ancestry and his "liberal" views to the contrary, Rojack is the last surviving white man as conquering hero. Mailer's *An American Dream* is a rallying cry for a sexual politics in which diplomacy has failed and war is the last political resort of a ruling caste that feels its position in deadly peril.

III

A few days later, when I met him near the docks Armand ordered me to follow him. Almost without speaking, he took me to his room. With the same apparent scorn he subjected me to his pleasure.

Dominated by his strength and age, I gave the work my utmost care. Crushed by that mass of flesh, which was devoid of the slightest spirituality, I experienced the giddiness of finally meeting the perfect brute, indifferent to my happiness. I discovered the sweetness that could be contained in a thick fleece on torso, belly and thighs and what force it could transmit. I finally let myself be buried in that stormy night. Out of gratitude or fear I placed a kiss on Armand's hairy arm.

"What's eating you? Are you nuts or something?"

"I didn't do any harm."

I remained at his side in order to serve his nocturnal pleasure. When he went to bed, Armand whipped his leather belt from the loops of his trousers and made it snap. It was flogging an invisible victim, a shape of transparent flesh. The air bled. If he frightened me then, it was because of his powerlessness to be the Armand I see, who is heavy and mean. The snapping accompanied and supported him. His rage and despair at not being *him* made him tremble like a horse subdued by darkness, made him tremble more and more. He would not, however, have tolerated my living idly. He advised me to prowl around the station or the zoo and pick up customers. Knowing the terror inspired in me by his person, he didn't deign to keep any eye on me. The money I earned I brought back intact.

This quotation, from Jean Genet's autobiographical novel *The Thief's Journal*, is the first passage in which the author's identification is with the "female figure." Jean Genet is both male and female. Young, poor, a criminal and a beggar, he was also initially the despised drag queen, the *maricone* (faggot), contemptible because he was the female partner in homosexual acts. Older, distinguished by fame, wealthy and secure, he became a male; though never ascending to the full elevation of the pimp (or supermale).

Sexual role is not a matter of biological identity but of class or caste in the hierocratic homosexual society projected in Genet's novels. Because of the perfection with which they ape and exaggerate the "masculine" and "feminine" of heterosexual society, his homosexual characters represent the best contemporary insight into its constitution and beliefs. Granted that their caricature is grotesque, and Genet himself is fully aware of the morbidity of this pastiche, his homosexuals nonetheless have unerringly penetrated to the essence of what heterosexual society imagines to be the character of "masculine" and "feminine," and which it mistakes for the nature of male and female, thereby preserving the traditional relation of the sexes. Sartre's brilliant psychoanalytic biography of Genet describes the sexual life of the pimps and queens, male and female figures, in terms that bear out these distinctions of character and prestige:

This is murder: submissive to a corpse, neglected, unnoticed, gazed at unmindfully and manipulated from behind, the girl queen is metamorphosed into a contemptible female object. She does not even have for the pimp the importance that the sadist attributes to his victim. The latter, though tortured and humiliated, at least remains the focal point of her tormentor's concern. It is indeed she whom he wishes to reach, in her particularity, in the depths of her consciousness. But the fairy is only a receptacle, a vase, a spittoon,

which one uses and thinks no more of and which one dis-
cards by the very use one makes of it. The pimp masturbates
in her. At the very instant when an irresistible force knocks
her down, turns her over and punctures her, a dizzying word
swoops down upon her, a power hammer that strikes her
as if she were a medal: *"Encule!"* (Faggot)

This is mainly a description of what it is to be female as reflected in the mirror society of homosexuality. But the passage
also implies what it is to be male. It is to be master, hero, brute,
and pimp. Which is also to be irremediably stupid and cowardly.
In this feudal relationship of male and female, pimp and queen,
one might expect exchange of servitude for protection. But the
typical pimp never protects his slave, and allows him/her to be
beaten, betrayed, or even killed, responding only with ambiguous
amusement. One is naturally curious to discover just what the
queen does receive in return. The answer appears to be an intensity of humiliation which constitutes identity for those who
despise themselves. This, in turn, leads us to the reasons for such
self-despair.

    With Genet they are quite explicit, and Sartre has little diffi-
culty outlining them. A bastard, Genet was repudiated at birth
and left at an orphanage; the double rejection of what can only
be described as an error from inception. Adopted then by a family
of narrow Morvan peasants, he was found stealing and sent to
grow up in a children's prison. There he experiences his final
ostracism in being subjected to rape by older and stronger males.
He has now achieved the lowest status in the world as he saw it;
a perfection of opprobrium in being criminal, queer, and female.
It remained only to study and refine his role, thus the wallowing
in self-hatred which both Sartre and Genet describe as the "femininity" of the passive homosexual. He is feminine because he was
ravished and subjugated by the male; therefore he must study the
slavish gestures of "femininity" that he may better exalt his
master. As a criminal he is obliged to controvert every decency
of the property-owning class not only through a life of larceny
(material) but through one of betrayal (moral) as well. And as
an outcast, his life's demeanor must be plotted both to imitate

and contradict every notion of the world beyond whose boundaries he lives in exile.

But having gone this far, having plunged this low, Genet studies the values of those who live above him so that he may further desecrate them. In doing so he acquires the pride of the utterly abject, a condition which turns out to be next door to saintliness. As a young beggar and whore in the Barrio Chino of Barcelona, Genet attained this sanctity and the unshakable self-respect of one who has truly nothing more to lose. Out of this sprang a wily urge to live. And for those who continue in downright ignominy, the will to live may very plausibly become the will to triumph. This whole cast of thought is generously supported by the French tradition wherein martyrdom is still the highest boon open to the religious imagination. In Catholic Europe sainthood remains, even among the renegades, the loftiest state of grace. That is why Divine, the hero/heroine of *Our Lady of the Flowers*, who is also Genet, is uncontestably a larger spirit than Darling, Gorgui, Armand, Stilitano, and all the other pimps. Not only has she greater courage, humor, imagination, and sensibility than the male oppressors before whom she prostrates herself; she alone has a soul. She has suffered, while they have not, because the consciousness required for suffering is inaccessible to them. And in Divine's mortification, both in the flesh and in the spirit, lies the victory of the saint.

Thus Genet's two great novels, *Our Lady of the Flowers* and *The Thief's Journal*, are tales of an odium converted to grandeur. But together with the rest of his prose fiction they also constitute a painstaking exegesis of the barbarian vassalage of the sexual orders, the power structure of "masculine" and "feminine" as revealed by a homosexual, criminal world that mimics with brutal frankness the bourgeois heterosexual society.

In this way the explication of the homosexual code becomes a satire on the heterosexual one. By virtue of their earnestness, Genet's community of pimps and fairies call into ridicule the behavior they so fervently imitate:

As for slang Divine did not use it, any more than did her cronies, the other Nellys. . . .

Slang was for men. It was the male tongue. Like the
language of men among the Caribees, it became a secondary
sexual attribute. It was like the colored plumage of male
birds, like the multi-colored silk garments which are the
prerogatives of the warriors of the tribe. It was a crest and
spurs. Everyone could understand it, but the only ones who
could speak it were the men who at birth received as a gift
the gestures, the carriage of the hips, legs and arms, the
eyes, the chest, with which one can speak it. One day at one
of our bars, when Mimosa ventured the following words in
the course of a sentence ". . . his screwy stories . . . ,"
the men frowned. Someone said with a threat in his voice:
"Broad acting tough."

The virility of the pimp is a transparent egotism posing as
strength. His "masculinity" is in fact the most specious of petty
self-inflations and is systematically undermined by the true
heroes of these adventures, the queens. Though Genet is a great
romantic and has created in Divine what is perhaps the last and
possibly the most illustrious of those archetypal great-hearted
whores so dear to the French tradition, Genet is just as certainly
a cold-blooded rationalist whose formidable analytic mind has
fastened upon the most fundamental of society's arbitrary follies,
its view of sex as a caste structure ratified by nature.

Beginning with the dissection of sexual attitudes in his prose
fiction, Genet has gone on in his plays to survey the parent world
of the parasitic homosexual community—that larger society where
most of us imagine we are at home. Emerging from the little
world of homosexual crime which still concerned him in *Death-
watch* and *The Maids,* he brought the truths he had learned
there to bear on the complacencies of the "normal" world which
for so long had banished and condemned him. His most scathing
critique of sexual politics is found in his most recent works for
the theater, *The Blacks, The Balcony,* and *The Screens.*

What he has to tell this snug and pious enclave will hardly
furnish it with the reassuring bromides they have begun to feel
the need of and take as a balm from old retainers like Norman
Mailer and Henry Miller. Genet submits the entire social code

of "masculine" and "feminine" to a disinterested scrutiny and concludes that it is odious.

If Armand is but a brute and a fool, there is really, as Genet demonstrates, no cause for surprise. He was schooled to be such through every element in his education and was clearly given to understand that these traits were no less than the fulfillment of his very nature as a male. All he has learned has taught him to identify "masculine" with force, cruelty, indifference, egotism, and property. It is no wonder that he regards his penis as a talisman: both an instrument to oppress and the very symbol, in fact the reality, of his status: "My cock," he once said, "is worth its weight in gold. . . ." At other times he boasts that he can lift a heavy man on the end of it. Armand automatically associates sexuality with power, with his solitary pleasure, and with the pain and humiliation of his partner, who is nothing but an object to him in the most literal sense. Intercourse is an assertion of mastery, one that announces his own higher caste and proves it upon a victim who is expected to surrender, serve, and be satisfied.

Armand, for all his turpitude, is at once both more primitive and more logical than a "gentleman," more honest and direct than the respectable bourgeois whose real convictions he has simply put into practice, and who, by no accident, enjoys reading such passages for the vicarious illusion of mastery which he fancies is offered therein.

The Balcony is Genet's theory of revolution and counter-revolution. The play is set in a brothel and concerns a revolution which ends in failure, preempted by the patrons and staff of the Balcony who assume the roles of the former government. Having studied human relationships in the world of pimp and faggot, Genet has come to understand how sexual caste supersedes all other forms of inegalitarianism: racial, political, or economic. *The Balcony* demonstrates the futility of all forms of revolution which preserve intact the basic unit of exploitation and oppression, that between the sexes, male and female, or any of the substitutes for them. Taking the fundamental human connection, that of sexuality, to be the nuclear model of all the more elaborate social constructs growing out of it, Genet perceives that it is in itself not only hopelessly tainted but the very prototype of institutionalized inequality. He is convinced that by dividing humanity into two groups and appointing one to rule over the other by virtue of birthright, the social order has already established and ratified a system of oppression which will underlie and corrupt all other human relationships as well as every area of thought and experience.

The first scene, which takes place between a prostitute and a bishop, epitomizes the play much as it does the society it describes. The cleric holds power only through the myth of religion, itself dependent on the fallacy of sin, in turn conditional on the lie that the female is sexuality itself and therefore an evil worthy of the bishop's condign punishment. By such devious routes does power circle round and round the hopeless mess we have made of sexuality. And money: for it is with money that the woman is purchased, and economic dependency is but another sign of her bondage to a system whose coercive agents are not only mythical but actual. Delusions about sex foster delusions of power, and both depend on the reification of woman.

That the Bishop is actually a gasman visiting the bordello's "chambers of illusions" so that he can vicariously share in the power of the church only clarifies this satire on the sexual class system. Those males relegated to reading gas meters may still participate in the joys of mastery through the one human being any male can buy—a female as whore. And the whore, one wonders, what profits her? Nothing. Her "role" in the ritual theater where sexual, political, and social institutions are so felicitously combined is merely to accommodate the ruling passion of each of her rentiers.

In the second scene, the whore is a thief and a criminal (versions of Genet himself) so that a bank clerk may play at justice and morality. Her judge may order her whipped by a muscular executioner or grant her mercy in a transcendent imitation of the powers-that-be, powers reserved to other more fortunate males. The General of Scene III, following his own notions of masculine majesty, converts his whore into his mount and plays at hero while her mouth bleeds from the bit. No matter with which of the three leading roles of sinner, malefactor, or animal the male client may choose to mime his delusions of grandeur, the presence of the woman is utterly essential. To each masquerading male the female is a mirror in which he beholds himself. And the penultimate moment in his illusory but purchasable power fantasy is the moment when whether as Bishop, Judge, or General, he "fucks" her as woman, as subject, as chattel.

The political wisdom implicit in Genet's statement in the play is that unless the ideology of real or fantasized virility is abandoned, unless the clinging to male supremacy as a birthright is finally foregone, all systems of oppression will continue to function simply by virtue of their logical and emotional mandate in the primary human situation. But what of the madame herself? Irma, the Balcony's able and dedicated administrator, makes money by selling other women, wherein it may be observed how no institution holds sway without collaborators and overseers. Chosen as queen under the counterrevolution Irma does nothing at all, for queens do not rule. In fact, they do not even exist in themselves; they die as persons once they assume their function, as the Envoy graciously explains. Their function is to serve as figureheads and abstractions to males, just as Chantal, a talented former whore who moves for a moment toward human realization by means of her hope in the revolution, wavers and then is sold anew and converted into the sexual figurehead for the uprising when it becomes corrupt and betrays its radical ideals under the usual excuse of expediency. "In order to win" it adopts the demented consciousness of its opponent and establishes a rotten new version of all it had once stood against. In no time it turns the rebellion into a suicidal carnival, an orgy of blood connected to the old phallic fantasy of "shoot and screw." Its totem is the ritual scapegoat provided by every army's beauty queen since Troy. Once Chantal enters upon the mythical territory of a primitive standard and prize over whom males will tear each other apart, the revolution passes irrevocably into counterrevolution.

Throughout *The Balcony* Genet explores the pathology of virility, the chimera of sexual congress as a paradigm of power over other human beings. He appears to be the only living male writer of first-class literary gifts to have transcended the sexual myths of our era. His critique of the heterosexual politic points the way toward a true sexual revolution, a path which must be explored if any radical social change is to come about. In Genet's analysis, it is fundamentally impossible to change society without changing personality, and sexual personality as it has generally existed must undergo the most drastic overhaul.

If we are to be free at last, Genet proposes in the last scenes of the play, we must first break those chains of our own making through our blind acceptance of common ideas. The three great cages in which we are immured must be dismantled. The first is the potential power of the "Great Figures"—the cleric, the judge, and the warrior—elements of myth which have enslaved consciousness in a coil of self-imposed absurdity. The second is the omnipotence of the police state, the only virtual power in a corrupt society, all other forms of coercion being largely psychological. Last, and most insidious of all, is the cage of sex, the cage in which all others are enclosed: for is not the totem of Police Chief George a six-foot, rubber phallus, a "prick of great stature"? And the old myth of sin and virtue, the myth of guilt and innocence, the myth of heroism and cowardice on which the Great Figures repose, old pillars of an old and decadent structure, are also built on the sexual fallacy. (Or as one is tempted to pun, phallacy.) By attempting to replace this corrupt and tottering edifice while preserving its foundations, the revolution's own bid for social transformation inevitably fails and turns into the counterrevolution where the Grand Balcony, a first-class whorehouse, furnishes both costumes and actors for the new pseudo government.

Genet's play ends as it had begun. Irma turning out the lights informs us we may go home, where all is falser than the theater's rites. The brothel will open again tomorrow for an identical ritual. The sounds of revolution begin again offstage, but unless the Police Chief is permanently imprisoned in his tomb and unless the new rebels have truly forsworn the customary idiocy of the old sexual politics, there will be no revolution. Sex is deep at the heart of our troubles, Genet is urging, and unless we eliminate the most pernicious of our systems of oppression, unless we go to the very center of the sexual politic and its sick delirium of power and violence, all our efforts at liberation will only land us again in the same primordial stews.

NORMAN O. BROWN

THE RESURRECTION OF THE BODY

The path of sublimation, which mankind has religiously followed at least since the foundation of the first cities, is no way out of the human neurosis, but, on the contrary, leads to its aggravation. Psychoanalytical theory and the bitter facts of contemporary history suggest that mankind is reaching the end of this road. Psychoanalytical theory declares that the end of the road is the dominion of death-in-life. History has brought mankind to that pinnacle on which the total obliteration of mankind is at last a practical possibility. At this moment of history the friends of the life instinct must warn that the victory of death is by no means impossible; the malignant death instinct can unleash those hydrogen bombs. For if we discard our fond illusion that the human race has a privileged or providential status in the life of the universe, it seems plain that the malignant death instinct is a built-in guarantee that the human experiment, if it fails to attain its possible perfection, will cancel itself out, as the dinosaur experiment

253

canceled itself out. But jeremiads are useless unless we can point to a better way. Therefore the question confronting mankind is the abolition of repression—in traditional Christian language, the resurrection of the body.

We have already done what we could to extract from psychoanalytical theory a model of what the resurrected body would be like. The life instinct, or sexual instinct, demands activity of a kind that, in contrast to our current mode of activity, can only be called play. The life instinct also demands a union with others and with the world around us based not an anxiety and aggression but on narcissism and erotic exuberance.

But the death instinct also demands satisfaction; as Hegel says in the *Phenomenology*, "The life and knowledge of God may doubtless be described as love playing with itself; but this idea sinks into triviality, if the seriousness, the pain, the patience and the labor of the Negative are omitted." [1] The death instinct is reconciled with the life instinct only in a life which is not repressed, which leaves no "unlived lines" in the human body, the death instinct then being affirmed in a body which is willing to die. And, because the body is satisfied, the death instinct no longer drives it to change itself and make history, and therefore, as Christian theology divined, its activity is in eternity.

At the same time—and here again Christian theology and psychoanalysis agree—the resurrected body is the transfigured body. The abolition of repression would abolish the unnatural concentrations engineered by the negativity of the morbid death instinct, and constituting the bodily base of the neurotic character disorders in the human ego. In the words of Thoreau: "We need pray for no higher heaven than the pure senses can furnish, a purely sensuous life. Our present senses are but rudiments of what they are destined to become." [2] The human body would become polymorphously perverse, delighting in that full life of all the body which it now fears. The consciousness strong enough to endure full life would be no longer Apollonian but Dionysian —consciousness which does not observe the limit, but overflows; consciousness which does not negate any more.

If the question facing mankind is the abolition of repression, psychoanalysis is not the only point of view from which the question can and should be raised. We have already indicated that the question is intrinsic to Christian theology. The time has come to ask Christian theologians, especially the neo-orthodox, what they mean by the resurrection of the body and by eternal life. Is this a promise of immortality after death? In other words, is the psychological premise of Christianity the impossibility of reconciling life and death either in "this" world or the "next," so that flight from death—with all its morbid consequences—is our eternal fate in "this world" and in "the next"? For we have seen that the perfect body, promised by Christian theology, enjoying that perfect felicity promised by Christian theology, is a body reconciled with death.

In the last analysis Christian theology must either accept death as part of life or abandon the body. For two thousand years Christianity has kept alive the mystical hope of an ultimate victory of Life over Death, during a phase of human history when Life was at war with Death and hope could only be mystical. But if we are approaching the last days, Christian theology might ask itself whether it is only the religion of fallen humanity, or whether it might be asleep when the bridegroom comes. Certain it is that if Christianity wishes to help mankind toward that erasure of the traces of original sin which Baudelaire said was the true definition of progress,[3] there are priceless insights in its tradition—insights which have to be transformed into a system of practical therapy, something like psychoanalysis, before they are useful or even meaningful.

The speciality of Christian eschatology lies precisely in its rejection of the Platonic hostility to the human body and to "matter," its refusal to identify the Platonic path of sublimation with ultimate salvation, and its affirmation that eternal life can only be life in a body. Christian asceticism can carry punishment of the fallen body to heights inconceivable to Plato; but Christian hope is for the redemption of that fallen body. Hence the affirmation of Tertullian: *Resurget igitur caro, et quidem omnis, et quidem ipsa, et quidem integra*—The body will rise again, all of the body, the identical body, the entire body.[4] The medieval Catholic synthesis between Christianity and Greek philosophy, with its notion of an immortal soul, compromised and confused the issue; only Protestantism carries the full burden of the peculiar Christian faith. Luther's break with the doctrine of sublimation (good works) is decisive; but the theologian of the resurrected body is the cobbler of Görlitz, Jacob Boehme. When Tillich and Barth finally get round to the substance of things hoped for, their eschatology, they will have to reckon with Boehme. Meanwhile, as neo-orthodox theology plunges deeper into the nature of sin and death, Boehme's *theologia ex idea vitae deducta* is neglected except by the lonely mystic and revolutionary Berdyaev.[5]

Whatever the Christian churches do with him, Boehme's position in the Western tradition of mystic hope of better things is central and assured. Backward he is linked, through Paracelsus and alchemy, to the tradition of Christian gnosticism and Jewish cabalism; forward he is linked, through his influence on the romantics Blake, Novalis, and Hegel, with Freud. We have argued that psychoanalysis has not psychoanalyzed itself until it places itself inside the history of Western thought—inside the general neurosis of mankind. So seen, psychoanalysis is the heir to a mystical tradition which it must affirm.

Mysticism, in the mind of the general public, is identified with that flight from the material world and from life preached by such popularizers as Evelyn Underhill and Aldous Huxley[6]—which, from the psychoanalytical point of view, may be termed Apollonian or sublimation mysticism. But there is in the Western tradition another kind of mysticism, which can be called Dionysian or body mysticism, which stays with life, which is the body, and seeks to transform and perfect it. Western body mysticism—a tradition which urgently needs re-examination—contains three main strands: the Christian (Pauline) notion of the "spiritual" body, the Jewish (cabalistic) notion of Adam's perfect body before the Fall, and the alchemical notion of the subtle body.[7] All of these strands unite in Boehme, and even a little knowledge of the real Boehme—for example Ernst Benz' first-rate book, not available in English[8]—makes it plain that Boehme and Freud have too much in common to be able to dispense with each other.

Boehme, like Freud, understands death not as a mere nothing but as a positive force either in dialectical conflict with life (in fallen man), or dialectically unified with life (in God's perfection). Thus, says Benz, "Our life remains a struggle between life and death, and as long as this conflict lasts, anxiety lasts also." [9] In Boehme's concept of life, the concept of play, or love-play, is as central as it is in Freud's; and his concept of the spiritual or paradisical body of Adam before the Fall recognizes the potent demand in our unconscious both for an androgynous mode of being and for a narcissistic mode of self-expression, as well as the corruption in our current use of the oral, anal, and genital functions. It is true that Boehme does not yet accept the brutal death of the individual physical body, and therefore makes his paradisical body ambiguously immaterial, without oral, anal, and genital organs; and yet he clings obstinately to the body and to bodily pleasure, and therefore says that Adam was "magically" able to eat and enjoy the "essence" of things, and "magically" able to reproduce and to have sexual pleasure in the act of reproduction. Boehme is caught in these dilemmas because of his insight into the corruption of the human body, his insight that all life is life in the body, and, on the other hand, his inability to accept a body which dies. No Protestant theologian has gone further; or rather, later Protestantism has preferred to repress the problem and to repress Boehme.

Oriental mysticism also, to judge from Needham's survey of Taoism or Eliade's study of Yoga,[10] has reached the same point. Needham (quoting Maspero) is right in stressing that the Taoist quest for a more perfect body transcends the Platonic dualism of soul and matter. But Needham's enthusiasm for Taoism as a human and organismic response to life in the world must be qualified by recognizing that the Taoist perfect body is immortal: Taoism does not accept death as part of life.

Psychoanalysis accepts the death of the body; but psychoanalysis has something to learn from body mysticism, occidental and oriental, over and above the wealth of psychoanalytical insights contained in it. For these mystics take seriously, and traditional psychoanalysis does not, the possibility of human perfectibility and the hope of finding a way out of the human neurosis into that simple health that animals enjoy, but not man.

As Protestantism degenerated from Luther and Boehme, it

abandoned its religious function of criticizing the existing order and keeping alive the mystical hope of better things; in psychoanalytical terminology, it lost contact with the unconscious and with the immortal repressed desires of the unconscious. The torch passed to the poets and philosophers of the romantic movement. The heirs of Boehme are Blake, Novalis, Hegel, and, as Professor Gray has recently shown, Goethe.[11] These are the poets whom Freud credited with being the real discoverers of the unconscious.[12]

Not only toward the mystics but also toward the poets psychoanalysis must quit its pretension of supramundane superiority. Instead of exposing the neuroses of the poets, the psychoanalysts might learn from them, and abandon the naive idea that there is an immense gap, in mental health and intellectual objectivity, between themselves and the rest of the world. In the world's opinion, in the eyes of common sense, Novalis is crazy, and Ferenczi also: the world will find it easier to believe that we are all mad than to believe that the psychoanalysts are not. And further, it does not seem to be the case that the psychoanalytical mode of reaching the unconscious has superannuated the poetic, or artistic, mode of attaining the same objective. Anyone conversant both with modern literature and with psychoanalysis knows that modern literature is full of psychoanalytical insights not yet grasped, or not so clearly grasped, by "scientific" psychoanalysis. And anyone who loves art knows that psychoanalysis has no monopoly on the power to heal. What the times call for is an end to the war between psychoanalysis and art—a war kept alive by the sterile "debunking" approach of psychoanalysis to art—and the beginning of cooperation between the two in the work of therapy and in the task of making the unconscious. A little more Eros and less strife.

Modern poetry, like psychoanalysis and Protestant theology, faces the problem of the resurrection of the body. Art and poetry have always been altering our ways of sensing and feeling—that is to say, altering the human body. And Whitehead rightly discerns as the essence of the "Romantic Reaction" a revulsion against abstraction (in psychoanalytical terms, sublimation) in favor of the concrete sensual organism, the human body.[13]

"Energy is the only life, and is from the Body . . . Energy is Eternal Delight," says Blake.

A young critic, whose first book represents a new mode of criticism—a criticism for which poetry is an experience both mystical and bodily—has traced the persistent quest in modern poetry for the resurrection of the body and the perfection of the body.[14] Wordsworth, in contrast with the sublime (and sublimating) tendency of Milton, "considers that his revelation can be expressed in the forms and symbols of daily life" and "sees Paradise possible in any sweet though bare nook of the earth." Hopkins "is engaged in a theodicy, and has taken for his province the stubborn senses and the neglected physical world"; "no one has gone further than Hopkins in presenting Christ as the direct and omnipresent object of perception, so deeply ingrained in the eyes, the flesh, and the bone (and the personal sense of having eyes, flesh, and bone), that the sense of self and the sense of being in Christ can no longer be distinguished." Rilke's plaint throughout his career is that "we do not know the body any more than we know nature": Rilke believes (in his own words) that "the qualities are to be taken away from God, the no longer utterable, and returned to creation, to love and death"; so that the outcome of his poetry is that "for Rilke, the body becomes a spiritual fact." Valery's poetry "may be considered as the Odyssey of Consciousness in search of its true body"; and "the intellectual pursuit of Valery is to this end, that the body may be seen as what it virtually is, a magnificent revelation and instrument of the soul. Could it be viewed as such, the eyes would not be symbol, but reality." [15]

The "magical" body which the poet seeks is the "subtle" or "spiritual" or "translucent" body of occidental mysticism, and the "diamond" body of oriental mysticism, and, in psychoanalysis, the polymorphously perverse body of childhood. Thus, for example, psychoanalysis declares the fundamentally bisexual character of human nature; Boehme insists on the androgynous character of human perfection; Taoist mysticism invokes feminine passivity to counteract masculine aggressivity; and Rilke's poetic quest is a quest for a hermaphroditic body.[16] There is an urgent need for elucidation of the interrelations between these disparate modes of articulating the desires of the unconscious. Jung is aware of these interrelations, and orthodox psychoanalysts have not been aware of them. But no elucidation results from incorporation of the data into the Jungian system, not so much because of the intellectual disorder in the system, but rather because of the fundamental orientation of Jung, which is flight from the problem of the body, flight from the concept of repression, and a return to the path of sublimation. Freudianism must face the issue, and Freud himself said: "Certain practices of the mystics may succeed in upsetting the normal relations between the different regions of the mind, so that, for example, the perceptual system becomes able to grasp relations in the deeper layers of the ego and in the id which would otherwise be inaccessible to it." [17]

Joseph Needham's interest in what we have called body mysticism, an interest which underlies his epoch-making work *Science and Civilization in China*, reminds us that the resurrection of the body has been placed on the agenda not only by psychoanalysis, mysticism, and poetry, but also by the philosophical criticism of modern science. Whitehead's criticism of scientific abstraction is, in psychoanalytical terms, a criticism of sublimation. His protest against "The Fallacy of Misplaced Concreteness" is a protest on behalf of the living body as a whole: "But the living organ of experience is the living body as a whole"; and his protest "on behalf of value" insists that the real structure of the human body, of human cognition, and of the events cognized is both sensuous and erotic, "self-enjoyment." [18] Whitehead himself recognized the affinity between himself and the romantic poets; and Needham of course recognizes the affinity between the philosophy of organism and mysticism. Actually Needham may be exaggerating the uniqueness of Taoism. The whole Western alchemical tradition, which urgently needs re-examination, is surely "Whiteheadian" in spirit, and Goethe, the last of the alchemists, in his "Essay on the Metamorphosis of Plants" produced the last, or the first, Whiteheadian scientific treatise. Goethe, says a modern biologist, "reached out to the reconciliation of the antithesis between the senses and the intellect, an antithesis with which traditional science does not attempt to cope." [19]

Needham has recognized the crucial role of psychology in the philosophy of science. The refutation of Descartes, he has said, will come from psychology, not biology.[20] And yet he seems to be unaware of the profound affinities between the Tao, which he so much admires, and psychoanalysis. He seems to be unaware of Ferenczi's brilliant essay attempting to reorganize the whole theory of biological evolution in the light of psychoanalysis.[21] But the function of psychoanalysis in relation to Whitehead and Needham's critique of science is not that of supplementing their ideology with sympathetic support; rather it is indispensable if their critique of science is to amount to more than mere ideology. For what they are calling in question is the subjective attitude of the scientist, and if their critique is to amount to more than mere dislike, it must be supplemented by a psychoanalysis of the subject. In fact a psychoanalysis of the subject (the "observer") seems necessary if science is to remain "objective." The essential point has been seen by Ferenczi, who coined the term "utraquism" to indicate the required combination of analysis of the subject and analysis of the object: "If science is really to remain objective, it must work alternately as pure psychology and pure natural science, and must verify both our inner and outer experience by analogies taken from both points of view. . . . I called this the 'utraquism' of all true scientific work." [22]

Ferenczi's formulations date from 1923–1926: today we would presumably think of "integration" rather than alternation. Ferenczi saw psychoanalysis as marking a significant step forward in general scientific methodology, a step which he defined as "a return to a certain extent to the methods of ancient animistic science" and the "re-establishment of an animism no longer anthropomorphic." [23] But the re-establishment of an animism is precisely the outcome of Whitehead and Needham's line of thought. And Ferenczi argues that psychoanalysis is necessary in order to differentiate the new "purified" animism from the old naive animism: [24]

Insofar as Freud attempts to solve problems of biology as well as of sexual activity by means of psychoanalytic experience, he returns to a certain extent to the methods of ancient animistic science. There is a safeguard, however, against the psychoanalyst falling into the error of such naive animism. Naive animism transferred human psychic life *en bloc* without analysis onto natural objects. Psychoanalysis, however, dissected human psychic activity, pursued it to the limit where psychic and physical came into contact, down to the instincts, and thus freed psychology from anthropocentrism, and only then did it trust itself to evaluate this purified animism in terms of biology. To have been the first in the history of science to make this attempt is the achievement of Freud.

We therefore conclude with a plea for "utraquistic" integration between psychoanalysis and the philosophy of science. Ferenczi, in his important analysis of Ernst Mach entitled "The Psychogenesis of Mechanism," put it this way: "When will the physicist, who finds the soul in the mechanism, and the psychoanalyst, who perceives mechanisms in the soul, join hands and work with united forces at a Weltanschauung free from one-sidedness and 'idealizations'?" [25]

Perhaps there are even deeper issues raised by the confrontation between psychoanalysis and the philosophy of organism. Whitehead and Needham are protesting against the inhuman attitude of modern science; in psychoanalytical terms, they are calling for a science based on an erotic sense of reality, rather than an aggressive dominating attitude toward reality. From this point of view alchemy (and Goethe's essay on plants) might be said to be the last effort of Western man to produce a science based on an erotic sense of reality. And conversely, modern science, as criticized by Whitehead, is one aspect of a total cultural situation which may be described as the dominion of death-in-life. The mentality which was able to reduce nature to "a dull affair, soundless, scentless, colourless; merely the hurrying of material endlessly, meaninglessly"—Whitehead's description [26]— is lethal. It is an awe-inspiring attack on the life of the universe;

in more technical psychoanalytical terms, its anal-sadistic intent is plain. And further, the only historian of science who uses psychoanalysis, Gaston Bachelard, concludes that it is of the essence of the scientific spirit to be mercilessly ascetic, to eliminate human enjoyment from our relation to nature, to eliminate the human senses, and finally to eliminate the human brain: [27]

It does seem that with the twentieth century there begins a kind of scientific thought in opposition to the senses, and that it is necessary to construct a theory of objectivity in opposition to the object. . . . It follows that the entire use of the brain is being called into question. From now on the brain is strictly no longer adequate as an instrument for scientific thought; that is to say, the brain is the obstacle to scientific thought. It is an obstacle in the sense that it is the coordinating center for human movements and appetites. It is necessary to think in opposition to the brain.

Thus modern science confirms Ferenczi's aphorism: *"Pure intelligence* is thus a product of dying, or at least of becoming mentally insensitive, and is therefore *in principle madness."* [28]

What Whitehead and Needham are combating is not an error but a disease in consciousness. In more technical psychoanalytical terms, the issue is not the conscious premises of science; the trouble is in the unconscious straits of the scientific ego, in the scientific character-structure. Whitehead called the modern scientific point of view, in spite of its world-conquering successes, "quite unbelievable." [29] Psychoanalysis adds the crucial point of view. It is unlikely that problems generated in the mechanistic system will lead to organismic solutions. The two points of view represent different instinctual orientations, different fusions of life and death. It is even doubtful that the adoption of an organismic point of view under present conditions would be a gain; it might be a relapse into naive animism. Thus the kind of thinking which Needham hails as Taoist wisdom (alchemy, etc.), is attacked by Bachelard as unconscious projection, dreaming, and naive mythologizing; he sees science (and psychoanalysis) as sternly committed to the task of demythologizing our view of nature. It would seem therefore, in line with Ferenczi's argument, that Taoist ideology without psychoanalytical consciousness could be a relapse into naive animism. And psychoanalytical consciousness means psychoanalytical therapy also. Psychoanalytical therapy involves a solution to the problem of repression; what is needed is not an organismic ideology, but to change the human body so that it can become for the first time an organism —the resurrection of the body. An organism whose own sexual life is as disordered as man's is is in no position to construct objective theories about the Yin and the Yang and the sex life of the universe.

The resurrection of the body is a social project facing mankind as a whole, and it will become a practical political problem when the statesmen of the world are called upon to deliver happiness instead of power, when political economy becomes a science of use-values instead of exchange-values—a science of enjoyment instead of a science of accumulation. In the face of this tremendous human problem, contemporary social theory, both capitalist and socialist, has nothing to say. Contemporary social theory (again we must honor Veblen as an exception) has been completely taken in by the inhuman abstractions of the path of sublimation, and has no contact with concrete human beings, with their concrete bodies, their concrete though repressed desires, and their concrete neuroses.

To find social theorists who are thinking about the real problem of our age, we have to go back to the Marx of 1844, or even to the philosophers influencing Marx in 1844, Fourier and Feuerbach. From Fourier's psychological analysis of the antithesis of work and pleasure Marx obtained the concept of play, and used it, in a halfhearted way to be sure, in some of his early utopian speculations. From Feuerbach Marx learned the necessity of moving from Hegelian abstractions to the concrete senses and the concrete human body. Marx' "philosophic-economic manuscripts" of 1844 contain remarkable formulations calling for the resurrection of human nature, the appropriation of the human body, the transformation of the human senses, and the realization of a state of self-enjoyment. Thus, for example, "Man appropriates himself as an all-sided being in an all-sided way, hence as total man.

[This appropriation lies in] every one of his human relationships to the world—seeing, hearing, smell, taste, feeling, thought, perception, experience, wishing, activity, loving, in short, all organs of his individuality." [30] The human physical senses must be emancipated from the sense of possession, and then the humanity of the senses and the human enjoyment of the senses will be achieved for the first time. Here is the point of contact between Marx and Freud: I do not see how the profundities and obscurities of the "philosophic-economic manuscripts" can be elucidated except with the aid of psychoanalysis.

Psychoanalysis, mysticism, poetry, the philosophy of organism, Feuerbach, and Marx—this is a miscellaneous assemblage; but, as Heraclitus said the unseen harmony is stronger than the seen. Common to all of them is a mode of consciousness that can be called—although the term causes fresh difficulties—the dialectical imagination. By "dialectical" I mean an activity of consciousness struggling to circumvent the limitations imposed by the formal-logical law of contradiction. Marxism, of course, has no monopoly of "dialectics." Needham has shown the dialectical character of Whitehead's philosophy, and he constantly draws attention to dialectical patterns in mystical thought.[31] The goal of Indian body mysticism, according to Eliade, is the "conjunction of contrarieties" (*coincidentia oppositorum*). Scholem, in his survey of Jewish mysticism, says, "Mysticism, intent on formulating the paradoxes of religious experience, uses the instrument of dialectics to express its meaning. The Kabbalists are by no means the only witnesses to this affinity between mystical and dialectical thinking." [32]

As for poetry, are not those basic poetic devices emphasized by recent criticism—paradox, ambiguity, irony, tension—devices whereby the poetic imagination subverts the "reasonableness" of language, the chains it imposes? And from the psychoanalytical point of view, if we, with Trilling, accept the substantial identity between poetic logic (with its symbolism, condensation of meaning, and displacement of accent) and dream logic, then the connection between poetry and dialectics, as defined, is more substantially grounded. Dreams are certainly an activity of the mind struggling to circumvent the formal-logical law of contradiction.[33]

Psychoanalytical thinking has a double relation to the dialectical imagination. It is, on the one hand (actually or potentially), a mode of dialectical consciousness; on the other hand, it contains, or ought to contain, a theory about the nature of the dialectical imagination. I say "actually or potentially" because psychoanalysis, either as a body of doctrine or an experience of the analysand, is no total revelation of the unconscious repressed. The struggle of consciousness to circumvent the limitations of formal logic, of language, and of "common sense" is under conditions of general repression never ending (see Freud's essay, "Analysis Terminable and Interminable").[34] "Dialectical" are those psychoanalysts who continue this struggle; for the rest, psychoanalytical terminology can be a prison house of Byzantine scholasticism in which "word-consciousness" is substituting for consciousness of the unconscious.

And even if we take Freud as the model of psychoanalytical consciousness, we have argued that at such crucial points as the relation between the two instincts and the relation between humanity and animality, Freud is trapped because he is not sufficiently "dialectical." Nevertheless, the basic structure of Freud's thought is committed to dialectics, because it is committed to the vision of mental life as basically an arena of conflict; and his finest insights (for example, that when the patient denies something, he affirms it) [35] are incurably "dialectical." Hence the attempt to make psychoanalysis out to be "scientific" (in the positivist sense) is not only vain but destructive.[36] Empirical verification, the positivist test of science, can apply only to that which is fully in consciousness; but psychoanalysis is a mode of contacting the unconscious under conditions of general repression, when the unconscious remains in some sense repressed. To put the matter another way, the "poetry" in Freud's thought cannot be purged away, or rather such an expurgation is exactly what is accomplished in "scientific" textbooks of psychology; but Freud's writings remain unexpurgatable. The same "poetical" imagination marks the work of Roheim and Ferenczi and explains why they are superior. The whole nature of the "dialectical" or "poetical" imagination is another problem urgently needing examination; and there is a particular need for psychoanalysis, as part of the psychoanalysis of psychoanalysis, to become conscious of the dialectical, poetical, mystical stream that runs in its blood.

The key to the nature of dialectical thinking may lie in psychoanalysis, more specifically in Freud's psychoanalysis of negation. There is first the theorem that "there is nothing in the id which can be compared to negation," and that the law of contradiction does not hold in the id. Similarly, the dream does not seem to recognize the word "no." [37] Instead of the law of contradiction we find a unity of opposites: "Dreams show a special tendency to reduce two opposites to a unity"; "Any thing in a dream may mean its opposite." [38] We must therefore entertain the hypothesis that there is an important connection between being "dialectical" and dreaming, just as there is between dreaming and poetry or mysticism. Furthermore, in his essay "The Antithetical Sense of Primal Words" [39] Freud compares the linguistic phenomenon of a hidden (in the etymological root) identity between words with antithetical meanings; he reveals the significant fact that it was the linguistic phenomenon that gave him the clue to the dream phenomenon, and not vice versa. It is plain that both psychoanalysis and the study of language (philosophical and philological) need a marriage or at least a meeting.

And, on the other hand, Freud's essay "On Negation" [40] may throw a light on the nature of the "dialectical" dissatisfaction with formal logic. Negation is the primal act of repression; but it at the same time liberates the mind to think about the repressed under the general condition that it is denied and thus remains essentially repressed. With Spinoza's formula *omnis determinatio est negatio* in mind, examine the following formulations of Freud: "A negative judgement is the intellectual substitute for repression; the 'No' in which it is expressed is the hall-mark of repression. . . . By the help of the symbol of negation, the thinking process frees itself with the subject-matter without which it could not work efficiently." But: "Negation only assists in undoing one of the consequences of repression—the fact that the subject-matter of the image in question is unable to enter consciousness. The result is a kind of intellectual acceptance of what is repressed, though in all essentials the repression persists." [41]

We may therefore entertain the hypothesis that formal logic and the law of contradiction are the rules whereby the mind submits to operate under general conditions of repression. As with the concept of time, Kant's categories of rationality would then turn out to be the categories of repression. And conversely, "dialectical" would be the struggle of the mind to circumvent repression and make the unconscious conscious. But by the same token, it would be the struggle of the mind to overcome the split and conflict within itself. It could then be identified with that "synthesizing" tendency in the ego of which Freud spoke,[42] and with that attempt to cure, inside the neurosis itself, on which Freud came finally to place his hope for therapy.[43] As an attempt to unify and to cure, the "dialectical" consciousness would be a manifestation of Eros. And, as consciousness trying to throw off the fetters of negation, the "dialectical" consciousness would be a step toward that Dionysian ego which does not negate any more.[44]

What the great world needs, of course, is a little more Eros and less strife; but the intellectual world needs it just as much. A little more Eros would make conscious the unconscious harmony between "dialectical" dreamers of all kinds—psychoanalysts, political idealists, mystics, poets, philosophers—and abate the sterile and ignorant polemics. Since the ignorance seems to be mostly a matter of self-ignorance, a little more psychoanalytical consciousness on all sides (including the psychoanalysts) might help—a little more self-knowledge, humility, humanity, and Eros. We may therefore conclude with the concluding words of Freud's *Civilization and Its Discontents:* [45]

> Men have brought their powers of subduing the forces of nature to such a pitch that by using them they could now very easily exterminate one another to the last man. They know this—hence arises a great part of their current unrest, their dejection, their mood of apprehension. And now it may be expected that the other of the two "heavenly forces," eternal Eros, will put forth his strength so as to maintain himself alongside of his equally immortal adversary.

And perhaps our children will live to live a full life, and so see what Freud could not see—in the old adversary, a friend.

NOTES

1. Hegel, *Phenomenology of Mind,* p. 81.
2. Thoreau, *A Week on the Concord and Merrimack Rivers;* cf. Read, *Icon and Idea,* p. 139.
3. Baudelaire, *Mon coeur mis à nu.* Cf. Marcuse, *Eros and Civilization,* p. 153.
4. Tertullian, *De Carnis Resurrectione,* p. 63. Cf. Mead, *The Doctrine of the Subtle Body in Western Tradition,* p. 111.
5. See above, chap. IX, note 58.
6. Underhill, *Mysticism;* Huxley, *The Perennial Philosophy.*
7. Mead, *The Doctrine of the Subtle Body in Western Tradition:* Scholem, *Major Trends in Jewish Mysticism:* Gray, *Goethe the Alchemist.* Cf. Savage, "Jung, Alchemy and Self," pp. 14–37.
8. Benz, *Der vollkommene Mensch nach Jacob Boehme.*
9. Benz, *op. cit.,* p. 138.
10. Needham, *Science and Civilization in China,* II, 139–54. Needham seems to underestimate Occidental body mysticism; cf. *op. cit.,* p. 464, the only reference to Boehme. See also Watts, "Asian Psychology and Modern Psychiatry," pp. 25–30.
11. Gray, *Goethe the Alchemist.*
12. See above, chap. V, note 22.
13. Whitehead, *Science and the Modern World,* pp. 93–118.
14. Hartman, *The Unmediated Vision.*
15. Hartman, *op. cit.,* pp. 27–28, 57, 64, 94, 96, 107, 109.
16. See above, chap. IX, notes 56–60.
17. NIL, 106.
18. See above, chap. XV, note 9.
19. Cf. Gray, *Goethe the Alchemist,* pp. 98–99.
20. Needham, "Mechanistic Biology," in *Science, Religion and Reality,* p. 257.
21. Ferenczi, *Thalassa.*
22. Ferenczi, *Further Contributions,* p. 373.
23. Ferenczi, *Further Contributions,* p. 256; *Thalassa,* p. 2.
24. Ferenczi, *Further Contributions,* p. 256.
25. Ferenczi, *Further Contributions,* p. 393.
26. Whitehead, *Science and the Modern World,* p. 69.
27. Bachelard, *La formation de l'esprit scientifique,* pp. 250–51.
28. Ferenczi, *Further Contributions,* p. 246.
29. Whitehead, *Science and the Modern World,* p. 69.

30. Marx, Engels, *Kleine ökonomische Schriften,* p. 131; cf. pp. 127–37.

31. Needham, "A Biologist's View of Whitehead's Philosophy," in Schilpp (ed.), *The Philosophy of Alfred North Whitehead,* pp. 241–72; Needham, *Science and Civilization in China,* II, 75–77, 291, 454, 467.

32. Eliade, *Le Yoga,* pp. 110, 258, 269; Scholem, *Major Trends in Jewish Mysticism,* p. 218.

33. Cf. the role of paradox in philosophy: Wisdom, *Philosophy and Psychoanalysis,* pp. 169–81, 248–82.

34. CP V, 316–57.

35. CP V, 181–82.

36. For the positivist approach to psychoanalysis, see Kris, "The Nature of Psychoanalytical Propositions and Their Validation," pp. 239–59; Frenkel-Brunswik, "Psychoanalysis and the Unity of Science," pp. 273–347; Pumpian-Mindlin (ed.), *Psychoanalysis and Science.*

37. BW (Dreams), 345–46; NIL, 99; CP III, 559n; CP IV, 119, 184; CP V, 185.

38. CP IV, 184; BW (Dreams), 346n.

39. CP IV, 184–91. Cf. BW (Dreams), 346n.

40. CP V, 181–5.

41. CP V, 182. Cf. CP III, 559n; CP IV, 119.

42. See above, chap. VII, note 13.

43. CP V, 369–71.

44. See above, chap. XII, note 70.

45. *Civ.* 144.

GEORGES BATAILLE

THE ENIGMA OF INCEST

How indeed could we not define incest with [obscenity] as a starting point? We cannot say that such and such a thing is obscene. Obscenity is relative. There is no "obscenity" in the sense that there is "fire" or "blood," but only in the way that an "outrage to modesty" exists. Such and such a thing is obscene if this or that person thinks it is and says so; it is not exactly an object, but a relationship between an object and the mind of a person. In this sense we can define situations of which given aspects are or at least seem to be obscene. Moreover, these situations are unstable and always presuppose certain ill-defined elements; or else what stability they have has an arbitrary character. Similarly they often have to be adapted to fit the necessities of life. Incest is a situation of this kind which has its arbitrary existence only within the mind of man.

This way of seeing it is so necessary and unavoidable that if we were unable to affirm the universality of incest we should hardly be able to demonstrate the universal character of the taboo on obscenity. Incest is the first proof of the fundamental connection between man and the denial of sensuality, of the carnal and animal.

Man has never managed to shut out sexuality except superficially or through a lack of individual vigour. Even the saints at least have their temptations. We can do nothing about it except fence off certain areas to be kept free of sexual activity. Times, occasions and people are marked off in this way: every aspect of sexuality is obscene in this place, or in these circumstances, or in the presence of these people. The different aspects, just like the places, times and persons, are variable and always arbitrarily defined. Thus nakedness is not obscene in itself. It has become obscene almost everywhere but unequally so. Genesis refers to nakedness, linking the birth of modesty with the transition from the animal to the human and this is only the feeling of obscenity in other words. But actions which outraged modesty even at the beginning of our own century do so no longer today, or much less at any rate. The relative nakedness of women on the beach is still shocking in Spain but not in France; but in a town even in France bathing suits still upset a certain number of people. In the same way a low-cut dress will not do in broad daylight but is correct wear in the evening. And the most intimate kind of nakedness is not obscene in a doctor's surgery.

In the same sort of way the reservations affecting people may shift. Theoretically the sexual contacts of people living together are limited to the inevitable conjugal relationship of the father and mother. But like the taboos on aspects of sensuality, on times and places, the limits are very uncertain and very changeable. In the first place, the expression "living together" can be used on one condition only: it must never be given a precise meaning. In this domain there are to be found as much that is arbitrary and as many adaptations as we saw there to be with nakedness. In particular the importance of convenience must be stressed. Levi-Strauss's analysis makes this very clear. The arbitrary division between relations with whom marriage is permissible and those with whom it is forbidden varies with the need to guarantee cycles of exchange. When these organised cycles cease to be of use the scope of incest diminishes. If utility no longer enters into consideration men will end by ignoring obstacles which have come to seem hopelessly arbitrary, but to counter this tendency, when the taboo has been firmly grounded it has gained in strength: its intrinsic power has been felt more forcibly. Each time it is convenient, what is more, the limits can be extended; thus with divorce proceedings in the Middle Ages where theoretical cases of incest with no basis in contemporary custom were used as a pretext for the legal dissolution of princely marriages. No matter; the point is always to set against the disorder of the animal world the essentially and unconditionally human: this mode is not without its resemblance to the English lady of Victorian days who affected to believe that the flesh and the animal urges did not really exist. Thoroughgoing social humanity cuts out the disorder of the sense altogether; it denies its own natural principle, it refuses to accept it as a fact and only admits the space of a clean and tidy house through which move worthy people at once naive and inviolable, tender and inaccessible. This symbol does not only indicate the boundaries that make the mother sacrosanct to the son, the daughter to the father. It is in a general way the image— or the sanctuary—of humanity unsexed, holding its values aloft safe from violence and sullying passion.

Let us come back to the fact that these remarks are in no sort of contradiction with Levi-Strauss's theory. The idea of an absolute denial (as absolute as possible) of the carnal and animal is inevitably situated at the very point where the two avenues explored by Levi-Strauss converge, where in fact marriage itself begins. In one sense marriage combines economic interest and purity, sensuality and the taboo on sensuality, generosity and avarice. But its first movement puts it at the other extreme; it is a gift. Levi-Strauss has shed clear light on this point. He has analysed the process so well that his interpretations show clearly what the essence of a gift is. The gift itself is a renunciation, the refusal of an immediate animal satisfaction with no strings attached. Marriage is a matter less for the partners than for the man who gives the woman away, the man whether father or brother who might have freely enjoyed the woman, daughter or sister, yet who bestows her on someone else. This gift is perhaps a substitute for the sexual act; for the exuberance of giving has a significance akin to that of the act itself: it is also a spending of resources. But the renunciation based on taboo that allows this kind of expenditure is the one thing that makes such giving possible. Even if there is some relief in giving as there is in the sexual act it is not at all a physical, animal relief; its transcendent nature belongs essentially to man. For a close relation to renounce his right, to forego the enjoyment of his own property: this is what defines human beings in complete contrast to the greedy animals. As I have said, such renunciation enhances the value of the thing renounced. But this is also a contribution to the creation of the human world in which respect, difficulty and reservations are victorious over violence. It complements eroticism which heightens the value of the object of desire. Without the counterbalance of the respect for forbidden objects of value there would be no eroticism. (There would be no complete respect if the lapse into eroticism were not both possible and full of delightful promise.)

Respect is really nothing but a devious route taken by violence. On the one hand respect keeps order in the sphere where violence is forbidden; on the other it makes it possible for violence to irrupt incongruously in fields where it has ceased to be permissible. The taboo does not alter the violence of sexual activity, but for disciplined mankind it opens a door closed to animal nature, namely the transgression of the law.

The sudden upsurge of transgression (or free eroticism) on this side, and on that the existence of an environment where sexuality is not allowed are the extreme forms of a situation where there are many middle ways. In general the sexual act is not taken to be sinful and the places in which only husbands from outside can have anything to do with the local women echoes a very old practice indeed. More often than not moderate eroticism is tolerated and where there is condemnation of sexuality, even when it appears to be stringent, it only affects the facade, the act of transgression itself being allowed as long as it is not made public. Yet only the extremes have much significance. The essential point is that circumstances do exist, however limited they may be, when eroticism is quite unthinkable, and equally there are moments of transgression when eroticism is a complete upheaval.

It would be difficult to imagine these two extremes without taking into consideration the constant flux of circumstances. Hence, the element of giving that comes into marriage (since gifts are part and parcel of celebrations and giving is a luxury, an exuberance, an absence of calculation)—this element associated with the turbulence of the feast has a strong flavour of transgression about it. But this side has certainly become blurred. Marriage is a compromise between sexual activity and respect. More and more it is coming to mean the latter. The act of marriage, the transition, has retained some of the quality of transgression it originally possessed. But in a world of mothers and sisters conjugal life stifles and to a certain extent neutralises the excesses of reproductive activity. In the process the purity on which the taboo is based, which is characteristic of the mother or the sister, slowly passes on to the wife, now a mother. Thus the state of marriage enables man to live a human life in which respect for taboo contrasts with the untrammelled satisfaction of animal needs.

LAWRENCE LIPTON

THE EROTIC REVOLUTION

What would you put in place of the old morality? There is nothing that can be put in place of the old except experimenting with
the new. And hoping that something humanly good will come
of it. In the meantime there are some measures which I would
recommend as desirable because they would help to make experiment safer and more intelligent.

Repeal all the laws and statutes regulating premarital sex.
Make legal marriage optional, as religious marriage is now
optional. Those desiring contract marriage, providing for
husband or wife in case the marriage fails, or for the children of such a marriage, should be able to make such con-
tracts and seek legal adjudication in case differences arise.
Repeal all laws making homosexuality, male or female,
illegal.
Repeal all laws making any sexual act, the so-called "unna-

tural" acts, illegal. Nature knows no unnatural sexual acts.

Make all contraceptives and abortions legal everywhere and free to all who are unable to pay.

Make all forms of mating legal if there is mutual agreement between the parties concerned.

These would do for a starter. Questions like divorce, rape, psychoneurotic sexual behavior, inheritance, and related questions like wife-swapping, infidelity, incest, and illegitimacy would appear in a new setting. If the measures I recommend were adopted, action could then be taken on them in the light of changed conditions.

The assertion that changes in the law must wait on changes in custom and consensus is only a half truth. The assertion that changes in custom must wait on changes in the law is also a half truth. The two taken together do not add up to a whole truth; neither do they add up to a whole lie. History offers abundant evidence that law and custom are interactive, at all times, in intricate and often unexpected ways. What is unthinkable today may be inevitable tomorrow.

Among the unthinkables is the notion that one of the inalienable rights of man is the right to probe, explore and experiment sexually and, together with others like him, male and female, establish any sexual relationships that satisfy their needs, as long as they do not attempt to force their ideas on others or interfere with the corresponding right of others to follow their own sexways.

AFTERWORD

One of the ways we recognize a new age is by its clumsiness. Another way is by its determination to be new perhaps at all costs. I have sought to clear the field of punitive obstacles and wrong expectations so that whatever is genuinely new and threatening can appear with the fullness of its radical difference. But two nagging concerns persist. The first has to do with the determination to remain clumsy and thus to jeopardize the tasking contribution of art. The second has to do with a disturbing affinity to violence. Because both are fearful and because both really are versions of each other, I have chosen as my first and now my last selection the consideration of the art of the Marquis de Sade. It is not with God or Freud that we finally must make peace; it is with the Devil and Sade.

Irving H. Buchen

ANTHONY BURGESS

OUR BEDFELLOW,
THE MARQUIS DE SADE

Only two writers in the whole of world literature have, solely on
the strength of the philosophies they preached, been elevated
into monstrous figures of evil. The first was Niccolò Machiavelli,
whose book on statecraft, *Il Principe* (The Prince), was not well
understood by his chief traducers, the Elizabethan English. The
popular view of "Old Nick" (yes, that's where the diabolic
sobriquet comes from) was of a bogeyman dedicated to the subversion of good, the liquidation of religion, and the promotion of
death and violence for their own sake. A close reading of *Il
Principe* shows that Machiavelli went, in fact, nowhere near so
far: he was concerned with a very laudable end—that of maintaining order in a community threatened by enemies without
and traitors within. What earned him such extravagent odium
was his lack of scruple about the means by which that end should
be fulfilled. Every state, even the most liberal and democratic,
has in time of emergency had to use Machiavellian devices: yet

mention the term, or preferably whisper it ("Machiavellian!"), and the response is a shuddering one. The word has been loaded for centuries.

The second of these writers is the Marquis de Sade, and till recently, the term sadism has not carried the full load of horror available to it. The most popular joke that admits the perversion and its complement is about the sadist and the masochist who share adjoining beds in a psychiatric ward. "Beat me, beat me!" cries the masochist. "No," says the sadist. But that is not it at all: there is nothing negative in sadism. And the small torturer, the boy who pulls wings off flies, the husband who drops burning brown paper on his wife's bare body—these don't go far enough. The extravagance of evil falsely attributed to Machiavelli should, by rights, be transferred to the Marquis. But few people have read his works, and few imaginations are capable of reaching the ingenuities of his fancies. It is only fairly recently that this devil has been given his due.

The world that George Orwell presents in *Nineteen Eighty-Four* owes a great deal to Sade. The ruling oligarchy knows what it is doing: it wants power, and it intends, behind the immortal, because mythical, facade of Big Brother, to keep power till the end of time. This power is the ultimate pleasure, the final human fulfillment. Its image is of a jackboot poised voluptuously over a terrified human face. The exercise of power means the exercise of cruelty, for it is only through cruelty that you can show your victim the extent of your total domination over him.

Sade's actions and, more patently, Sade's literary fantasies represented power as an aspect of the sexual impulse. The sexual act is shown not as a reciprocity of pleasure giving, but as the enforcing of strange desires on an unwilling victim. To share pleasure, said Sade, is to weaken it. The victim (like Winston Smith in *Nineteen Eighty-Four*) must be impotent to strike back and must be of a preordained persecutable type. In the sexual field it is women who are made for persecution: physiologically they are natural victims. Sade's major work, the unfinished *120 Days of Sodom,* is a detailed catalogue of sexual perversion, all

of which involve torture and some of them death. The form of
the book is fictional. The setting is a castle in the Black Forest,
totally impregnable, and in it four debauchées from Paris—a
banker, a bishop, a duke, and a judge—spend seventeen weeks
in perverse pleasures that are graduated from the merely revolting to the ineffably and transcendently evil. It was Sade's intention to describe six hundred perversions, but he only managed to
get through the first thirty days—though he made very detailed
notes for the other ninety. Thus the seventy-ninth perversion in
the "Third Class of Criminal Passions" entails strapping a naked
girl face down to a table and having "a piping hot omelette
served upon her buttocks." The eater "uses an exceedingly sharp
fork." This is comparatively mild. The ultimate horror has fifteen
girls (none older than seventeen) all tortured simultaneously in
fifteen different ways, while the *grand seigneur* who arranges
this elaborate *grand guignol* watches and waits for orgasm. It
does not come easily, despite the monstrous stimulus: it has to
be effected through masturbation and the exhibition of two male
bottoms.

It is evident that Sade, in conceiving these nightmares (nightmares to us; delicious dreams to him), was in a state of sexual
frustration so intense that it drove him to a kind of clearheaded
mania. The deprivations of prison life were an obvious factor, but
they must be only a small part of the story. For Sade's dreams
are essentially dreams of impotence, just as the recorded orgies
on which some of the dreams are based are attempts to find
satisfaction when the normal means have failed. The situation is
not all that unusual. Eighteenth-century France was notable for
its lecherous aristocracy, and Sade's youthful roistering was not
more spectacular than that of many of his peers and superiors.
But the normal sexual vein was overworked; the palate demanded
sharper sauces. Or put it another way: the familiar intoxication
could only, as with drug takers, be attained by stimulants that
grew stronger and stronger.

The first stimulant was sodomy—one that has never been as
rare as the law, which represses it mercilessly, would have us
believe. Heterosexual sodomy (read the *Kamasutra* on this) is
a regular age-old practice among Tamils, and it carries little

flavor of the perverse. But sodomy is selfish, and it can also be cruel. Sade was fascinated by it, and he is led through it to a genuinely nauseating preoccupation with the anus: he plays with feces like an infant.

When what may be termed pure sodomy fails to bring satisfaction, the next stage of cruelty is reached: the imposition of pain unconnected with coition and not necessarily centered on the erogenous zones. To inflict suffering is enough, by whatever means. But the more elementary forms—burning the flesh, cutting, flaying, even poisoning—must pall sooner or later, and then the sadist is led on to the more ingenious tortures, most of them slowly lethal. Where is the limit? The limit is reached, it would seem, when heterosexual fantasies are swallowed up in apocalyptic visions of mass destruction—Hitlerian visions whose sexual content is not immediately apparent. Sade's destructive fantasies are curiously modern—the blasting of whole towns, a sort of fête in which "children are blown up by rockets and bombs." Edmund Wilson, to whose long essay on the Sade documents I am deeply indebted, says apropos of this: "How gratified Sade would have been if he could have foreseen the scale on which we were later to indulge in this pastime! Or would he perhaps have been appalled, as he was by the Terror?"

Sade was capable of being appalled; his sadism was not so thoroughgoing as, for total philosophical consistency, it ought to have been. But once you divide the world into victims and persecutors, you are faced with the problem of a frontier where roles may change: sadism tends to embrace its opposite, masochism. Leopold von Sacher-Masoch was born twenty-two years after Sade's death, but his stories about the pleasure of being hurt, degraded, dominated, are to some extent anticipated in the older master. While in prison at Vincennes, Sade regularly flagellated himself. The girls involved in the Marseilles orgy testified that the inflictions of cruelty were not all onesided. Nowadays, informed by the sexologist of whom Sade was the true forerunner, we recognize in ourselves the dichotomy of our response to one of these magazine photographs we're always seeing—a girl in top boots with a whip or gun. "Kinky," we say, and shudder with two kinds of anticipatory pleasure: we identify with the torturer; we see ourselves as the victim.

That the sadomasochistic impulse is in all of us we no longer doubt. There is some obscure neural liaison in the brain between the sexual urge and the desire for domination—and the latter phrase I have deliberately left ambiguous. We are, quite rightly, scared of letting the sadomasochistic get out of hand: it is all too easy. We're all pretty bad inside; it's what we do outside that counts.

Sade, in his actions, and even more in his books, extrapolated on a Wagnerian scale what society insists on keeping locked in the crypts of the mind. Though vicious and perhaps demented, he does not belong to a race very different from our own. That is why he fascinates. But the fascination does not long survive the actual opening of one of his books. Nauseated by his anal fixations, we soon become bored with his ingenuities. Nobody is real; he seems to be playing with automata. He was interested in the art of the novel, and he wanted to contribute to the pornographic branch of it (in this he was merely one among many); but he was not sufficiently interested in people as people. There is no give and take, none of the dialectic of character that we find in competent fiction; there is only the wearying but unwearied catalogue of atrocities. The people who publish extracts from Sade in paperback are misrepresenting him: they are picking out the plums and putting in the wastebasket the dollops of farinaceous inedibility. Sade has to be given us entire, so that we may yawn over the long pages of eighteenth-century moralizing and become irritated by the self-contradictions. The public ought not to be titillated by half-censorship: the works of the Marquis de Sade ought to be freely available, and that would cure the smut hounds.

Has he any value in the history of literature or philosophy? His literary interest is slight though not entirely negligible. His philosophy of Nature is untenable but stimulating. Where he has to be taken seriously is in his role as pioneer sexologist. He was the first modern Western man to list the varieties of erotic perversion, and the list is pretty well exhaustive. Moreover, his view of sex is not limited to the European ethos. He was something of an anthropologist and argued that there was not one sexual practice regarded as perverse by the West that was not accepted as normal in some remoter society. Most important of all, he saw with terrible clarity the sexual springs of cruelty, no matter how cruelty was disguised as a device of politics or of ecclesiastical discipline. Even in his recognition of the sexual elements that lie below family relationships and manifest themselves long before the age of puberty, he anticipated the Viennese school of psychology. He knew what we have taken a long time to learn—that sex is not just something that happens in a bedroom.

His profound misanthropy, while justified by the events of European history through which he lived, was not in conformity with the optimistic philosophies of his time. The chains of man could be broken, said Rousseau; reason could triumph, said the Encyclopedists. Sade never expected anything but the worst from mankind, so he could never be disappointed. He did not overestimate the rational capacities of man; however—following the custom of the age—he did invoke reason in his writings. Nowadays there are millions of people who find cause, far better cause than Sade had, to despair of the human race. Sade merely dreamed of chemists who could blow up whole cities; we have seen the reality of conventional high explosives and the thermonuclear bomb. His visions, like those of science fiction in our own day, were ahead of their time.

It is sourly amusing to observe where his true influence lies. The great dictators, bemused by dreams of national glory, have found him abhorrent (Napoleon was the first to be shocked). Schoolmasters with canes and parents with flat, hard hands have scarcely thought about him. It is the popular writers who have diluted his message and made it palatable to suburban minds. Ian Fleming, for instance:

". . . I can tell you that the entire population of Fort Knox will be dead or incapacitated by midnight. . . . The substance that will be inserted in the water supply, outside the filter plant, will be a highly concentrated form of GB."

"You're mad! You don't really mean you're going to kill sixty thousand people!"

"Why not? American motorists do it every two years."

Bond stared into Goldfinger's face in fascinated horror. It couldn't be true! He couldn't mean it! He said tersely, "What's this GB?"

"GB is the most powerful of the Trilone group of nerve poisons. It was perfected by the Wehrmacht in 1943, but never used for fear of reprisals. In fact, it is a more effective instrument of destruction than the hydrogen bomb. . . . Introduction through the water supply is an ideal method of applying it to a densely populated area."

How the Marquis de Sade would have reveled in the technological triumphs that now, in literature, merely serve the end of a popular frisson.

In literature less popular, the misanthropy of Sade has become totally acceptable. I'm thinking particularly of William Golding's novel *The Inheritors*, where Homo sapiens, supervening on the gentle Neanderthals, destroys a worthier race because it is in his nature to destroy. Evil, Golding seems to say, is built into man. What do we do about that: acquiesce in it, as Sade did, or seek, however hopelessly, some form of regeneration? Mankind is not doing very well at the moment, but mankind has never done very well. Always expect the worst, and then you can never be depressed by your morning paper. As for action, note that history has a few lonely figures who did good or, fearing to do evil, did nothing. The impulses we share with the diabolic Marquis are best left to him, to be worked out in fantasy. We can never rid ourselves of these impulses by merely banning the books that most thoroughly express them. They are merely a spectacular symptom of one of the big human diseases. Whether the disease is curable is something we have still to find out.

BIBLIOGRAPHY

Adolf, Helen. "The Amazon Type in Literature." *Comp. Lit. S.* I (1960), 256–62.

Allendy, R. F. *Capitalisme et sexualité*. Paris: Denoël et Steele, 1932.

Bataille, Georges. *Death and Sensuality: A Study of Eroticism and the Taboo*. New York: Ballantine, 1969.

Bengler, Edmund. "On Obscene Words." *Psychoanalytical Quarterly* V (1936), 226–48.

Bentley, Eric. "The Naked American." *New Republic* 161 (Aug. 9, 1969), 31–34.

Bentley, Joseph. "Satire and the Rhetoric of Sadism." *The Centennial Review* XI (Summer, 1967), 387–404.

Bettelheim, Bruno. "Portnoy Psychoanalyzed." *Midstream* (June–July, 1969), 3–10.

Blöcker, Günter. *Die Neuen Wirklichkeit*. Berlin: Argon, 1957.

Booth, Wayne. "Censorship and the Values of Fiction." *English Journal* (March, 1964), 6–12.

Boyers, Robert. "Attitudes toward Sex in American 'High Culture.'" *Annals American Academy of Political and Social Science* 376 (March, 1968), 36–52.

Brophy, Brigid. "Our Impermissive Society." *Mosaic* I, ii (1968), 1–15.

Brophy, Brigid. "The Perversity of Aubrey Beardsley." *Atlantic* 221 (Feb., 1968), 61–67.

Brown, Norman O. *Love's Body.* New York: Random House, 1966.

Brustein, Robert. "The Third Theater Revisited." *New York Review of Books* XII (Feb. 13, 1969), 25–27.

Brustein, Robert. "Monkey Business." *New York Review of Books* XII (April 24, 1969), 43–46.

Burgess, Anthony. "Our Bedfellow, the Marquis de Sade." *Horizon* XI (Winter, 1969), 105–9.

Burgess, Anthony. *Urgent Copy.* New York: Norton and Company, 1968.

Bush, Douglas. "Sex in the Modern Novel." *Atlantic* 203 (Jan., 1959), 73–75.

Callois, Roger. *Babel: Orgueil, Confusion et Ruine de la Littérature.* Paris: Gallimard, 1948.

Calverton, V. F. and Schmalhausen, Samuel D., eds. *Sex in Civilization.* Garden City: Garden City Publishing Co., 1929.

Capouya, Emile. "The Varieties of Love." *Nation* 197 (Dec. 28, 1967), 457–59.

Chandos, John, ed. *To Deprave and to Corrupt.* New York: Association Press, 1962.

Cioran, E. M. *Précis de Décomposition.* Paris: Gallimard, 1949.

Clark, Kenneth. *The Nude.* Garden City: Doubleday, 1959.

Comfort, Alex. *Darwin and the Naked Lady.* New York: George Brazillier, 1962.

Coulteray, George de. *Sadism in the Movies.* Trans. Steve Hult. New York: Medical Press, 1965.

Cox, Arthur Jean. "The Boredom of Fantasy." *Riverside Quarterly* I (1964–65), 26–31.

Cox, C. B., *et al.* "Pornography and Obscenity." *Critical Quarterly* III (1961), 99–122.

Craig, Alec. *The Banned Books of England and Other Countries.* London: Allen and Unwin, 1962.

Dell, F. "Sex in American Fiction." *American Mercury* 66 (Jan., 1948), 84–90.

DeMott, Benjamin. *Supergrow.* New York: Dutton, 1969.

DeVoto, Bernard. "Dull Novels Make Dull Reading." *Harpers* 202 (June, 1951), 67–70.

Doheny, John. "The Novel Is the Book of Life: D. H. Lawrence and a Revised Version of Polymorphous Perversity." *Punch* 26 (April, 1966), 40–59.

Drury, David. "Sex Goes Public: A Talk with Henry Miller." *Esquire* LXV (May, 1966), 118ff., 170, 172.

Durbach, Errol. "Form and Vision in Erotic Tragedy from Aphrodite to Freud." *Mosaic* I, iv (1968), 35–52.

Elliott, George P. "Against Pornography." *Harpers* 230 (March, 1965), 51–60.

Elsen, Claude. *Homo eroticus: Esquisse d'une psychologie de l'érotisme*. Paris: Gallimard, 1953.

Feynman, Alberta E. "The Fetal Quality of 'Character' in Plays of the Absurd." *Modern Drama* IX (1966), 18–25.

Fiedler, Leslie. *Love and Death in the American Novel*. New York: Criterion Books, 1960.

Foster, Jeanette H. *Sex Variant Women in Literature*. New York: Vantage Press, 1956.

Fowler, Albert. "Sensibility Since Sade," *Southwest Review* XLV (1960), 240–50.

Gerson, Walter M. and Sander, H. Lund. "*Playboy* Magazine: Sophisticated Smut or Social Revolution." *Journal of Popular Culture* I (1967), 218–27.

Gilman, Richard. "There's a Wave of Pornography. . . ." *New York Times* Magazine (Sept. 8, 1968), 36–37.

Ginzburg, Ralph. *An Unhurried View of Erotica*. New York: The Helmsman Press, 1958.

Glicksberg, Charles I. "Sex in Contemporary Literature." *Colorado Quarterly* IX (1961), 277–87.

Gold, Herbert. "The Sexual Stalemate." *Nation* 187 (Nov. 1, 1958), 309–11.

Goodman, Paul. *Five Years*. New York: Brussel and Brussel, 1966.

Goodman, Paul. *Utopian Essays and Practical Proposals*. New York: Random House, 1962.

Gorer, Geoffrey. *Death, Grief and Mourning*. Garden City: Doubleday and Co., 1945.

Harrison, Harry. "We Are Sitting on Our . . ." *SF Horizons* (Oxford) I (1964), 39–42.

Hassan, Ihab. "Sade: Prisoner of Consciousness." *TriQuarterly* 15 (Spring, 1969), 23–44.

Hentoff, Margot. "Notes from Above Ground." *New York Review of Books* XII (May 22, 1969), 12–14.

Hermann, Imre. "The Giant Mother, the Phallic Mother, Obscenity." *Psychoanalytical Review* XXXVI (1949), 302–6.

Hoffman, Stanton. "The Cities of Night: John Rechy's *City of Night* and the American Literature of Homosexuality." *Chicago Review* XVII (1964), 195–206.

Huizinga, J. *Homo Ludens: A Study of the Play-Element in Culture.* New York: Roy, 1950.

Hyman, Stanley Edgar. *Standards: A Chronicle of Books for Our Time.* New York: Horizon Press, 1966.

Issacs, Neil D. "The Autoerotic Metaphor in Joyce, Sterne, Lawrence Stevens and Whitman." *Literature and Psychology* XV (Spring, 1965), 92–106.

Kaplan, Abraham. "Obscenity as an Aesthetic Category." *Law and Contemporary Problems* XX (1955), 544–59.

Kaplan, David M. "Homosexuality and American Theater: A Psychoanalytical Comment." *Tulane Drama Review* IX (1965), 25–55.

Kronhausen, Everhard and Phyllis. *Pornography and the Law.* New York: Ballantine, 1959.

Legman, Gershon. *The Hornbook: Studies in Erotic Folklore and Bibliography.* New Hyde Park, New York: University Books, 1964.

Lipman, Matthew. "The Aesthetic Presence of the Body." *Journal of Aesthetics and Art Criticism* XV (1957), 425–34.

McNamee, M. B. "Esthetic Distance and Sex." *America* 102 (Dec. 19, 1959), 372–73.

Marcus, Steven. *The Other Victorians.* New York: Basic Books, 1966.

Marcuse, Herbert. *Eros and Civilization.* Boston: Beacon Press, 1955.

Marcuse, Ludwig. "Freud's Aesthetics." *Journal of Aesthetics and Art Criticism* XVII (1958), 1–21.

Marcuse, Ludwig. *Obscene: The History of an Indignation.* Trans. Karen Gershon. London: MacGibbon and Kee, 1965.

Meager, R. "The Sublime and the Obscene." *British Journal of Aesthetics* IV (1964), 214–27.

Meeske, Marilyn. "Memoirs of a Female Pornographer." *Esquire* LXII (April, 1965), 112–15.

Millett, Kate. "Sexual Politics: Miller, Mailer, Genet." *New American Review*, No. 7. New York: New American Library, 1969.

Moravia, Alberto. *Man as an End.* New York: Farrar, Straus and Giroux, 1965.

Packard, Vance. *The Sexual Wilderness.* New York: McKay, 1969.

Pearsall, Ronald. *The Worm in the Bud: The World of Victorian Sexuality.* New York: The Macmillan Co., 1969.

Perrin, Noel. *Dr. Bowdler's Legacy*. New York: Atheneum, 1969.

Phillips, William. "Writing about Sex." *Partisan Review* 34 (1967), 552–63.

Pisanus Fraxi (H. S. Ashbee). *Bibliography of Prohibited Books*. 3 vols. New York: Orion, 1962.

Plimpton, George. "Philip Roth's Exact Intent—Interview." New York *Times Book Review* (Feb. 23, 1969), 2, 23–25.

Purdy, Strother. "On the Psychology of Erotic Literature." *Literature and Psychology* XXI (March, 1970), 22–29.

Redman, B. R. "Sex and Literary Art." *American Mercury* 63 (October, 1946), 412–17.

Reisner, Robert. *Show Me the Good Parts: The Reader's Guide to Sex in Literature*. New York: The Citadel Press, 1964.

Rembar, Charles. *The End of Obscenity*. New York: Random House, 1968.

Richardson, Jack. "Groping toward Freedom: The Living Theatre." *Commentary* 47 (May, 1969), 79–81.

Schechner, Richard. "Pornography and the New Expression." *Atlantic* 219 (January, 1967), 74–78.

Smylie, J. H. "Prudes, Lewds and Polysyllables." *Commonweal* 89 (Feb. 28, 1969), 671–73.

Sontag, Susan. "The Pornographic Imagination." *Partisan Review* 34 (1967), 181–212.

Steiner, George. "Night Words: High Pornography and Human Privacy." *Encounter* XXV (October, 1965), 14–19.

Stoehr, Taylor. "Pornography, Masturbation and the Novel." *Salmagundi* 2, ii (1967–68), 28–56.

Tanner, Tony. "The New Demonology." *Partisan Review* XXXIII (1966), 547–72.

Thody, P. M. W. *Four Cases of Literary Censorship: An Inaugural Lecture*. Leeds: Leeds University Press, 1968.

Thompson, John. "Pornography and Propaganda." *Commentary* 48 (August, 1969), 52–57.

Thorslev, Peter L., Jr. "Incest as Romantic Symbol." *Comparative Literature Studies* II (1965), 41–58.

Vidal, Gore. *Reflections on a Sinking Ship*. Boston: Little, Brown, 1969.

Waldrop, Bernard Keith. "Aesthetic Uses of Obscenity in Literature." DA XXV (1965).

Wren-Lewis, John. "The Passing of a Puritanism." *Critical Quarterly* V (1963), 295–305.

NOTES ON CONTRIBUTORS

Georges Bataille, French novelist and essayist, is founder of many journals including *Documents* and *La Critique Sociale*.

Joseph Bentley teaches English at the University of South Florida in Tampa.

Robert Boyers is a member of the English faculty at Skidmore College and the editor of *Salmagundi*.

Norman O. Brown, formerly professor of Classics at Wesleyan University, is the author of *Life against Death* and *Love's Body*.

Robert Brustein is on the faculty of the Yale School of Drama.

Anthony Burgess's most recent work of fiction is *Enderby* (1968); his most recent collection of criticism is *Urgent Copy* (1969).

Benjamin DeMott is a critic, essayist and novelist and Professor of English at Amherst College.

Geoffrey Gorer, British satirist and social anthropologist, is the author of *The Life and Ideas of the Marquis de Sade* (rev. ed. 1964) and *Death, Grief and Mourning* (1965).

Ihab Hassan is at the Center for the Humanities of Wesleyan University. His *The Literature of Silence: Henry Miller and Samuel Beckett* appeared in 1967.

Stanton Hoffman is a member of the English faculty of Sir George Williams University in Montreal and a regular contributor to the *Chicago Review*.

Lawrence Lipton is a novelist, essayist and poet. A regular lecturer at UCLA, he is perhaps best known for his *The Holy Barbarians*.

Kate Millett is on the faculty at Barnard and is a member of the radical feminist movement.

William Phillips is the editor of *Partisan Review*.

George Plimpton is the author of *Out of My League* (1961) and an editor of *Paris Review*.

Strother Purdy teaches English at Marquette University.

Richard Schechner is professor of Drama at New York University and the editor of *Drama Review*.

Gore Vidal's most recent novel is *Myra Breckinridge;* his most recent collection of essays is *Reflections on a Sinking Ship*.

Wayland Young is a British journalist, member of Parliament and editor of *Disarmament and Arms Control*.

DATE DUE